RUSSELL —
THANKS SO MU

[handwritten signature]

D0592740

FRANKLY SPEAKING

(FOUR DECADES ON THE AIR AND OFF)

— A MEMOIR —

Frank Reed

Foreword by B. Eric Rhoads

Frankly Speaking... Four Decades on the Air and Off A Memoir
by Frank Reed

Printed in the United States of America

ISBN 9781628397796

This is a work of creative nonfiction. The events are portrayed to the best of the author's memory. While all the stories in the book are true, some names and identifying details have been changed to protect the privacy of the people involved. The conversations in the book come from the author's recollections, though they are not written to represent word-for-word transcripts. Rather, the author has retold them in a way that evokes the feeling and meaning what was said and in all instances, the essence of the dialogue is accurate.

Frank Reed
Host, 94.9 KLTY Family-Friendly Morning Show
www.klty.com
Find me on Facebook and follow me on Twitter @frank949klty

www.xulonpress.com

What others are saying about 'Frankly Speaking'

Frank Reed and I share a long history together. For over 20 years it's always been a pleasure to join Frank on the radio, or have him introduce me in concert. He's been a supportive friend and the consummate professional. I always love when Frank shares his stories and now they're all captured here, in 'Frankly Speaking.' His journey through secular radio, to finding Christ, his wife Patti, and his on air 'home' at KLTY in Dallas-Ft. Worth. It's an address I hope he keeps for years to come! Within these pages you have the opportunity to look into the heart of the man behind the microphone, my good friend Frank Reed.

Steven Curtis Chapman,
Nashville, Tennessee

I first heard Frank Reed's name when I was living in San Antonio working as a radio station manager. A colleague of mine told me about the new guy he just hired to host his morning show on his Christian radio station in New York. "He used to work at NBC," my friend said. "Middays. Between Don Imus and Howard Stern." My first thought? I hope he really loves Jesus. This is the compelling story of a guy who learned that you can be working at a top station in the #1 market in the USA and, as Bono said, "you still haven't found what you're looking for." Along the way, he learned that his love for Jesus and his love for the magic of radio can fit perfectly together. And in the process, he's touched a lot of people's lives. I loved reading his story. I think you will too.

Bob Lepine, Family Life Today,
Little Rock, Arkansas

Frank Reed has shown his gift of storytelling for decades on the radio. It is obvious from this book he can tell a compelling story with the keyboard too! As I read his words, I could visualize the lake house he built in Orlando, his best friend Josh, the limo driver that was waiting for him at LaGuardia and what it must have been like for a young guy from Florida to be living in Manhattan, as part of one of the most accomplished air staffs in the radio industry. If you've ever thought about what it would be like to have your 'dream job,' and how faith can play an integral part, read this book!

Tim Dukes, Chief Operating Officer,
Halftime Ministries, Dallas, Texas

I've always known that Frank had a way with words. For twenty-plus years I've laughed and cried as his rich voice inspired and informed listeners of all ages on KLTY Radio in Dallas. So it's no surprise that the man who has held my attention behind the microphone carried that same authenticity and character to the written page. Yet, here I found more to the man than just the incredible 'radio' voice-celebrity. In the pages of his book, I found a jazzy wordsmith willing to share his authentic and sometimes painful journey. And once again, I found myself laughing, crying, and learning as he shared his journey of career, family, and faith. At some point, (as is often the case with many of my morning drives listening) I found myself wishing it didn't have to end so soon.

Dan Dean, Phillips, Craig and Dean,
Colleyville, Texas

It's the early 80s and I am sitting at my desk when the receptionist comes to my door and says, "Frank Reed is on the phone." I say, "Yeah, right," thinking it is a joke. Why would the midday host at WNBC call me? A week later he is in my living room listening to CCM music with me and my wife, Ellen. That began a friendship that lasts to this day. It has been a joy to follow Frank in his professional and spiritual journey as he has impacted thousands of lives along the way. Those who listen to him daily on KLTY in Dallas will find that his easy-going, conversational on-air manner translates beautifully to print, so 'Frankly Speaking' is like having him over for coffee. I urge you to spend some time with this book and get to know my friend Frank. He has a wonderful story that just may surprise you.

Lloyd Parker, Chief Operating Officer,
WAY Media, Inc. Colorado Springs, Colorado

I've known Frank Reed for twenty five years and I am privileged to call him my friend. There is one word that describes him; genuine. There is nothing phony about him. He is genuine through and through. He knows his sins have been forgiven and he knows God's love for him never fails. His story is all about this wonderful good news of Jesus Christ being lived out in daily life. Read this book and at the end you will feel like Frank is your personal friend. You will laugh and cry with him along his journey. You will also be inspired and encouraged by him, inspired to take God at his word, and encouraged to trust Christ in every area of your life.

**Bob Christopher, Host of Basic Gospel Radio,
author of 'Love Is', Denton, Texas**

Frank Reed is the consummate storyteller. Sometimes he uses his own words, sometimes songs or the stories of others. But you don't have to dig very deep to find Frank's greatest passion, his love for Christ and His people. So make a full pot of coffee and curl up somewhere quiet and enjoy this journey.

**Sheila Walsh, author of 'The Storm Inside',
Frisco, Texas**

It's always been a pleasure to share life and music with Frank during our many visits together through the years. 'Frankly Speaking' has given me the opportunity to get to know more about the life of my friend behind the microphone. If you enjoy Frank on the air, I'm certain you will enjoy Frank the author. And what a great surprise to hear that Frank was playing my songs on WNBC in New York! I'm certain you will be inspired as you follow his journey of faith. 'Frankly Speaking' is very much like Frank himself; honest, transparent, and real.

**Michael W. Smith, Singer/Songwriter,
Franklin, Tennessee**

Table of Contents

Foreword

I 'm not sure the exact moment I met Frank Reed, but the year was 1975. Frank had joined our radio station as the midday disc jockey and he was one of the better radio personalities I had ever heard. Over time, with the direction of our boss, Jerry Clifton, Frank got better and better and became a world class air personality. Frankly, he got so good on the air that he was no longer suited to be in Miami, but was destined for New York, where he became a star on WNBC, which was winning in New York with Frank's help. Some big names in the radio industry were part of that radio station and Frank was on the road to even bigger and better things. His star was soaring. But something happened to Frank that few others could relate to. Frank became a 'Jesus Freak,' as our friends called him.

When Frank and I worked together in Miami, I did not know him Christian to Christian. Though he struck me as having the heart of a Christian because of his sincerity and kindness, his behavior and lifestyle made it clear that Frank had not yet found Christ. I'll save the gory details of that lifestyle for the pages that follow, in which Frank held nothing back. Unlike most, he has not rewritten his story to suit a PR objective. This missive about his life and adventures tells the unvarnished truth, which isn't easy to hear and is harder to reveal.

I suppose like all young people, we have moments when we drift from our core foundational principles. I know I did. I'm not proud of some of the things associated with my past. I started out with those foundations as a Christian. I knew better, yet drifted and eventually returned. Frank had a slight foundation from his youth and the early 70s, but while in New York his life was truly transformed. He suddenly lived for Christ. It's something that is rare. Total transformation usually includes some clinging to the past ways of life, but when Frank accepted Christ totally, he was willing to give up the trappings of the world he was accustomed to. Being on the radio is fuel for those starved for attention. Our egos soar when 'groupies' call the request line at the rate of dozens and sometimes hundreds a day. It's addictive to be the center of attention for an entire city that listens daily. It's nearly impossible to lose one's self and turn it over to God when one is in the spotlight and has the fame to go with being on the radio. Those of us in radio thrive on the attention, the access to rock stars, being pointed out in crowds for recognition, being on stage and on the air and being the center of attention. Frank saw this on a massive scale in New York (much more than I ever did in Miami) and yet, when he found Christ, he lost himself and instantly abandoned that seductive lifestyle. He left WNBC, and in a few years would move to a Christian teaching and music station that, while profitable, had few listeners. Yet Frank believed he needed to dedicate his God-given skills to a life in Christian radio, which meant giving God the glory and avoiding it personally. It meant smaller audiences (at least in those early days) and meant giving up New York-level money and a giant fixture in the secular media industry to follow what he believed God's plan to be. Frank was driven to put Christ-centered radio on the map. In those days it barely existed. There were very few Christian music acts and it was difficult to find enough 'Contemporary Christian' content to fill up all the songs on a radio station. Frank was a pioneer. He fought hard to work on radio for

Christ, which he and his colleagues thought would transform the world. It was unheard of for Christian hit music stations to be on the air, and believed to be impossible for them to compete against high-powered, well-funded secular radio stations, yet Frank and friends succeeded in a big way. The success of KLTY is legendary in Christian music circles and has left Dallas' secular radio industry scratching its head that a Christian station could be so strong in the ratings. Of course, Frank had a huge role in that success, yet he humbly gives the glory to God.

You may know Frank Reed from the radio, but this is a chance to get a look inside the mind and the life of a man who was on a crash course with disaster. Though I loved Frank's heart, I never pegged him as one who would become a believer and accept Christ's great gift. Not only did he transform his own life, he is on a mission to use his radio pulpit to help others find a fresh, new life by learning about Christ. Frank is transparent about his past and fully willing to be an example of someone who shows that if he can be saved, anyone can be. While we've all seen TV preachers start with no fame, gain fame, get addicted to it and lose their way, Frank is the opposite. He gave up his fame to follow Christ's path.

I learned things about Frank I never knew, in spite of our friendship that spans almost forty years. He is an inspiration to me personally, and has been a wonderful supportive friend. I don't think I know anyone who is as uplifting and positive and always seeking ways to make me feel better about myself. Frank is never about Frank, he is all about his God, his family, and his mission to lift people up and help them find the same God who changed his life.

B. Eric Rhoads, Publisher/CEO, Radio Ink Magazine
and RadioInk.com.

Introduction

———— ⌇ ————

I n the many years that I've been hosting 'The Family Friendly Morning Show,' on 94.9 KLTY, Dallas-Ft. Worth, I've always been on the lookout for 'the story.' It's that compelling moment on the air that you just have to listen to. The one that makes you late rushing into work, because you can't turn the radio off. (Sorry if I've made you late!) Those are the moments that I live for. Don't misunderstand, I love playing all the great songs we play; songs that get you moving and make a difference. I love having fun on the air with my team, Starlene, Perri, and Cowboy Chris. Every weekday morning we work hard to bring you the information you need to start your day, and we try to share things that will make life for you and your family just a little bit easier. We love to put a smile on your child's face, and your face too. It's a blast to give away lots of free stuff, like the trips, the cash, the romantic getaways, and unique things like a private breakfast with your favorite artist. But for me, the absolute *best* thing is facilitating 'the story'!

There have been hundreds of them; Matthew West explaining about the mom who lost her daughter to a drunk driver, amazingly over time found forgiveness in her heart, and how she and the young man have ministered together on the same stage. Toby Mac being so in love that he left the DC Talk tour, flew to Jamaica, and finally won over Amanda, the lady who would become his wife. Chris Tomlin explaining that it all started with a guitar given to him by his dad in a little town called Grand Saline, Texas. The unemployed dad, who was having a hard time making ends meet, gets out of bed and prays for a miracle, and then wins $5,000 in our Secret Sound contest. Blake Shelton hopping in a rental car at DFW International, hitting scan, and hearing 'God Gave Me You,' which he would record for Miranda Lambert. The single mom who went to the Women of Faith Conference with her daughter, who felt led to tell her mom she must go back to the guy holding the sign at the entrance and give him her business card. A year later he would hold a sign at the exact same spot, but when she approached, this one said, "Will you marry me?" And the morning that Mary Beth, Steven Curtis Chapman's wife, boldly shared how her faith sustained her in the tragic loss of their daughter, while Steven looked on quietly with eyes that said, "I love this woman."

I love the fact that you will hear stories on our show that you won't hear anywhere else. They set us apart, are often inexplicable, and point to the reality of a loving God being involved in our everyday lives. We have a saying we often say in unison when we have one of these God moments on the air: "You just can't make this stuff up!" (YJCMTSU!)

I believe stories like this have a dual purpose. If you are a Christian, they inspire and energize your faith. They give you hope. They keep you moving forward. There is a deep spiritual connection going on inside of you that says, "Yes! What I am hearing right now is true!" And if you are not a Christian, if you are a seeker, you can't help but wonder or be intrigued by what is coming out of the radio. You keep seeking. You want to hear more. When those two dynamics are happening, I am in my element. I am totally alive. And I am doing what I was created to do, for a time such as this.

My hope and prayer is that my book, 'Frankly Speaking,' will have the same dual purpose. If you are a believer, I hope you will be inspired to keep growing in your faith, that you would be assured and secure in your salvation, and that you would come away with the desire to let God use you, just the way you are. And if you are a skeptic or a seeker, I'm praying you will conclude that in spite of anything you have heard or thought about Christianity in the past, the claims of Christ are something you need to investigate further. Because everything you are about to read is true. You really *can't* make this stuff up!

May I state for the record I am not a theologian or Bible teacher. I'm just a simple guy who was fortunate to find some success in a profession I love, and it has allowed me a platform to share what I believe. For me, it is no coincidence.

For many years I lived for myself. I was in total control, and I was on my way to self-destruction. Then, while working for one of America's biggest radio stations, I was rescued. I became a Christ follower. Frankly speaking, it is without a doubt the most exciting, satisfying, fulfilling, and radical way to live, ever. I speak from experience, because I've lived my life two different ways: my way, and God's way. I've spent many years bringing you other people's stories. Now, I'd like to bring you mine. I'm Frank Reed, and this is my story.

Dedication

For Patti, Ryan, and Hope. And to the loyal listeners of 94.9 KLTY Radio. Every morning you have a choice of who you are going to listen to, and for many years, you have chosen us. We consider it an honor and privilege to serve you. Thank you!

ONE

Beginnings

———— ❧ ————

"**W**ay to hit that ball!" Coach Beck yelled so loud everybody in the bleachers and on the field heard him. Unfortunately, my line shot to right center was caught for the last out. It was the end of my Little League season, 1962.

Memories, like the corners of my mind. Like quotes from my Mom. I remember them well. "If you're well enough to play ball on Sunday afternoon, you're well enough to be in church on Sunday morning," and "Son, I don't care if you become a ditch digger, you be the best ditch digger you can be." Of course, "If there's a job worth doing, it's worth doing right," and one that has served me very, very well down through the years: "If you can't say something nice about somebody, don't say anything at all." We all have influencers in our life. In our house, Mom ruled.

Her name was Thelma, and she was the dominant figure in our household. My Dad, Leo, was the passive, non-confrontational, laid back bread winner. We were a middle class family in suburban Baltimore. My sister, Kathryn, known as Kitty, is six years my senior. My Dad is Polish, and Mom is a coal miner's daughter from St. Charles, Virginia, which is in the middle of the Blue Ridge Mountains. During World War II, Mom traveled to the big city to find work, and Dad was her supervisor at Glenn L. Martin Company, which at the time built sea planes. They fell in love and married. An interesting fact that I didn't find out about until a few years ago was that it almost never happened. Mom's dad and my future grandfather, Maynard Thompson, found out about the wedding and drove from Virginia to Baltimore with his brother to stop the ceremony! They didn't get there in time. God obviously had other plans. I was one of them.

We were a very typical middle class household, with Mom staying at home taking care of me and my sister, and Dad working a nine-hour day. Baltimore was Dad's home, and he came from a huge family. This meant I had aunts and uncles and cousins all over town. In the 50s and 60s, everything seemed to revolve around family. Saturday morning visits downtown with my Dad to visit my grandmother were commonplace. Recreation often meant going swimming somewhere. Dad loved the water, and my earliest remembrance is going to a placed called Holly Beach, which was on the Chesapeake Bay. It must have been the summer of '56, because I remember the adults dancing in the picnic area to a song they played over and over again; 'Rock around the Clock,' by Bill Hayley and the Comets. Some of my fondest memories are of a place known in our family as 'the shore,' which was a big house my Aunt Mary owned on Bird River, which was also connected to the Chesapeake. The family would gather on weekends for swimming, steamed crabs, Esskay hotdogs, Rolling Rock Beer, and the Baltimore Orioles on the radio. As long as I can remember, I loved swimming and playing in the water, and anything to do with it. Boats, fishing, crabbing, I was all over it most weekends in the summer. I would hope and pray one of my uncles who had an outboard motor would show up so we could attach it to one of the rowboats. Like a normal kid, I had an interest in anything that was motorized. I also had an early interest in the Rolling Rock! I looked for ways to sneak into the rickety old garage and see if I could drink a whole one on my own.

Years later, I would connect the dots and discover that addiction runs in both sides of my family. It would one day become an issue with me, but at the time I was just a kid trying to secretly imitate what the grownups did. Drinking and smoking at the time was very commonplace and very acceptable.

It must have been some time in 1960 when my sister came to the conclusion one Sunday morning that Jesus died for her sins. The reality of that became very apparent, when driving home from church one particular Sunday morning, she and Mom were in the front seat, sobbing. I was about ten at the time, and there's nothing more awkward than being a kid in the back seat of a car with a couple of women just crying and crying. The reality was, my sister had 'gotten it.' The gospel, that is. It clicked, the light went on, whatever. So Kitty made the decision to 'walk the aisle' during the invitation the next Sunday, and was going to be baptized.

Mom, sensing an opportunity, I guess, explained that my sister had decided to ask Jesus to come into her heart, and wouldn't I like to do the same thing? Knowing that Mom was the controlling figure in the family, and knowing that I would probably be going to church for the rest of my life (as long as I lived with her!), I think I probably said something like, "Sure, why not?" Though I certainly didn't have any reason to doubt the truth of the gospel, (I grew up with all the Bible stories), the decision was probably made more to satisfy an overbearing mom, rather than a sincere desire of my heart. For whatever reason, my Dad in those days never joined us at church. His background was Catholic, but as far as I could tell, he had no interest in spiritual things. He didn't seem to be anti-religious, like most things he just seemed to be very passive.

Ironically, after I 'got dunked,' as one of my friends called it, I got caught up in shoplifting. We lived about a twenty-minute walk from

Hillendale Shopping Center, and it had lots of stores, and a bowling alley. I was in a bowling league, and I had a custom ball and shoes, and a bowling bag. It was easy for me to go browsing thru Read's Drug Store and just slip a whole bunch of candy bars into my bag! Little portable flashlights from the five and dime store were also a favorite. My partners in crime and I would bury them in the woods in plastic, as if we had to hide the evidence. During this short season of my life, my grandmother on my Mom's side suffered a stroke. This was the first time I heard of this happening to somebody, and I could tell it was a big deal. I was absolutely convinced in my mind she had a stroke because of my shoplifting! I told God I was sorry, that it would never happen again. My kleptomaniac days ended just like that. Grandma recovered. Funny how, from the very beginning, my concept of Christianity was very performance-oriented. Do good, everything is okay. Do bad, and people you love have strokes! Like so many of us, I believed that good deeds would be all you needed to get into heaven.

Since my Dad worked for a defense contractor, it was very cool to be his son. Dad would bring home pictures and artist's renderings of the latest projects they were working on at 'the plant.' I almost failed the 4th grade at Loch Raven Elementary School, because I spent all my time in class drawing airplanes and rockets. The teacher and I did not connect at all, and it was probably my first taste of rejection from an adult. Mrs. Wessner was my teacher from hell. I think my Mom picked up on it. My grades were bad enough that there were some conversations about holding me back for a year. Mom convinced the school principal that "Frank knows the 4th grade," and they moved me on. The 5th and 6th grades were pretty normal and uneventful.

I lived for Little League baseball. Dad had some natural talent, and passed it on to me. I played 3rd base and also pitched. I had a very strong arm for a kid my age, and every season I made the all-star team. Mom made just about every game to cheer me on, and Dad would be there if he got home from work in time. My self-worth as a kid definitely came from my success on the ball field. After a night that I pitched, Dad would rub down my shoulder and pitching arm with rubbing alcohol, just as if I was in the big leagues. I dreamed of playing 3rd base just like Brooks Robinson, or pitching, and of course the team would be the Orioles.

In the middle of the 6th grade, Dad made a major family announcement. His company was merging with another, it would now be known as Martin-Marietta, (which would eventually become Lockheed-Martin) and we were being transferred to Orlando, Florida. Dad would head down there immediately, and we would move at the end of the school year. For a kid growing up in the suburbs of Baltimore, the only thing I knew about Florida was this: they had beaches and flamingoes. Arthur Godfrey did his TV show from Miami Beach and sure looked like he was having fun. Rich people got to go to Florida for vacation. And me? I was getting to move there for the rest of my life!

The Friday before we moved, I was pitching for the Red Sox. I had a good game, but the thing I remember best was my last time at bat. I hit that line shot to right center. There's nothing better than the feeling of knowing that you nailed it, even though it was caught. Since the season wasn't over, Coach Beck asked Mom if somehow I could stay around a few more weeks. It was a nice compliment to have him want me to stick around for a few more games, but with the moving van packed and ready to go, it was a moot point. We hit the road that weekend.

TWO

Florida

———— ✑ ————

Since Martin-Marietta was paying for our relocation, they put us up in a motel for two weeks. Jamaica Inn, on West Highway 50, was a great place for a kid to live if you had to be in a motel. It had a huge swimming pool with diving board, and a full-service restaurant. They had Tiki lamps that were lit every night among the grounds and gardens within the complex. Palm trees were everywhere. It felt like perpetual vacation in paradise. It was the month of June, and it seemed like every day was "mostly sunny, in the upper 80s with a chance of afternoon thunderstorms." And the thunderstorms, when they did happen, were downpours. It would rain for thirty or forty minutes, and then turn sunny again. I soon began to learn about the Florida rainy season. That first summer you could almost set your clock by the afternoon thunderstorms. Of course, we had to find a place to live. A lot of the employees were moving to the west part of Orlando in an area called Pine Hills. It was only about twenty minutes from 'the plant,' which was a straight shot down Kirkman Road.

We settled into a subdivision called Hiawassee Highlands, which was a collection of very typical Florida ranch-style homes. A typical home there consisted of terrazzo floors, usually three bedrooms and two baths, maybe a sunroom, and a garage, but more likely a carport. On average, probably about 1,500 square feet. One eating, and one living area. I had my own bedroom, and my sister and cousin Pat (who had come to live with us) shared a bedroom. I remember Mom and Dad having an adjoining bath next to their bedroom and thinking that was pretty cool. That first home on Villano Avenue was a rental, and I found myself gravitating over to a neighbor's house a block away whenever possible. They had a built-in swimming pool, so I concluded they were probably rich! The first summer in Florida was very hot, and our home, while very adequate, did not have air conditioning. We bought a couple of box fans, and the jalousie windows were always open. At times I had trouble sleeping because of the heat, but all in all, life was good.

A really neat thing we discovered that summer were the Florida beaches. Dad would drive us over to either Cocoa Beach, Daytona, or New Smyrna. You could drive on the beach back then for free. At the most it was about a ninety-minute trip. We'd take sandwiches or cookout burgers, play in the ocean all day, and drive home exhausted. Once when we went to Cocoa Beach, we drove south on A1A to Patrick Air Force Base. Out front were displays of various missiles and rockets, and some of the Martin weapons were on display. It was a source of pride knowing my Dad had a small part in some of those rockets. We also discovered great places like Rock Springs, only about thirty or forty minutes to the north by Apopka. The water was crystal clear, and very cold, but with a mask and snorkel, you didn't really care. I fell in love with Florida virtually overnight. Orlando was called 'The City Beautiful,' probably because of all of the lakes. It seemed like there was water everywhere, and I loved it.

Summer in paradise in 1962 was interrupted by a phone call from Indiana. My grandmother had died suddenly from another stroke. It seemed like we had just made the trip from Baltimore to Florida, and now we were on the road again, as the funeral and burial would be in

Pennington Gap, Virginia. We made the trip in two days, but it was terribly awkward and uncomfortable. Mom and Dad in the front seat, Kit, Pat and I across the back, and it seemed like all Mom did was cry. Of course I was sad, but I had never experienced somebody going through that kind of grief, it was a first for me. I tried to suggest, "Let's stop and visit Ruby Falls in Chattanooga!" and was told very sternly, "This isn't a pleasure trip!"

We got to St. Charles, Virginia, and the whole family, aunts, uncles, and cousins were gathered at my Aunt Helen's. I got to hang out with my cousin Jeff, who was a year younger than me, so we made the most of it and had typical boy fun. I guess my parents concluded this was as good a time as any to begin to share 'grownup' issues like death and funerals. I remember Jeff and I were considered too young to go to the funeral and burial, but we were taken to the funeral home during visitation hours. We sheepishly approached the coffin, stood there looking at our grandmother, feeling uncomfortable. I think Mom said something like, "See, it's just like she's sleeping." A moment later it was time to leave, and that was it. We stayed for another day and headed back. I distinctly remember stopping by the graveyard on the way out of town. Kit, Pat and I waited in the car as Mom and Dad walked arm in arm down the hill to the gravesite. I think my Dad was probably a good comforter. He was never one for a lot of words, but I get the feeling he was very steady, stable, and consistent. Mom was definitely more emotional, while Dad was more laid back, quiet and even keeled. That's probably why they lasted so long together as husband and wife.

That summer I had to register for school, and I was going to be in the 7th grade. The nearest school was Maynard Evans Junior and Senior High, a few miles away, but because of some crazy zoning law I would be going to Ocoee Junior and Senior, in the town of Ocoee, which was about ten miles west. Evans was definitely more suburban, and Ocoee was definitely what you would call rural. It seemed like the city of Ocoee was cut right out of an orange grove. They didn't call it Orange County Florida for nothing. Before the freezes of the 80s, which wiped out a lot of citrus growers, there were citrus trees everywhere. The Ocoee High driveway where the bus would drop us off was right next to a grove, and you could smell the orange blossoms, or at times the smell of rotting fruit that didn't get picked and was decomposing on the ground.

We started school in September, and one thing I noticed was that some of the younger kids were riding motor scooters and motorcycles to school. After some research, I found that in the state of Florida, you could get your restricted driver's license at age fourteen, and operate a motor scooter or motorcycle up to five horsepower. So this included scooters like Vespa and Lambretta, and small motorcycles by Honda and Yamaha. I thought this was a great law! I befriended a guy named James Abbott who lived up the street, and he owned a Cushman Scooter. James looked a little bit like he came out of the movie 'Grease,' and the thunder coming out of his loud exhaust pipe on his scooter fit him to a tee. He would drive by, exhaust pipe roaring, and there was definitely envy there on my part. He was a year ahead of me, in the 8th grade, and we would often ride the bus together if he wasn't on his scooter. And of course whenever he was on his scooter, I was looking to hitch a ride. Even though I was just twelve when I started the 7th grade (my birthday falls in December), I began to plot and scheme in my mind how I could have my license and a scooter when I turned fourteen! I noticed that one kid had a Honda 150, which I knew was probably ten or fifteen horsepower, so I wondered how closely the local law enforcement monitored the five horsepower law. Often times before we took the school bus home, we would go by where the bikes were parked and watch their owners crank 'em up. The Honda 150 had electric start, no kick-starting. Of course as he zoomed away on his bike, that kid was the envy of all of us underlings who were relegated to riding on the bus.

Seventh grade at Ocoee was relatively uneventful. I would occasionally get into trouble, but nothing very serious. In the early 60s in Florida schools corporal punishment was still around, and I remember getting 'licks' a few times. Since Ocoee was an older school, many rooms were not air conditioned, so big oscillating fans in the classrooms were the norm. I met my first girlfriend, Connie Lusk, who lived across the street from my friend, Don Vickers. We all rode the bus together. Don's house became a regular hangout, since he also was a ballplayer, and had a bunch of brothers. We also built a homemade go-cart with an old lawnmower engine. It was kind of primitive, wasn't anything to look at, but it was a thrill to motor our creation up and down his street. It wasn't a scooter or a cycle, but it had an engine, and for me, that was really all that mattered. I gravitated toward anything that was motorized. We would scrape up fifty cents, get a couple of gallons of gas in a can, and we were good to go.

That spring I played Little League in Ocoee, and once again was a starting pitcher. The opening day of the season they had a parade, and Connie led the parade, sitting up in the backseat of a convertible, just like out of a Miss America parade. Looking back, this may have been the beginning of enjoying what others thought of me, or, trying to impress people. There was definitely a feeling of pride. I mean, here's this pretty girl in a convertible leading the Little League parade, and she's my girlfriend! I had a so-so season playing ball, and was excited that Orange County was building a new junior high school in Pine Hills. Robinswood Junior High would be ready for the next school year. And I was psyched, because they would have their own basketball and baseball teams. I was determined to make both.

After renting for a year in Hiawassee Highlands, we began to look for a home to buy. I thought this was great fun. To this day I still love looking at houses, and if I could have a second career, I think it would have to do with waterfront real estate or home building. We looked at a subdivision within a stone's throw of the Martin plant, called Tangelo Park, but didn't find anything we liked. We also looked at a very modest house in a town called Windermere, and it was on a lake! I'll never forget that as we were touring the house, the lady who lived there walked up from the lake, displaying what had to have been at least a five-pound bass that she had just caught. Of course I'm thinking to myself, "This is it!" After some long discussions, Mom vetoed the idea, saying something like, "What if there is a hurricane and the water comes up and floods the house?" Even though I had not yet really discovered all of the ins and outs of my parents' marriage, I remember thinking at the time, "Hey Dad, come on, you've got to be kidding me, we could have a blast here! Tell her this is it!" As usual, Mom won out.

And in hindsight, they missed a tremendous opportunity. Windermere is now a premiere address, the home of Tiger Woods and other wealthy athletes, and surrounded by one of the most pristine and beautiful chains of lakes, the Butler chain. The house we walked through was for sale for about $15,000. My guess is the house is gone, and a mansion has replaced it, probably worth millions. One of my early dreams in life after that was to have a home someday on the Butler chain of lakes. Little did I know that one day that dream would come very close to coming true.

My sister ended up marrying her high school sweetheart, John, that summer. He really was (and is) an exceptional guy and their wedding was a real event. We drove back to Baltimore for the wedding and got to spend a few more days down at the shore. (My sister and brother-in-law are to this day two of my heroes. They've raised three awesome kids. I'm Uncle Frank to Johnny, Jeff, and Lena. Kit and John always welcomed me into their home without reservation, all I had to do was call and say I was coming to visit. I'm grateful they are family.)

We ended up buying a three-bedroom two-bath home on Hastings Street in a neighborhood called Robinswood. Dad's commute was still about twenty minutes, and I could ride my bike to the new junior high School. New friends were Mary, who lived right behind us, and a couple of guys my age, Terry and Bill, down the street. Terry had a basketball hoop in the driveway, so I started to get interested in basketball, especially since Robinswood would have a team.

Something else was also interesting about our home on Hastings Street. Whenever you were on the phone at our house, very faintly in the background you could hear a radio station over the phone line. WHOO radio was at 990 on the AM dial, and their radio towers were no more than a half-mile away, a few blocks over and through some woods. Since the woods were a great place for a kid to camp out, my first exposure to a radio station was at WHOO. It was pretty common to head over there during a camp out, and try to talk the overnight announcer into letting us come in and watch him work. Sometimes it was yes, and sometimes it was no. When it was yes and we were granted access, I found it fascinating. Of course, at this age I wasn't thinking about career choices, I was just a kid camping out, looking for fun things to do. And camping out and visiting the local radio station in the middle of the night was definitely fun.

Being the first new students in an all-new school was great. We didn't have a cafeteria yet, so we would bring our own lunch, or McDonalds made hamburgers available for twenty cents each. The new campus was air conditioned, but we didn't have showers yet for the locker rooms.

One of my first remembrances was of Coach Jim Dzurus, who was my PE instructor, and he was also the basketball and baseball coach. Put bluntly, the guy was a stud. Probably 6'2", in great shape, and just out of the University of Florida, where he played baseball. He had a whiteboard on the way into the locker room, and he was a great cartoonist. It was always fun to see what he had drawn on the board on your way in to get changed.

I tried out for the basketball team, but got cut; I think I was probably in the second tier of guys. I was also short, probably 5'2 or 3. I was a late bloomer, and even though now I'm 6'2", I didn't really grow that much all the way through high school. I volunteered as the team manager, or ball guy. This was great since I got to travel with the team to away games. Even though I wasn't a player, I had the cool white Converse sneakers with the blue laces. I did make the baseball team that year, though I didn't start. Being one of the smaller guys, this was a feeling of great accomplishment. I was playing ball with some of the more popular guys in school. There was definitely a group that was considered 'the jocks,' and I was now included in that group. My girlfriend for a while in the 8th grade was a cheerleader named Brenda Kelly. Like most kids I wanted to fit in, so having a cheerleader as a girlfriend was a plus. I didn't get that much playing time that year on the team, but I did have a great outing pitching against the Lyman High School Junior Varsity team. We played them up in Apopka, and these guys were huge. I shut them down for five innings, and the game was called because it was getting dark. I didn't have much power against these guys, but I had a wicked curveball, and I had them pretty frustrated. The season ended a couple of games later, and I felt confident the next year I could either pitch or maybe play second base. My grades were pretty good, my girlfriend was a cheerleader, and I got a letter for baseball. I was also playing Little League that summer. I bought an LP called 'Meet the Beatles.' It was the end of 8th grade, 1964, and life was great. That would all change in the next year.

Looking back on my childhood, it's interesting the way things shaped us. Like most kids in junior high, I had a desire to be popular and well-liked. I was always bugging Mom to buy me the latest clothes so I would be cool. I became more fashion-conscious. Things like wanting penny loafers, or the original 'Bass Weejuns' for my shoes. It's obvious in retrospect I was looking toward athletics to gain acceptance among my peers. I guess you could say my identity was wrapped up in being a ballplayer. And a pitcher, of course.

My freshman year I took the normal courses, and I also took Algebra II with a teacher named Mrs. Ann Schneider. As I remember, Mrs. Schneider was a little more outgoing and more engaging than your average everyday teacher. She looked a little bit like she could have been a movie star. She had a certain flair about her, blonde and buxom. She actually lived right across the street from us, had a very handsome husband, and two beautiful little kids, a boy and a girl, both blonde. As a family they had the appearance of happiness and success. She had a habit of always passing out a piece of hard candy before a test or a quiz. I guess she thought a little sugar buzz would help your performance. I struggled with Algebra, and by the time baseball season came around, I was failing the course. My Mom, being the enforcer in the household, basically said, "No pass, no play." I went out for the team, but was told it wouldn't matter, I wouldn't be playing. I think I tried to brush it off, but looking back, the decision left me devastated. Coach Dzurus contacted Mom to ask her, "Are you sure?" It was a done deal. A few months later, Mrs. Schneider found out and confided in me she would have changed my grade, had she known I wouldn't be playing ball! This was a shock, as I had no idea back then that a teacher would even think about doing something like that for a student, much less me.

Before my Mom died in 1986, she told me this was one instance she wished my Dad had taken a stand with her and overruled the decision.

I've always known my Dad was a good guy. But he didn't become a Christian till later in life. Also, since his own father died when he was six, he had no real reference on being a dad. Rather than take a biblical leadership role in the family, Mom ruled, she made the decision I wouldn't play, and that was basically the end of the story. I also noticed that spring I was having problems with my pitching arm. I had pain when I threw, but tried to ignore it, figuring over time it would get better. It never did. Looking back, it was probably a bad decision to be throwing so many curveballs at such a young age. I didn't really have the power to blow people away with fastballs, so I always got by on my 'junk' pitches. I've always been a fierce competitor at whatever I did. Experimenting with other pitches besides the basic fastball seemed to give me an edge. In the mid 60s we weren't concerned with pitch counts and the other things that coaches and dads watch out for today. It was a moot point, as my playing days were over.

I got through the 9th grade with just okay grades, and would now be going to Maynard Evans High School. I started spending the summers mowing yards wherever I could find work. Usually two to three bucks was the going rate. One thing I remember distinctly growing up was developing a good work ethic. Mom and Dad had made it clear that anything with an engine, I would be paying for it. Okay, fine, I'll work. Mom would actually drive me to different mowing jobs if they weren't close, and we'd have the lawnmower sticking out of the back of the trunk. She'd help me get it in and out. One day she dropped the thing on a finger, getting it out, and it got really smashed up. She was actually crying from the pain, and had to go to the clinic. Looking back, it seems it would have been a lot easier just to give me the two dollars! I was taught from an early age that work is a good thing. I found out later in life it is also a God thing.

Our world was rocked that summer when police cars and ambulances converged on our neighborhood, and ended up right across the street at Mrs. Schneider's house. The next morning she was on the front page of the Orlando Sentinel, as she had taken her own life as well as the lives of her two precious children. All gunshot wounds to the head. I was shocked, as was everybody in the neighborhood and everybody from school. Evidently it was problems with their marriage. 'Batman' was the big TV series at the time, but this was real life drama with a lady who was kind enough to care about one of her struggling students not being on the baseball team. I can only think that mentally she must have been 'off' to take her own life and the life of her precious kids. All I knew at the time was she was an adult who had taken quite a personal interest in me, and she was suddenly and violently gone. I was very distraught over it, and I knew I would miss her.

THREE

High School Blues

⸺◦⁓◦⸺

Maynard Evans High School was a big school with a student population of probably about 2,000. They always had a great basketball team, but we were terrible at football. Let me be blunt. High school was misery for me. I was very self-conscious of the way I looked, which was short and a little fat. I was developing a pretty good shot as a basketball player, but didn't have a prayer of making the team, being as short as I was. My grades were just average or a little below, and I had few friends.

Like most of the kids of the day, I began to get caught up in the excitement of the music that was coming out of the radio. At the time we had two Top 40 radio stations battling each other, WHOO at 990 on AM, and WLOF at 950. WLOF eventually beat their competition, even though they had an inferior signal. Everybody listened to WLOF. They were fun to listen to, and they were nationally known for 'breaking' the hits, in other words, playing new songs first that would become hits. They always had stuff going on, like sponsoring 'The Battle of the Bands' at shopping centers. It seemed like in the mid 60s everybody wanted to start a band or be in a band. Weekends I would get a ride to the Orlando Youth Center, where we could shoot pool, and dance to local bands. They would usually cover the national hits of the day, stuff by the Stones, The Kinks, The Beatles, the Animals, and so forth. Since I was too shy to really approach a girl and ask her to dance, I would spend my time hanging out, listening to the music, shooting pool, and just trying to look cool.

While Saturday night might have been at the youth center, my Sunday mornings were still at church. Dad still stayed home, and Mom and I went to Hyland Baptist Church, the home of Reverend George Brown. I guess you could say I put in my time there on Sunday mornings. Reverend Brown had two sons; Lonnie, who was probably seventeen or eighteen, and Kenny, who was my age. The three of us would be on the back pews of the church, trying to sneak in a nap. Only thing was, Reverend Brown had a tendency to scream and shout from the pulpit, so it was pretty hard to sleep. One thing was clear to me during those teen years: the church was not relevant to me. I was there because I had to be, no other reason. Kenny actually became a lead singer with one of those bands at the Youth Center, and I'm sure he was also just putting in his time just like me because he had to, since his dad was the pastor.

The summer of 1966 I was fifteen, and though I was running about a year behind schedule, I got my restricted driver's license, took my savings from cutting lawns, and bought a used Lambretta motor scooter for $125. I think my mother was shocked that I actually pulled this off. Dad went with me to pick out the scooter, and it was red and white. What I didn't figure in my plans was insurance. Mom and Dad covered that and I now had wheels. There was no helmet law in Florida, and you very seldom saw a kid on a scooter or motorcycle wearing a helmet. (A few years later I would purchase a very fast Kawasaki 350 motorcycle, have a very scary wreck, and wearing a helmet would save my life.)

I landed my first 'real' job, at the newly opened Burger Chef just a block away from school. Burger Chef was a franchise that was a knockoff of McDonalds. Really about the only difference was our burgers were charbroiled. Mr. and Mrs. Haberkamp were the owners (Mrs. Haberkamp and her son, Tim are still there to this day, it is now a Hardees), and I made ninety cents an hour. I was the fry guy, making the French fries and fillet of fish. The Haberkamp's were nice folks but absolutely no nonsense, so they reinforced the work ethic I was developing with my lawn business. At Burger Chef, if you have time to lean, you have time to clean!

My senior year at Evans was probably my worst of the three years there. I flunked out of chemistry, and also had a hard time with geometry. I ended up taking 'business arithmetic.' I was convinced this must be the math class for the very slow students, but since it was pretty easy for me, I was glad just to find a class I did okay in. I also began to spend more time cutting class, hopping in a car with a friend or two and heading to Daytona Beach for a few hours, or up to Wekiva Springs, or over to Burger Chef for lunch. I got caught a lot, and spent a lot of time in the school office. Mom would have to come in, we would have visits with the guidance counselor, and the standard line was, "Frank is a smart kid, he just needs to apply himself."

I had a few friends I hung out with, but I definitely felt insecure and unsure of myself. At Evans we had 'service clubs' that were sort of like fraternities. There was The Interact Club, The Key Club, and The Optimist Club. Of course, you had to be asked to join, and it was painful to be left out. I had little emotional support from my parents in dealing with my insecurities. Don't get me wrong; they weren't bad parents. In those days they just didn't have the resources that involved parents have available today. Reflecting back to those years, my parents and I just did not communicate that much. Not having athletics or anything else to fall back on, and certainly not grounded in any sort of faith experience, I was pretty miserable.

One guy I did hang out with, Mike Mazur, had a part-time job at radio station WLOF. I didn't realize it at the time, but before the government deregulated radio, you had to have an FCC (Federal Communications Commission) operator's license to operate a radio station. Mike found out that WLOF had what was called directional antennas, which required people operating the station to have a first class FCC license. Getting a first class license wasn't the easiest thing to do, and Mike had attended an electronics school in Sarasota where you could cram the questions and answers for five weeks and learn enough to test with the FCC in Miami and get your license. His first class license got him a part-time job taking the transmitter readings at WLOF, which eventually led to him getting an overnight air shift on the weekends. I began to hang out there whenever he worked, and thought that was just about the neatest job anybody could have in the world. Rock and roll music, buttons, dials, meters, posters on the walls, and girls calling in on the request line, which seemed to ring non-stop. The guys who worked at WLOF full-time seemed like big time celebrities to me. Names like Peter Jay, Pat O'Day, Johhny Gee, and Bill Vermillion. And now my friend Mike was connected to that group. I began to think that radio might be a fun way to make a living, but never really imagined that somebody like me could pull it off.

While Mike was working at WLOF, I had left Burger Chef for greener pastures, washing dishes at the grill at Walgreens ($1.10 an hour, up from ninety cents), and then moved on to a job at Jamaica Inn (the place where we stayed when we moved to Florida) as a bellhop. My friend, Dana was also working there and he told me the tips were good. The PGA tour came through town, and I carried luggage and got ice for pros like Tom Weiskopf and Bert Yancey. Mr. Weiskopf was a good tipper. Not so Mr. Yancey. I think he stiffed me! The job was boring when it was slow, but I liked walking the grounds, lighting the torches, and helping people whenever I could. I think from an early age I just liked working in general. To this day I've always felt maybe I wasn't always the most talented at certain things, but I've always been tenacious and persistent. Somebody else might have more talent, but that's okay, to get ahead I'll just work harder! Mom and Dad weren't rich by any means, but they were both consistent in getting up every day and doing whatever needed to be done. In a certain way, I guess that rubbed off on me. While I had little interest in school, I had lots of interest in work and making money. My concern was: Could I get a decent job somewhere without college? I knew my grades weren't that great, and I certainly wasn't scholarship material. I began to realize that certain colleges might not accept me at all because of my poor grades. The more I hung out over at WLOF, the more I started thinking I might want to give radio a try. I just didn't know how to go about it. The door opened for Mike because he had that first class license. I didn't have a license, but I did have a lot of dreams, desire, determination, and a boatload of ambition.

During my senior year of high school we got a new pastor at church. His name was Neil Shirey, and his background was being a chaplain in the Navy. He was much more laid back then the screaming Reverend Brown. He was personable, and genuinely a nice guy. To me, church was still pretty much a waste of time, but the neat thing was, Neil would stop by often and just visit my Dad. Dad's background was Catholic, and I don't ever remember him going to church with us. My only recollection of him being in a church at all was once in Baltimore, I think we were there with his mom and family. I just remember the smell of incense, candles, and everybody was very somber, serious, and they did that cross your heart thing. Everybody had a very sad face like somebody had just died. I thought it was all rather morose and spooky!

Dad was really into yard work, and I think our lawn at 5801 Hornet Drive was award-winning. We had thick, lush St. Augustine grass. After it was mowed and edged, it really looked awesome. Neil would stop by and I'd see Dad stop his yard work and they would chat. I really didn't think anything of it, until one day, Mom announced to me that Neil had led my Dad to Christ. He began going to church with us, and though I didn't realize it at the time, my Mom had been praying for him for a long, long time. She never nagged him, and never as far as I could tell even talked to him much about spiritual issues. She just prayed and prayed. And sure enough after about twenty-five years, God answered her prayers. After all of those years of staying home on Sunday, Dad began attending church.

With a few months to go before graduation, it became clear I didn't have enough credits to graduate with my class. I wouldn't be doing the graduation ceremony with the cap and gown, and even though it was my fault I didn't take care of business with school, I still took it as another rejection. I would be done after taking a class in summer school, so basically I had to go to school another ten weeks or so. A popular teacher named Mr. Barber taught an Americanism vs Communism class, and that would give me enough credits to be finished. I jokingly tell people I graduated from Maynard Evans High School, class of 1968 and a half!

Most seniors in 1968 were either moving on to college in the fall, or going into some kind of construction work to help build Disney World, and some guys enlisted in the service. Of course, Vietnam was going on at this time, and many guys went to school to get a student deferment, which would keep you out of the draft. There was always the possibility of me getting drafted, but my thought was, "I'll deal with that when and if it comes up." I was fairly informed about the war, and soon I would hear of a friend who had died there, but my life at the time was pretty out of touch politically and very self-centered.

I got a full-time job through a friend at the Goodyear Tire retread plant. I worked in the cleanup department with a nice black guy named Marvin. After the tires came off the press, we'd put the tire on a machine that spun the tires and we would clean off the excess rubber, put some black stain on the tire, and then we had a machine that whitened the white walls. It was hard work, but I was making about $60 a week, still living at home, so for a while anyway this was a pretty good deal. I began to gravitate a little more toward the counterculture. Growing long hair was easy to do, and a few of us began to go surfing on a regular basis over at Cocoa Beach, about an hour away. I began to occasionally smoke pot and drink, mostly beers. I found acceptance with a few friends from school who were getting into the drug scene. My life right out of high school basically consisted of working hard Monday thru Friday, surfing on the weekend, occasionally getting high, and starting the cycle over again on Monday morning. I bought a 1953 Ford station wagon just because I thought it looked like a neat surf-mobile. It was easy to put down the backseat and sleep in the back at the beach in a sleeping bag. Always wanting to fit in, I would cruise through the Steak n Shake on Saturday nights, surfboards on top. Of course, I thought I was very cool.

During this time, my parents, who were both now attending church on a regular basis, pretty much let me do my own thing. I guess they thought even though I was living at home, I was now out of high school, and would be moving out soon, or moving on to something somewhere. I don't think they had any idea about the drugs, and out of respect to them, if I would be coming home a little out of it, I made sure it was after they went to bed.

One day, Mom told me that the reason she had taken a job a year earlier being night manager at a restaurant was to help save money for me to go to college. I really had no idea that financially they had been making plans if I wanted to go to school. Looking back, it is odd that she shared this news with me after I was out of high school. With that news, I began to think, "Okay, seriously, it looks like I've got some money available to get some sort of education, what exactly would I like to do?" I was still seeing Mike occasionally over at WLOF, and I found out that there was such a thing as 'broadcasting school.' I did some research, and found out about a school in Atlanta called Career Academy.

Looking back, I think a lot of trade schools popped up around the country to take advantage of the servicemen coming back from Vietnam with their GI bill money. A lot of those guys wanted to go to school when they returned, and schools like Career Academy had courses for things like radio, sportscasting, and would you believe the same school could teach you how to be a dental assistant! Since Mom and Dad had some money saved, and since I wasn't really going anywhere recapping tires, I proudly made the announcement to them: "I think I'd like to get into radio!" I can only guess the reaction going through their minds at the time was, "Thank goodness you've decided you wanted to do SOMETHING. Now would you please leave as soon as possible?" I applied to the school, we made a down payment, and I was nervous that when they saw my transcripts from high school they would turn me down. Another rejection? Not likely. At Career Academy, if you had the cash, you were in! I finished out a few more months at Goodyear, said goodbye to my hardworking friend Marvin, and prepared to move to Georgia.

FOUR

Atlanta

———— ✺ ————

I t was January 1969, and Mom and Dad drove me to Atlanta, which is normally about an eight-hour trip from Orlando. Just hop on the Sunshine State Parkway, get I-75 at Wildwood and head north. They had a 1965 Dodge Dart, and we were towing my old Ford station wagon behind it with a tow bar. I could have probably made the trip myself, but I think they thought my old surf-mobile might not make it. Mom and Dad helped me unload my stuff, we had a hug and said goodbye. Mom cried (much like she did when my sister left home and married), and I was clueless of what the fuss was about. I had no problem leaving home or my surroundings, and felt like I was embarking on an exciting new adventure. I had no fear. I had no idea how this was going to work out, and didn't know if I could learn enough to get into the radio business, but I was at least going to give the school a good shot and my undivided attention. While high school seemed like a waste of my time, at least I could learn something here that could possibly put me on a career track. Some Career Academy grads had actually found real jobs in the radio business.

The school had most of the students rooming for a reduced rate at an old hotel on Ponce De Leon Avenue. I was rooming with a Vietnam vet,

Andy, who had lost his foot in the war. It seemed like a lot of vets bought electronics overseas and brought them home, and Andy had a very cool reel to reel tape recorder. He had one album on tape, The Beatles' White album. Even though he asked me not to mess with his stuff, I couldn't resist listening to the Beatles on his machine. Whenever he was away, I had a habit of secretly listening to 'Rocky Raccoon,' 'While My Guitar Gently Weeps,' 'Blackbird' and 'Julia,' over and over again.

Our hotel was a little southeast of downtown, and it was about a twenty-five-minute ride up through Piedmont Park to Northeast Peachtree Street where Career Academy was located in a bank building. Our routine consisted of getting up early enough to get some scrambled eggs and toast downstairs, which was served dormitory-style and was part of our package deal. Then I would carpool with three or four other guys to school. The head instructor at the broadcasting school was a guy named Dan Rotundo, and he looked like he was out of the Marines. Our days at school consisted of reading commercial scripts, re-writing and delivering newscasts, and of course learning how to run a control board. Since I wanted to be a disc jockey, I had a mock air shift where I played records, did the news, read commercials, the whole bit. Our call letters were WCAB (for Career Academy School of Broadcasting), and we really did try to run it like a real radio station. Of course we weren't really on the air, but everything was simulated pretty accurately. I wasn't there too long when I thought to myself, "Well, I don't know if I'm any good, but I do think I can do this."

Our down time away from class consisted of pickup basketball games, and it always seemed like there was a card game going in somebody's room. I wasn't legal drinking age yet, so I was always on the lookout to pick up a beer or two from somebody older. Often for lunch we would head to Lums Hot Dogs, and since a lot of the guys I was with looked older, I could order a beer there and was never asked for ID. Suffice it to say, I liked Lums a lot.

After about three months or so, I felt like I had learned everything I was going to learn at the school. It was a six-month course, and of course the hotel and everything was paid for in advance, so I felt like I needed to finish what I started. Mom and Dad were sending me some spending money, but of course like any nineteen-year-old, I felt it wasn't enough, so I got a job delivering pizzas at a take-out pizza shop over by Georgia Tech. Dominos wasn't around yet, but Pizza Quick was. It was run by a guy named Gary, and his girlfriend, Sharon. Gary took a liking to me, and I was making some pretty decent extra money delivering pizzas. The tips were good, and they even had a little red three-wheeler delivery truck I tooled around town in. I got to know Atlanta pretty well, and I liked it.

Since some of the guys at Career Academy wanted to be sportscasters, I made some trips with them to see the Braves when the season opened. Underground Atlanta, Georgia Tech, Piedmont Park, Six Flags, The Varsity drive-in, I liked it all. I also loved 89 WQXI, which was the big Top 40 powerhouse radio station in Atlanta. They had a terrific morning guy, Skinny Bobby Harper, who eventually became the inspiration for the Dr. Johnny Fever character on the TV show 'WKRP in Cincinnati.' We all listened to 'Quixie in Dixie' whenever we could, and one morning we talked Bobby into letting us come in and watch him work for about an hour. During a newscast, I watched as he ran up and down a big flight of stairs to pick up a coffee, then immediately sat down and did his on-air break as if nothing had happened. I was mesmerized by his control over everything going on around him; the music, the commercials, the newsman, the sports guy, the phone calls. It was as if he was in a world all his own, and I got to watch his world for a few minutes firsthand. It was impressive stuff. It was about ten levels above my little simulated world at WCAB.

Gary, my pizza friend, was going to open up a sporting goods store south of town off of I-75, and we drove out one afternoon to look at the site. I guess Gary recognized my work ethic, because he asked me if I'd like to help him launch the store and go to work for him full-time. I was flattered by his proposition, but my primary goal was to finish my radio course, head back home and look for a job in the business. On the way back to the pizza shop, we stopped at a new mall called Greenbriar. He told me he had to pick up something for Sharon. Inside the mall we walked up to a red and white walk up take-out restaurant that looked like it was built right into the wall. I'd never seen anything like it. We picked up some sandwiches and headed back to the shop. At the time, this was the only place you could pick them up. Sharon absolutely loved these sandwiches, and whenever he was close to the mall Gary would pick one up for her. I liked the sandwich too. It was a chicken breast on a bun, with a pickle. It was called Chick-fil-a.

In June 1969 I finished up my course at Career Academy. They had a little graduation ceremony at a hotel, and of course Mom and Dad drove up. I got a certificate, saying I had completed the course, and I think I had about a B average. It wasn't anything like having a college degree, but I felt I knew at least enough to get an entry-level job somewhere. Back then, to apply for a radio job you needed three things: a resume, an audition tape, and at least a third class FCC broadcast license. Getting your third was not a big deal. Study a few questions for a few hours and it was more like a glamorized driving test, except it was about radio stuff. Getting your second class or first class license was much more difficult. It was very technical with a lot of math and formulas. A third class was good enough to get you into a few doors, though getting that first class license could literally open doors for you. I had an audition tape of me doing my shift on the fictional WCAB, and I learned what a professional resume looked like.

I had no idea how much money this whole experience cost, but I'm grateful to Mom and Dad for at least having something set aside. I was particularly grateful to my Mom for taking the night shift manager's job at the restaurant. There were a couple of close calls where she felt like somebody was casing the place to rob it. Fortunately, it never happened while she was there. Being a parent myself, I 'get it' about wanting to provide as best as you can for your kids. My old surf-mobile broke down, and since it wasn't worth what it would cost to fix it, I abandoned it in the garage next to the old hotel on Ponce De Leon. When we got home, Mom and Dad had bought a new 1970 Ford, and passed on their Dodge Dart to me. It ran great, was in great shape, and was quite a gift just for getting through a six-month course. Realizing that their rule "if it has an engine you have to pay for it yourself!" had bitten the dust made their gift that much more special.

FIVE

On the air!

———— ❦ ————

When I got home to Orlando I hit the ground running. I figured since I had no real experience, I would apply at some of the small radio stations in smaller towns around Central Florida. Most decent size towns in those days had at least one radio station that would serve the local community with news, weather, and of course most played some form of music. Talk radio had not even begun to come into its own yet. FM stations were stepchildren of their AM counterparts, with most of them playing 'elevator music' or 'muzak.' AM radio was still king, and most stations played music of one kind or another. Of course my dream job was to work at WLOF, but I didn't even consider it. I knew those guys were in a league of their own. I started knocking on doors and dropping off tapes and resumes.

I hit the local station in Eustis, and there was a little station on the east coast, WMEL in Melbourne. I got a call back for an interview there, but it didn't develop into anything. I was about ready to hit the road again, dropping off more tapes, when I got a callback from WFIV in Kissimmee. I interviewed with a guy named Homer Rhoden, who was known on the air as Big Sarge. Big Sarge did it all. General Manager, Sales guy, Program Director, you name it, he did it. He was pretty much a one-man show running the station. WFIV was at 1080 on the dial, and had a very good 10,000 watt signal. It was a daytime station, meaning at sundown the station would sign off the air to protect other frequencies on 1080. Since it was not a directional station, my third class license would suffice for this job. They played traditional Country music like Jim Reeves, Ernest Tubb, Bill Anderson and Porter Wagoner. They even played a hymn every hour, but I didn't really care. I got the job and heard Big Sarge telling somebody that Frank would work out just fine, because he is coming from a very famous broadcasting school in Atlanta! I realized later he was just selling me, which of course is what salesmen do.

My first shift I actually ran the control board while Big Sarge did a remote broadcast from the Silver Spurs Rodeo in Kissimmee. Of course, this is before the days of cell phones, and we had no two-way communication between the rodeo and the station. I would listen to Big Sarge giving me directions off the air, on the cue speaker, and he would say things like, "Now Frank, if you are hearing me loud and clear and you're getting a good signal from me, I want you to fade the music down and then turn it back up again real fast." This was our little special signal. I would fade the music down, turn it back up, but I guess it wasn't obvious enough because he asked me to do it again. He basically walked me through the broadcast, and we got through it just fine. The problem came when the broadcast was over, and it was my turn to be on the air. I was absolutely scared to death. I stumbled through a couple of breaks when Big Sarge had arrived back from the rodeo. He came in to give me some direction, and I noticed he was whispering something to me. I took my headphones off and realized the music was playing on the air, but I couldn't hear any music coming out of the speakers in the studio. I started asking him in a panic, "What am I doing wrong? What am I doing wrong?" He got a little closer and whispered in my ear, "Frank, you forgot to turn the mic off!"

Once I made it through the first day, and survived, I wanted to learn everything that I possibly could. It was August 1969, and I was the new afternoon guy at WFIV in Kissimmee, known as 'The Mighty Five,' right smack dab in the middle of your radio dial. The lineup consisted of Big Sarge in the morning, a young, talented, handsome guy named Richard Chamberlain doing middays, I did afternoons, and Lee Moss 'The Country Hoss' did fill-ins. The station was about a forty-minute drive from home, and I stayed with Mom and Dad for the few months while I was working there. I was only making $1.60 per hour, so I was doing a night shift at Burger Chef on South Orange Avenue for extra cash. Weekends I began to head over to the beach again to surf occasionally, but often I had a weekend shift and the station began to take first place above everything. Big Sarge wanted me to also sell ad time, but I was terrible at it. Since I wasn't really crazy about rejection, I knew quickly it wasn't my thing, but I acted like I was interested to appease Big Sarge. Frankly, it was all an act. My goal was to learn everything I could, and then move on.

I had been working there for quite a few months when I told Big Sarge I just had to have this one particular weekend off. He was considerate enough to not press me for details, which was a good thing, because I have a feeling Big Sarge would not understand the importance of me having to drive up to the Atlanta Pop Festival. After all of the buzz about Woodstock, festivals seemed to be popping up everywhere. Jimi Hendrix, Grand Funk and others were going to play Atlanta, and I and a friend, Jon Marshall, decided we would drive up. It really was like something out of a movie, with thousands of kids gathered at the old Atlanta Raceway. I got back in time for my shift on Monday. It was quite a contrast, going from watching Jethro Tull live in concert, to playing Hank Williams and Ernest Tubb on the radio.

WFIV was a wonderful learning experience. Big Sarge and the owners were all decent people, and I was just very excited to be on the radio. I wasn't a big fan of Country music, but it didn't matter. I was on the air getting some experience and that was what it was all about. I began to search for my next career move, and it happened north of Orlando in a little town called Mt. Dora. WVGT was at 1580 on the dial, and musically was MOR, or Middle of the Road. This is where you would hear standards from Johnny Mathis, Andy Williams, Herb Alpert and the like. The program director, Sonny George, hired me to do middays and be the music director. This was great because the record companies would mail you free records! This was a big move for me financially, because I moved from the hourly wage to making a whopping sixty bucks a week. I moved away from home, and Sonny and I became roommates, paying $60 a month for the 2nd floor of a house in downtown Mt. Dora. Do the math. I've got no bills, and rent is thirty bucks. I bought a very fast Kawasaki 350 motorcycle from a friend, Steve, and also bought a new surfboard. It's 1970 and I'm living the good life.

I had a frightening experience Thanksgiving morning that year. I was with Mom and Dad for the holiday, and got up early that morning to go for a ride on my bike. I loved riding early in the morning when there was little traffic, and Thanksgiving morning is usually pretty quiet on the streets. My Kawasaki was one of the faster street production motorcycles at the time, and I loved accelerating quickly through the gears. I was accelerating after a light turned green, and when I hit about 40 mph, I was still gaining speed when a guy pulled out of a gas station and made a left turn right in front of me.

I'm sure it's instances like this that led to laws for motorcycles having their lights on at all times. The guy obviously didn't see me. I lurched to the right to avoid him, and then left to recover. That put me headed toward traffic coming from the other direction, so I lurched right again and lost control, running off the road and crashing. Fortunately, I was wearing a helmet. It had a fiberglass face guard that really got scratched up in the fall. Without it my face would have been a disaster. I was really banged up, and I guess my body went into shock because I could feel no pain. My whole body felt numb. I experienced some short-term memory loss, and when I couldn't explain what had happened, the Florida Highway Patrolman wanted to cite me for the wreck! I told him I knew there was no way this could be my fault, and he let me off the hook. I left the hospital on crutches, grateful to be alive. A split second either way and I would have smashed into a car, and I'm certain it would have been fatal. I didn't believe in angels at the time. Reflecting back on that event, I do now.

Things got tense the next year when I received my pre-induction notice from the United States Selective Service. They had the first draft lottery in 1970, which means they actually drew birth dates to see the order in which you might be drafted. My birth date, December 11th, came up number 39. Not good. Realizing I had no deferment, like being a full-time college student, I decided to inquire about enlisting in various branches of the service. I took the initiative to talk to as many recruiters as I could, and thought maybe I could get a commitment to some sort of broadcasting position in the service. No such luck. The Air Force, Navy, etc, all wanted a four-year commitment, and there were no guarantees once I got there I could find anything broadcast-related. So one very early cold Monday morning, I boarded a bus with a bunch of other guys on our way to Jacksonville for our pre-induction physical. A surfing buddy, Jake and I both graduated in '68, and we rode up together.

I began to ponder the fact that I could very well pass the physical, and be on the fast track to being drafted and on my way to Viet Nam.

I began to think about the ramifications of the war, the pros and cons. While I don't think I was radically anti-war, I was not excited about the possibility that I could be asked to go. I don't think I would have dodged the draft, but I had a hard time processing in my mind just exactly what I would do if I passed the physical. While I certainly loved my country, I was your basic self-centered nineteen-year-old kid. Joining the service or getting drafted was just in the way of what I now wanted: a career in the radio business. One of the first things they did when we arrived in Jacksonville was check your blood pressure.

"Do you have a problem with your blood pressure?" I was asked.

"Uh, no sir, not that I know of," I replied.

"Well, you might have one now," I was told.

I think it was probably because I was a nervous wreck! I went through the rest of all of the tests, probably a few hours' worth of moving from examination to examination. At the end of the physical they took my blood pressure again, and once again it was high. It was then I was told that the United States Government would gladly house me there in Jacksonville for three days, and they would take my blood pressure twice a day for three consecutive days to see if it stayed elevated.

Or, the guy in the uniform said, "You can take this form home to your family doctor, have him monitor you twice a day for three days, and mail it back." Easy decision. I took the form.

On the way home from Jacksonville, they broke us up into two groups, the ones who passed the physical, and the ones who failed. Jake (who had some health issues of his own) and I were on the 'happy' bus. Even though everybody on our bus had issues of one kind or another, people were upbeat on the three-hour trip home. The mood was a complete 180 compared to the trip on the way up. Though I had some concern that I might have a medical condition, it paled in comparison to the relief of knowing that I might not be getting drafted and heading to Southeast Asia.

Dr. James Carroll had an office directly across the street from Evans High. At the time, I didn't have a regular physician, but I remembered Dr. Carroll from getting physicals there as a kid. I figured he was as good a choice as any to take the form to. The appointment took about five minutes. He took my blood pressure and commented, "A little high," though he didn't say how much. What came next caught me completely off guard.

"Do you want to go to war?" he asked.

"Not really," I replied.

He filled out the form on the spot, logging six blood pressure measurements over three consecutive days, all with high readings. He scribbled his signature, dated it, handed the form back to me, and I was gone. I dropped the form in the mail the next day. My fears over getting drafted and going to war were over.

I used to spend a lot of energy rewinding the past in my mind. A person's history is just that, history. It's a done deal, and can't be rewritten. I used to waste way too much time lamenting on the past. Should have I enlisted? What if I insisted on Dr. Carroll really monitoring my condition and filling out the form legitimately? Was my condition really bad enough to keep me out of the service? Was I unpatriotic? It's taken many years to get there, but I have found peace with my past. In some of the pages ahead I'll be honestly sharing about some stupid mistakes. What I've concluded is this: I wouldn't be the person I am today without the baggage and mistakes of the past. The good news is that accepting the sacrifice of Christ for those mistakes allows you to move on. Without his sacrifice, I wouldn't be able to break free and have peace with myself and the past. And the Bible says if the son sets you free, you are free indeed.

Randolph Gredes was an attorney from Philadelphia, and part owner of WVGT. Randy was genuinely glad I wasn't getting drafted, and that

I would be continuing to work at the station. Sonny and I had a pretty good relationship, though he probably leaned a little more conservative socially. I had long hair; he was clean cut. I liked to have a beer; he opted for JW Dant Whiskey. He drove an Opal GT, which looked a little bit like a smaller version of a Corvette. It was a blast to drive, and that was a perk of hanging out with Sonny. I got to borrow a cool car! Mt. Dora wasn't more than a thirty-minute drive from home, so I would stop in often to see Mom and Dad, and grab a sandwich or a meal. I was still into the surfing scene on the east coast, so weekends that I didn't work often meant heading over to Cocoa Beach.

Whenever I was in the car, my preset was pretty much locked on WLOF at 950 on the AM dial, and when at the beach, WKKO, at 860. Both were high-energy Top 40 type stations. WLOF in 1970 was still dominating Orlando radio. I dreamed of working there someday. The hits heard on the radio in those days were so diverse. My favorites leaned more toward the 'progressive' sound. Songs like 'Ride Captain Ride' by Blues Image (I would meet the lead singer, Mike Pinera, a few years later in Miami), 'Get Ready' by Rare Earth, 'Venus' by The Shocking Blue, and 'Spirit in the Sky' by Norman Greenbaum. (For the record, I now prefer the version done by DC Talk!) Of course, since WLOF was playing the hits, you also hear songs like 'Close to You' by The Carpenters, 'Bridge Over Troubled Water' by Simon and Garfunkel, and 'Make it With You' by David Gates and Bread. In the meantime, every afternoon on WVGT I'm playing standards by Steve Lawrence and Edie Gorme, but I'm on the air learning all I can, and that's okay by me.

The years of 1969 and 1970, my body decided it was time to get tall. I went to 6'2" in what seemed like no time. Had I had this height in high school, I certainly could have been a jock, but that obviously was not meant to be. I was a jock all right, but the on-air kind.

WVGT began to run into financial difficulties. There were three full-time employees: Sonny, myself, and a nice office lady named Barb. To keep the ship afloat, we began to rotate weekly who would not get paid! Randy encouraged us week after week to hang in there, that "money is on the way." We suspected he was trying to sell, find an investor, or find a partner. Weeks turned into months. At the end of our rope, collectively, we made a big decision.

Randy arrived from Philadelphia one day, was in his office, and all three of us appeared at his door. Sonny was the spokesperson. His speech was short and to the point, and goes something like this: "We've cashed all of the back checks you owe us, and we are all resigning, effective now!" We drove away from the station and headed to Barb's to have a beer. I turned the station on, and since I was on the air, there was no one available to work. The record ran out, and there was nothing but silence. Just the sound of the record needle bumping the end of the vinyl on the record. Besides that, nothing but dead air. YJCMSTU! (You just can't make this stuff up!)

SIX

Gaining experience

————— ⌘ —————

People get into the radio business for various reasons. As for me, I was probably looking for acceptance from my peers. Now that I had a little bit of legitimate experience under my belt, I began to feel surer of myself personally, and professionally. Being on the radio was great for my self-esteem. I didn't know if I had much of a future in the business, but for now, this was all going pretty good. We had a very good part-timer at WVGT, Gabe Burton, who went by the name of Bobby Allen. His full-time gig was at WABR in Orlando, and he did a shift for us on the weekend just to make a few extra bucks. Prior to WABR, he also worked part-time at WLOF and was one of the many guys who went by the name of Peter Jay.

Gabe knew I was now out of work and introduced me to Bob Andrews, who was the Program Director and Chief Engineer at WABR. I got a job doing middays between a great guy named Rick Taylor in the morning, and Bobby, who did afternoons. The pay was a big step up; I think I was making $110 a week. While WFIV and WVGT seemed like little small town radio stations, WABR was a pretty big player at the time in the Orlando market and played Country music. Our on-air slogan was appropriately, 'Top Gun 1440 WABR.' The studios were in a converted old house right by Dubsdread Golf Club.

I ended up getting my first apartment alone, on Princeton Street in College Park, not more than ten minutes from the station. WABR was a great move. I was working with some real pros, and really felt like I was starting to learn the business. Even though we were in a competitive situation with WHOO, which switched to Country, we had some decent ratings, and we had a lot of commercial business on the air. I got reunited with my old high school buddy, Mike Mazur, who worked for us part-time.

Mike and Gabe were always playing practical jokes. The turntables when you were on the air were positioned to the right of where you sat, and the second turntable to the rear was just out of eyesight if you were looking ahead to run the control board. It was not uncommon for somebody to walk by while you were on the air and take the tone arm off of the cued up record. When you hit the remote switch on the board to start the record, nothing happened!

I've stayed in touch with Gabe down through the years, and he reminded me of a time I almost got both of us fired. On Saturday night, we used to broadcast a live Saturday night dance party from a club that played live Country music, called The Rainbow Ranch. I convinced Gabe it might be fun if we played a sound effects record of farm animals faintly in the background during the broadcast. It sounded on the air like the club was right in the middle of a cow pasture! Funny for us, but the client and Bob the boss were not amused.

Bob was easygoing to work for, and I learned a lot. I was reliable and hardworking, and I could tell he appreciated that. When Rick Taylor got hired away to WHOO, I got moved up to the morning shift, along with a nice raise. There is nothing better than working hard, being appreciated, and then getting ahead a little bit. This was also my first experience in learning about loyalty in what can be a very cutthroat business. Since

WABR was a directional station during part of the day, I knew I could have more flexibility with on-air shifts if I had that first class FCC license. Mike had told me about Radio Electronics Institute in Sarasota, where he studied to get his license when we were in high school. I checked it out, and needed about a five-week leave of absence to go get my 'first class ticket,' as they called it. Bob agreed this would be a very good thing for my career, as just having a first class license could open a lot of doors. Bob told me he would cover for me, and I stayed in a little motel in Sarasota while I took the course and studied for the test. Sure enough, almost five weeks to the day, I drove to Miami and took the test at the FCC office. The school had me totally prepared and I passed easily. With my 'ticket' secured, I headed back to resume work in Orlando.

Little did I know that while I was gone, the general manager of the station was trying to convince Bob to have me replaced! Bob basically told him, "If he goes, I go." We both stayed, and I learned what it's like when somebody has your back. As I look back over the past forty-plus years, loyalty has played a big part of my success and longevity in the business. When you do your absolute best for the boss, and stay loyal to them, the good ones don't forget it. One thing I've worked hard at doing is to keep my differences with the boss private. He or she needs to know that even though you may not agree on everything, you are on their team, and will do everything within your power to help them succeed. Bob is quite a legend in the Orlando area, and remained a dear friend. He recently passed away, but he stayed on the air at WLBE in Leesburg until illness prevented him from working.

Rest in peace, Bob. And thank you.

SEVEN

Pamela

—⟡—

W hen I moved back to Orlando, I started going back to church again. They had a new pastor at church, named Frank Loveless, and he and his family moved down from Oklahoma. Frank and his approach leaned on the contemporary side, and his high school son, David, had started a youth choir. There seemed to be more of an acceptance for young people at the church. It was pretty exciting. It seemed to connect with me. The Jesus movement was beginning to spread across the country, and I remember being impacted by a young evangelist named Arthur Blessitt at a big church downtown. All of a sudden it seemed like it was kind of cool to be Christian. I easily fell into hanging out with the young singles at church, and it felt comfortable. Sunday nights after church, visits to Frisch's Big Boy on Colonial Drive, became the norm.

A group of us traveled to Daytona one weekend for some street evangelism. I wasn't that crazy about talking to people but enjoyed hanging with the group. For some reason, it just felt right to me. I met a girl on that trip whose family had just joined the church. We drove back from the beach together. My world was about to officially be turned upside down. Her name was Pam.

'Your Song,' by Elton John. The relationships in my life have always been associated with a song. The first time I fell into a serious relationship, it was Elton John on the radio. And it was all about a beautiful girl named Pam. She was interested in me, I was interested in her, and it clicked. I've never fallen in love so easy, so quick, and so deep. Chicago was playing on my stereo; I liked them and also the soundtrack to 'Jesus Christ Superstar.' Another favorite was the album 'All Things Must Pass,' by George Harrison. This must be why you usually have an Oldies or Classic Hits station in just about every radio market. The songs bring back memories.

Pam worked at Combank and drove a Simca. She was it. If you've experienced head-over-heels-in-love, I don't have to describe the feelings and emotions. There was a convergence in my life between my relationship with Pam, and seeing God answer some prayers and seeming to be semi-involved in my life. For a while it seemed almost euphoric. David from church was also dating Pam's sister, a blonde named Donna. There was definitely something going on with the young people at the church. Pam and I even took part in a youth service, and a whole bunch of kids gave their lives to Christ. It felt good to think that maybe I had a small part in that. More than anything, though, it felt really good at this time in my life to be loved by a girl named Pam. We became inseparable.

Ownership change in radio is part of the business. The government has loosened the ownership rules in the last ten years, and now it seems like just a handful of companies own the majority of stations. But in 1971, the Peterson Family, who owned WABR, sold the station to a company called Rounsaville Radio. Rounsaville had a very famous Top 40 station in Miami called WFUN. When I got word that we might be sold, I began to think about my next move. Often times when new owners move in, the current station management could be on the way out. Rather than react to what might happen, I wanted to be proactive and see if there was a better position at another station. I put together a pretty decent audition tape and got an appointment with Pat O'Day, who did mornings and was the Program Director at the legendary WLOF. He listened to the tape, was cordial, but just flat out told me I had no future in the business. I couldn't tell if he was just being a jerk, or if what he said really had merit. I left his office undeterred. If anything, I left more determined than ever. There was also something down deep inside of me that wanted to someday prove him wrong.

Meanwhile there was a new Top 40 station in Cocoa competing with WKKO. WRKT was at 1300 on the AM dial, and they simulcast the AM station on their FM, WKPE. I got in to see the Program Director, Scott Connelly, and he was interested. I had at least three meetings with him when he finally got the okay from his boss to hire me. WRKT had a twenty-four-hour license, but signed off at midnight. The game plan was to hire me for overnights, and they would be a twenty-four-hour a day operation. I gave two weeks notice at WABR, and they even threw me a nice little going away party. I gave notice at my apartment on Princeton Street, and got ready to move to the beach and the Space Coast.

Cocoa is a smaller radio market than Orlando, and I was going to be doing the graveyard shift, but I was very, very excited to leave Country music and get into Top 40 radio. It's funny how in our lives we all have favorite songs that stick out. It's all about the memories. When you're crazy in love it seems like the memories from those songs during that time period are etched even deeper. I love the music of '71. Some of the hits that were a thrill to play on the radio that year were, 'It Don't Come Easy' by Ringo Starr, 'You've got a Friend' by James Taylor, 'Maggie Mae' and the flip side 'Reason to Believe' by Rod Stewart, and one of my all-time favorites even to this day, 'It's Too Late' by Carole King. The Jackson 5 and the Osmonds were getting their start. The music was still very diverse, from Marvin Gaye, to The Who, to a young Carly Simon. I was now renting a one-bedroom apartment a few blocks away from the ocean in Cocoa Beach. I was at the radio station a lot. I couldn't get enough of the business. My free time was spent with Pam, or at the beach, or listening to other radio stations.

Glen Hill, who was our music director, got word of an FM station in Miami that was doing a Top 40 format. In 1971 this was unheard of. AM radio stations still ruled, and most FM stations played 'beautiful music' that you would hear in the doctor's office waiting room. Of course, the majority of the cars in 1971 only had AM radios. There was a device you could buy at the time at Radio Shack called an FM converter. Hook it up to your AM, and you could listen to the FM stations in your market. Glenn and I would hop in the car and drive south on I-95 until we could pick up the signal from this station in Miami. Usually a couple of hours down the road, around Stuart or Jupiter, we could pick it up, and we were amazed at what we heard. Lots of music, nothing but the hits, and noticeably less commercials. The station was WMYQ, and I didn't realize it at the time, but fast forward a few years and I would be on the air there. It would be my last stop before I left Florida for the ultimate prize in my profession: a job in New York City.

"Chet, thanks for the job, but as soon as you can replace me, I'm leaving." Chet Pike was the General Manager of WRKT, and the only problem we ever had was that he didn't like the way I made the coffee. I got moved up to the morning drive shift and one of my jobs was to get the coffee machine going for the staff about 8am, and somehow I never got it to Chet's liking. He also didn't get the fact that I liked to be on the air barefoot, but as long as I did my job, he didn't seem to care. I think he probably thought I was just a little unusual. I've found many radio people are! My surfing buddy, Jake and I met a guy named Bill Underwood, and

Bill had this great idea we should just take a few months off and go to California and surf. I had a few dollars in the bank, I really didn't have any debt, so I was thinking, "Why not?"

We all left our jobs, loaded into Bill's Mustang, surfboards on top, and pulled a makeshift trailer that slept two. This was the era of 8-track tape players in the car, and we had one tape, by James Taylor. How many times can you hear 'I'm a steamroller, baby' going from Florida to Southern California? Don't ask! We spent the night on the beach in Galveston, and even went surfing at a manmade wave pool just outside of Phoenix called Big Surf. My uncle Larry, from my Mom's side of the family, lived in Long Beach, and I knew he would put us up at least for a few nights. We went surfing at a famous break called Trestles, but the swells were small. We found some very decent waves at Huntington Beach and did some of the tourist stuff, like Hollywood and Vine, and even went to Disneyland.

Before I left Florida, I dropped off some audition tapes and resumes at a few of the Orlando stations. I left my parents' home number as a contact number, and when I called Mom from Disneyland just to say hi, she told me I got a call back from WKIS. Our 'endless summer' surfing trip lasted all of two weeks. Bill missed his girlfriend, I missed Pam, and we were running out of money. The game plan was to work some odd jobs along the way. Great in theory, but not in reality. We drove straight back from California non-stop, rotating shifts sleeping and driving. As soon as I got back, I went in for the interview at WKIS.

EIGHT

Wonderful Kiss

———— ✑ ————

Johnny Mitchell was one happy guy. He was the Program Director at WKIS, and it seemed like this guy was always smiling. You could hear him smiling on the air! He hired me to do the seven-to-midnight shift, and I couldn't believe I got the job. I was making $140 per week and working for a pretty big outfit, Susquehanna Broadcasting Company. WKIS was at 740 on the AM dial, and musically they were a cross between Top 40 and Middle of the Road. Our promotional slogan was aptly named, 'Wonderful Kiss in Orlando.' So we were playing the softer Top 40 hits, like stuff from The Carpenters, Cat Stevens, and The Fifth Dimension. Probably the rockiest song we played was, 'You're So Vain,' by Carly Simon.

We also had a news commentator who was one of the best on-air communicators I've ever heard. Gene Burns moved to Orlando from WCBM in Baltimore, and this guy was obviously a cut above everybody in the market. (Gene recently passed away, and for many years was at one of America's great radio stations, KGO in San Francisco.) Gene originally had a talk show at night on WKIS, but he was moving into a commentary role, and for a while co-hosted the morning show. I remember while working there we had a fatal B-52 crash at McCoy Air Force base, which was just west of where Orlando International Airport now sits. Gene went into the newsroom and just took over. Journalist, newsperson, commentator, master of the English language, THAT was Gene Burns. One of the neat things of this business is to keep tabs on the careers of others that you've worked with. Watching the success and rise of Gene through the years has been really neat. I can say, "Hey I worked with that guy!"

Johnny the PD left shortly after he hired me, and the word was he was marrying somebody who was wealthy, so I'm thinking maybe that's why he was always smiling. Seriously, he just seemed like a very happy-go-lucky guy, and like many people in the business I've worked with, I have no idea whatever happened to him.

The business has a lot of turnover, and a lot of casualties, and I'm fortunate I've survived as long as I have. Johnny got replaced by a very good guy named Jim Boynton, JB for short, but he was soon replaced by a guy from Ohio named Larry Shannon. This guy was quite a showman. We connected and I became his Music Director, and we also became good friends. Larry was all about having fun on the radio, and it made coming to work a blast. Contests, promotions, and having fun were what radio was all about for Larry. We had the 'KIS Sticker Car,' which was a vehicle wrapped with hundreds of WKIS window stickers. Of course, this was way before cell phones, but somehow we had a mobile phone, and we would follow cars that had the sticker, pull them over if they were listening, and give them cash. We eventually gave the car away to a listener who guessed the closest on the number of stickers on the car. WLOF was still the big dog in town, but we sure did do our best to make some noise and give them a run for the money.

Larry and I broadcast the first ever 'Grad Night' live from the newly opened Walt Disney World. The park opened all night for graduating seniors, and we did our show all night from Cinderella's Castle. It was great stuff. Disney, especially that first year they opened, was a very exciting place. Pam got a job there as a tour guide, and I got access with her to a lot of the employee areas. Many people don't know it, but there is a whole other world going on below Main Street USA with a network of tunnels and underground areas. It really was a magical time for Central Florida. WKIS did their best to be right in the middle of it. There was a certain amount of pride being associated with this station. We weren't number one, but we were pretty darn good at what we were doing and were a major player in the market.

For anybody who has been in the business for any amount of time, there is always a "you are not going to believe this!" story or two. At WKIS, it was my telephone call to our chief engineer, John Loving. Engineers are definitely a different breed, and every one I've worked with had their own unique way of doing things. John was no exception, and one very stormy night, when I had just gotten through with my air shift, for some reason we were kicked off the air. I started looking at the transmitter on and off lights, meter readings, etc., and couldn't figure out what in the world was going on. About that time a person who had just been driving by the station was pounding on our side door. This person was yelling, and I almost couldn't believe what they were saying, but I took them at their word, and rushed outside in the darkness to look behind the building out to our tower field.

We had a directional signal with three towers, all in a row. I couldn't believe what I was seeing, and I realized I had to call John as soon as possible. I rushed back inside and made the call.

"Hello?"

"John, it's Frank."

"Hey Frank what's going on?"

"John, a tower just fell."

"What?"

I continued, "John, one of our towers just fell, we are off the air."

John screamed, "Are you XXXXing me?"

"John, I wouldn't lie about something like this," I explained. "A tower just fell over and we are off-the-air!"

He replied, "Okay, I'll be right there."

It's been quite a few years since I've talked to John, but every time I would talk to him, I would ask him how his towers were doing.

Pam and I began to drift apart. It was probably no coincidence that my relationship with God also began to drift. I was getting more consumed with the business, and became friends with the guy who was the seven-to-midnight jock at WLOF. Since we both got off the air at midnight, we began to hang out together after work, mostly talking shop. Warren Miller, known on the air as 'The Janitor,' was an absolute maniac on the radio. Totally unpredictable, and totally high energy. We found out there was a monthly service for air personalities called Programmer's Digest. This was basically a record album that came out monthly with nothing on it but air checks (or recordings of air personalities minus the music), from other radio stations all around the country. All of a sudden we had access to some of the best radio stations and air talent in the country. Folks on the air at powerhouses like WLS Chicago, KHJ Los Angeles, KCBQ San Diego, WABC New York, and somebody who really caught my ear, a morning man on the air at WNBC in New York. His name was Don Imus. Listening to him, I was thinking, "This guy is nuts, or a genius, or both." In a few years, I would find out firsthand.

In the 1970s, music radio stations were thriving all around the country. I began to follow the industry through trade magazines like *Billboard*, which at the time had a pretty extensive section devoted just to music radio. Due to the success of the major market music stations, clones and imitators began to pop up all around the country. Of course, more stations meant more jobs available for air personalities such as me.

Since the turnover rate in the business was so high, there were always job openings around in the business, provided you had no problem with relocating. Relocating with me was never an issue. And since I could tell my relationship with Pam was starting to unravel, I thought a geographic change would help me cope if we ended up splitting up.

I left WKIS, and before I moved on to my next job, I wanted to visit an old high school friend, Wanda Williamson, who had moved to New York. We weren't romantically involved; we had just remained good friends since 7th grade. Since New York was the #1 market, I thought it would be a fun thing to visit and just listen to radio for a week or two. WABC was legendary, and I could also check out this Imus guy who was making so much noise in the industry. I noticed in the classified section of the newspaper ads from a company looking for people to drive cars to different places. You delivered the car to a destination, and your cost was basically gas and tolls. My kind of deal. I found a car that had to get from Tampa to Totowa, New Jersey, which was just west of Manhattan. Lucky for me it was a new Cadillac with about 5,000 miles on it.

I knew that Wanda lived in the Bronx, and that I could probably get a subway there, but would have to get to midtown Manhattan. I delivered the car, and got a bus to Manhattan that dropped me off at the Port Authority Bus Terminal. I called Wanda's number, but the phone number had been changed, and her name was unlisted. She knew I was coming, so I was confused, and I was also stuck! I was right smack dab in the middle of New York City with no place to stay, and clueless on how to even get somewhere, plus I had no place to go. There was a guy who worked part-time for us at WKIS named Bill Donovan. I knew he lived in the New York area somewhere, and I had his number scribbled on a piece of paper somewhere in my wallet. He seemed like a good guy, and after working for us for a while he returned home to New York. I gave it a shot and called the number. He said sure he could put me up for a few days, that he lived in White Plains, and that I needed to get to Grand Central Station to get a commuter train up there.

I grabbed my duffel bag full of stuff, and began to walk up 42nd Street, heading east. He told me Grand Central would be just past Madison Avenue. What a hike! Also for a kid from Florida, the theaters and sex shops that lined the Times Square area at the time were pretty shocking. I got to Grand Central, caught my train, and Bill picked me up. He was gracious and really bailed me out. I connected with Wanda a few days later, but something significant happened during my visit with Bill.

One night we were hanging out, and he asked me if I wanted to go to a meeting. "What kind of meeting?" I asked. He said it was an AA meeting. I immediately told him, "Uh, I don't really have a drinking problem, Bill." He tells me that was okay, but he did, and I was welcome to tag along if I wanted to go. I told him sure, and we were off. I remember sitting in the back of a room at a table by myself, while the other people participated in the meeting. I thought nothing of it at the time, but one day down the road, God would end up using the memory of it, big time.

NINE

The World's Most Famous Beach

A guy I worked with in Cocoa, Tommy Walker, helped get me my next job at WDAT in Daytona. Another move, another station, but this one was definitely a step down. For one thing, the signal was a daytime-only signal, meaning we had to sign off the station every night at sundown. We were also competing with the number one music station in town, WMFJ, and they were pretty much cleaning our clock. The on-air studio was in a non-air conditioned back room at a country club. Commercials were recorded at the office across town, and then the tape cartridges with the ad were transported to the on-air studio at the country club. I did mornings, and many mornings tape recordings that were done late the night before were left on the doorstep for me to pick up in the morning, complete with moisture from the dew gathering on top of the cartridge! Big time radio, this was not.

All of the on-air guys pitched in and we bought a room air conditioner for about fifty bucks. We rigged some ductwork with a bunch of clear plastic winding through the entrance of our side of the building back to our little on-air studio. To get to where we were, you had to work your way though a maze of plastic that made it appear we were working inside of a plastic bubble. Bizarre, yes, but in the Florida heat, at least we provided some relief for ourselves while we were working.

WDAT was unusual in the fact that we mostly played the Top 40 hits, but in the late afternoon Tommy hosted a program called 'Collage,' which was more of an album rock type format. One of the groups you heard a lot on the show was the Allman Brothers Band, since Greg and Duane Allman were from Daytona Beach. Their mom was a regular listener to the show, and developed a relationship with Tommy. He even got invited over to her house, and I got to go along. Mama Allman was very sweet and gracious, and was glowing as she opened the garage and showed us the new powder blue Lincoln Continental that her sons had given her. It's funny how when you even have a small connection with an artist or a band, you listen to their stuff just a little more closely. I became a fan of the Allman Brothers.

Things came to a head with Pam and she drove over from Orlando to tell me it was over. I knew it, but wanted to deny it, and had a very hard time processing it. I had a meltdown, emotionally. If the first cut is the deepest, well, I don't know how you can go much deeper. This kind of pain was new to me, and I didn't know how to process it, much less handle it. One thing was for sure: though my Christian faith at times seemed real to me, it certainly didn't have any depth to it. I didn't have the wisdom or any prior experience to know how to deal with the situation; it was totally new territory for me.

Also, up to this time in my life I had become very self-sufficient. Though I probably could have used a good friend or counselor to talk to, I was basically doing my best to handle the situation on my own. Call it pride, or stubbornness, whatever, I was determined to deal with it on my own terms. For what would be a very long time, I shut down on anything Christian, or anything about faith. I was totally clueless on how to cope.

There was only one way I saw to escape the pain. I worked a lot and I drank a lot.

If I was consumed with the business before, the next chapter in my life would kick it up to the next level. I got difficult to work with at WDAT and developed an attitude. I've been fired twice in forty-four years, and the first time was at WDAT. It was totally deserved, and I was not surprised. Fortunately, I was making a name for myself in the short time I was in Daytona, and I immediately got hired to do mornings at the #1 station in town, WMFJ. My life consisted of doing mornings on the radio, and afternoons loading trucks at the 7-UP bottling company to make some extra money. Then back to the station, then to a bar in an industrial section of Daytona that became my hangout. Without the station noticing, I would plug the bar pretty often on the air and get to drink for free. For the next eighteen months, I escaped into work, the beach, and the bar, and that was pretty much my life.

The more I studied the business, the more I was determined to get ahead. It was now 1974, and I had been in the business four-and-a-half years. Around this time, a shift in my thinking occurred. I made the determination I wanted to really try to make it. I didn't want to stay in Daytona. I didn't want to go back to Orlando. My vision got much bigger. I realized the bigger the market and the bigger the station, the more money I could make. At this point in my life, making money and growing my career took center stage. Nothing else mattered. I stayed out of trouble at WMFJ, and one morning while I was on the air I got a call from a guy driving up I-95 who was listening to me. His name was Ray Lynn, and wanted to know if I'd be interested in moving up to a bigger market, Jacksonville.

"Ray," I said, "I think we should talk."

TEN

Jacksonville

———— ❧ ————

Well, the little talk I had with Ray ended with a new job at WIVY-FM in Jacksonville. There used to be a joke in the business that if you saw a single guy towing a U-Haul trailer on the interstate, it was probably a radio guy moving to his next job. For my first five years in the business, I was pretty much that guy. This was station #8, and I felt like I was starting to work my way up the ladder. I loaded up my belongings in my '69 VW bug and headed to Jacksonville. Ray had hired me along with Dave Edwards, who got hired away from WKKO in Cocoa. I was making $210 a week, which was very decent for the time.

WIVY was at 103 on the FM dial, and they simulcast their signal on WIVY AM, which was at 1280. Jacksonville at the time was the 3rd biggest market in the state, behind Miami-Ft. Lauderdale, and Tampa-St. Pete. Now *this* was exciting. WIVY's format was Adult Rock, and our chief competitor was the 50,000 watt powerhouse WAPE at 690 on AM, known on the air as 'The Big Ape.' Our approach on the air was more laid back and sophisticated, but The Ape continued to dominate the ratings.

Dave and I both lived in an apartment complex directly across the street from Jacksonville University. I lived one floor above him, and most nights we would get together and talk about the business and the station.

Radio folks, especially the single ones, seem to congregate. It's almost like a fraternity of sorts. Often, our conversation centered around our boss, Ray. He was a little hard to read, and Dave and I were convinced that any day we would be on our way out. After we had been at the station for three months, we realized one day that Ray wasn't around! He completely fell off the face of the earth. We heard he left the station, but nobody knew why, exactly when, or how. It was bizarre. One day this guy was in your life as your boss, and then next day, it was as if he never existed. It was odd, to say the least.

The radio station was in a shopping mall right below the Hilton Hotel, which was right on the St. John's River. It was an unusual setting, but a pretty neat place to have a radio station and a nice place to go to work every day. I began dating a girl who worked at a printing shop down the end of the mall. Her mom and dad were from St. Augustine and they owned the business. Judi was blonde, cute, and fun, and helped me feel confident about myself again. She did wonders for my self-esteem. We laughed a lot. I felt like I was rejoining the human race after being on another planet somewhere for a few years. There was a piano bar upstairs at the Hilton, and you could find us there often in the afternoon after work.

Billy Joel was breaking out on the radio, and our overnight guy declared to me, "Hey you need to listen to this guy, he is the next Dylan!" Judi and I went to see him in concert at the gymnasium at Jacksonville University. I was blown away and became a huge fan. Amazingly, tickets were two bucks. For the next few years, if Billy Joel was coming anywhere within a day's drive of where I was, I was there.

When Ray left, the station began the search for a new Program Director. My new boss was coming from Norfolk, where he programmed Top 40 WGH. Lee Fowler's assignment was to do whatever it took to beat WAPE. I liked him from the start and was on board with the idea.

I don't get what it is about me and winning. I've always been competitive. Maybe the insecurities I had when I was younger have driven me. If I was perceived as a winner, I guess I thought people would think more highly of me. There would be less chance for rejection. I've been in Christian radio for twenty-five years now, and though in many ways we have a higher calling and purpose, I still love to win at radio. I figure if you are going to do it, why not just do it better than everyone else? And if you do it better, and get more listeners, resulting in higher ratings, which gets results for your advertisers, and the sales department can sell the ads at a decent rate because you did your job, everybody wins. Listeners get a great listening experience, advertisers get results, the station makes money, and I get to keep my job. Simple. Add in the component of being involved with something that has eternal significance (like we do at KLTY), and it just doesn't get much better than that.

Back in Jacksonville, I was doing mornings for Lee and we flipped the format to a Top 40 approach and began playing the hits on the FM dial. We emphasized the fact that we were stereo, (WAPE was not) by calling ourselves 'WIVY, Rockin' Stereo 103.' Some FM music stations were beginning to have an impact in their market since more cars were now getting AM and FM receivers as standard equipment. Q-105 in Tampa, WMYQ and Y-100 in Miami began to make an impact in their markets. I ended up moving to Jacksonville Beach, and rented the bottom half of a house for $100 a month. I was living a block away from the ocean, so my mornings and middays were spent at the station, and a lot of afternoons were spent at the beach. With all of my windows open, I could fall asleep at night with the sound of the ocean in the background. Sort of like the McDonald's commercial: I'm lovin' it. The ratings came out, and when you combined our AM and FM ratings (since it was all the same station), we ended up beating The Ape. It was my first taste at winning in a decent sized market, and I loved it.

There was a really nice guy who worked behind the scenes at WIVY named Elliot Goshman. Elliot ended up getting a production job (these are the guys who put the commercials together) at WMYQ in Miami, the station that Glen Hill and I would drive south to listen to. In the radio business, as in life, it's all about relationships. There's great truth in the saying, "It's not WHAT you know, but WHO you know." I sent an audition tape to Elliott and asked him to pass it on to his boss. My next move would have a significant impact on my career. My friend passed on my info to the program director and I got a call. I took a quick flight from Jacksonville to Miami to interview for my next job.

ELEVEN

The Magic City

———— ⌇ ————

I t was now the summer of 1975, and the movie 'Jaws' was number one at the box office. Right before I flew to Miami, I had a nasty ingrown toenail removed from my left big toe. I had to wear sandals when I visited the station, and my toe was all wrapped up. As I was taken around the office, being introduced to people, naturally a lot of people asked me, "What happened to your toe?" Very seriously I would answer, "Shark bite!" That always got a laugh and broke the ice with a lot of people, and my demeanor and easygoing attitude seemed to fit right in.

WMYQ was a full-power FM station at 96.3 on the FM dial, and was programmed by a guy who was quickly becoming a legend in the business, Jerry Clifton. Of the many bosses I've had, Jerry was one of the most significant at impacting me professionally. He could be brutal, but the man knew how to program a major market radio station. I flew in on a Friday, hung out that weekend, and got offered the job on Sunday night. I was very excited. I was offered the midday show, 10am to 2pm, paying 300 bucks a week! That afforded me the opportunity to get an apartment in a very trendy area of town called Coconut Grove.

Jerry was the National Program Director for a company called Bartell. He was based in Miami at WMYQ, but he was also responsible for similar sounding sister stations we owned in San Diego (the very famous KCBQ), Milwaukee, Detroit, and St. Louis. He also had made a name for himself programming 99X FM in New York City, competing against powerhouse WABC. Our chief competitors in town were WQAM, which was on AM, and Y-100 on the FM dial. Y-100 was an excellent radio station programmed by a guy named Bill Tanner, who would go on to become very successful and is now a big time consultant.

WQAM, being on the AM dial, was fading in popularity, and was becoming less of a factor. In the mid-70s, it really came down to radio war in Miami between us and Y-100. Both had full-power 100,000 watt signals, and both were playing the hits. I began to eat, sleep and drink nothing but the radio station. It consumed me. We had some very talented people working with us: Lee Logan from WQXI Atlanta, who is now a successful consultant; Eric Rhoads, who would go on to own his own radio stations and also owns Radio Ink Magazine; the late Steve Rivers, who went on to become a major programmer; Gary Bridges, who is now a big voiceover talent out of Philadelphia; and Kid Curry, who continued to have great success programming in Miami until a few years ago, when he was sidelined by illness. We also had some assistants who were totally consumed with the station; future radio star Jackie Robbins, and Stuart 'Boy Wonder' Slotnick.

With most of us being single, everybody became like family. When we weren't working, it seemed like a constant party. We changed the call letters of the station to WMJX and began to call ourselves 96-X. All of our marketing was all about The X; We had listeners constantly on the air saying "I X in my car," and "I X in my home," it was all about the X! We had the X-Van that would show up in Y-100's parking lot and give away hundred dollar bills. We had our mascot, the Xa-Gator that would show up at events around town. It was guerrilla warfare, with no holds barred. Jerry was a master programmer and motivator. Sort of like the football coach that you loved and hated at the same time. We used to sometimes get out of the office to hold staff meetings, and he said something one day that really stuck with me. We were having a meeting on the rooftop of an old hotel right on the ocean in Miami Beach. As usual, we were having a few beers, and Jerry said something like this:

"Look, you know and I know that all of you guys are very good. That's why you're here. It's possible you are going to get a call one day to make a move to make a few dollars more to move to a station maybe in New Orleans, or Kansas City, or a place like Minneapolis. Do me a favor. No lateral career moves. We've got a good thing going here and we're going to win. The only way I want to see anybody leaving here is if you are going to one of three places: New York, Chicago, or Los Angeles."

I absolutely loved living and working in South Florida. There was water everywhere, and my business attire consisted of a t-shirt, shorts or jeans, sandals or sneakers. The weather, of course, was terrific. Naturally I became a Dolphins fan. The station used to cover high school football every Friday night, and all of us who were on the air would pick a game, and then call into the station with a quick recap and the score. We wanted to 'own' the Friday night football coverage, and we did. I was in the stands one night in Ft. Lauderdale, and sitting one row below me, just as an average dad watching his son David play, was the Dolphins' great head coach, Don Shula.

I discovered places like Haulover Beach, a beautiful place where you could park for free and take a swim in the ocean any time you wanted. South Beach was not yet developed, and that area at the time was mostly one big retirement community. One of my favorite places to get a bite to eat was Monte's in Coconut Grove. It was an open air bar and restaurant, outdoors, overlooking Biscayne Bay. At night there was usually live music, and it had the type of atmosphere where you expected Jimmy Buffet to appear at any moment.

My social network consisted of my radio family, and that was about it. Eric Rhoad's parents had a house directly on the ocean just north of The Strip in Ft. Lauderdale. Since his folks would spend the summers in Indiana, a lot of us would spend a lot of time at Eric's house! Somewhere deep in the back of my mind, I can recall God being semi-involved in my life, but during these years I felt like I was riding a great wave, and I didn't want to get off.

Kid Curry and I moved to an apartment complex in Hallandale, just off I-95 between Miami and Ft. Lauderdale. There was a church close by that I would occasionally drive by on Sunday mornings. I would stop for a moment and think about it, and keep driving. I liked my life the way I had it arranged, and feared any spiritual or God-type stuff would just cause interference. I was working with some great people, and having an absolute blast.

The station really began to catch on, and when we peaked, we were 1/10th of a rating point behind Y-100. Though we didn't actually beat them, just catching up with them was a great accomplishment. We had one very exciting, great sounding radio station.

When Jerry worked in New York, he worked with a great on-air talent named Walt 'Baby' Love. We lost our afternoon guy, and Walt Baby agreed to come work for us for a while until he figured out his next career move. Walt would often promote me on the air saying, "Reed is ready!" and then plug my midday time slot. Walt was always quick to compliment my air-work, and since this guy was from 'the big time,' I was appreciative of the kind comments. One day he shocked me as he was coming on to do his shift, when out of the blue he just said, "Man, you are sooo gooood, you are going to work in New York City one day!" I said thanks, was grateful for the kind words, and went about my business, not thinking much of it. I didn't know it at the time, but I would run into Walt Baby in the future, in a different town, in a totally different situation.

Radio stations, of course, are licensed by the Federal Communications Commission. Before deregulation in the 80s, the FCC kept a tight reign on rules, regulations, and licensing of stations. WMJX was up for license renewal, and we were being challenged. It seemed the commission got word of things that the station had done while owned by our company, Bartell Broadcasting, and it wasn't a pretty picture. Just prior to when I started working there, the morning guy at the time supposedly got 'lost' in the Bermuda Triangle. A publicity stunt gone wrong, the station reported it as a news story, and the morning guy was actually lost at, well, would you believe, a bar in Ft. Lauderdale? There were also some issues with double billing some clients, as well as some on-air promotional activity and contesting that didn't go over too well with the Feds. Many of us actually got served with subpoenas and got called into court. Of course, the station had attorneys representing the station, and they coached us on what to say, but the bottom line was they did not want us to commit perjury.

Eric was driving to the courthouse from Ft. Lauderdale, and since he was driving by Hallandale, he agreed to give me a ride since we both had to be in court on the same day. I was a nervous wreck. Would the station keep its license, and would I keep my job? The courthouse was in the Little Havana section of Miami, and since we were running late, Eric dropped me off in front of the building while he went to find a place to park. I rushed into the building, only to discover I was at the Dade County Courthouse, and I needed to be at the Federal Courthouse. I was about six blocks away, and here I was, this long-haired guy, in a pale green double knit suit and tie, running through Little Havana as fast as I could! People probably thought I just robbed a bank! I made it to the courthouse, got to the floor where the courtroom was, and the judge had already retired to his chambers because I wasn't there. Our attorneys told me to calm down, relax, it was not the end of the world, just tell the truth.

For the next few hours, that was just what I did. I had burned up a bunch of adrenaline with my sprint across town, which actually worked out well because I was calm and composed during the questioning. It really was like out of a movie. I spent about two hours on the witness stand, told them what I knew, and it was finally all behind me. I was relieved, but the fallout from the court proceedings was still ahead of all of us.

The license renewal of WMJX to Bartell was denied. We went through an ownership change immediately. The General Manager left, and Jerry was out. While turnover is common in the radio business, it's still no fun, especially when you feel you have a winning team, and of course when a friend is moving on.

We hired Joel Denver from WFIL in Philadelphia as the new Program Director. We got along fine, but for me, it just wasn't the same. Jerry had mentioned that we might get calls from other stations trying to hire us away, and sure enough, he was dead on. I got calls from Minneapolis, Kansas City, Washington, DC, and one in particular that caught my attention, a very famous station in Canada, CHUM in Toronto. I talked to the program director there, but knew it was very cold in Canada, and also knew in my heart that I wasn't going to make a 'lateral' move. My next move was anything but lateral. A better term would be radical. Very radical.

I announced to Joel that I was leaving. I had absolutely nothing lined up as far as a job went. In my opinion, the station had peaked, and if we were through with winning, the thrill and the joy of going to work just weren't there. I was single; I had no big obligations, and could pretty much do what I wanted to do. I gave two weeks notice, and was asked to stay a little longer, which I did. Another few weeks went by and I decided on a date for my final day. Kid Curry relieved me when my shift was over, and it was done. The last song I played on 96-X was a good one, 'Easy' by Lionel Richie and The Commodores.

Big Jim was, well, big. Probably six foot tall, and probably weighed about 275. Jim had done the construction work for us when we rebuilt the studios at 96-X, and he was a bit of a wild man. He was originally from Sarasota, and I had no idea how we hired him as a contractor. We developed a bit of a friendship, and he invited me to visit. I knew Sarasota had great beaches, as I remembered that from when I went to REI to get my first class FCC license. I went to hang out with Jim for a few days, and it turned out he was now hanging drywall in the Sarasota area with his uncle. I really had nothing going on, so I asked Jim if I could come work for him hanging drywall. I think he paid me maybe fifty bucks a week, if that. I ended up crashing on Jim's couch while I learned a little bit about the business. The hardest part of hanging drywall was holding the piece of sheetrock in place with your head, while you nailed the nails into the studs in the ceiling. I wasn't great as a drywall guy, but just like when I worked for Goodyear, the manual, physical part of the job felt good. It was the type of hot, sweaty work that left you pretty exhausted at the end of the day.

We would usually grab a six-pack after work, or hit one of the local bars where Jim hung out. Jim could get a little loud or obnoxious when he had too much to drink, but for the most part I think he was harmless. He certainly wasn't the type of person you'd want to get into a tussle with, though. Big Jim was as strong as he was big. My drywall career lasted about a month. I told Jim thanks for the experience and headed back to Miami, since I had gotten a call from Bill Tanner at Y-100.

Bill Tanner, of course, was the guy running the station that I wanted to destroy for about the last two years. Quincy McCoy, a very talented part of his staff was leaving, and they had a daytime opening. We met over at Bill's place and it was a fascinating visit because Bill had a macaw. I just thought it was neat this guy had this big tropical bird living in his house! It was definitely something you would only see in Miami. He also had a very neat Mercedes SL convertible, and we would drive around and talk about the job and the business. They were offering me a lot more money than I was making at the X. We met with the GM, and it all looked and sounded very good. I ran into Quincy in the men's room, and remembering him saying, "Frank, just take the job!"

Every bit of common sense said exactly that. It was more money, it was the #1 station, a great Program Director in Tanner, great facilities, I wasn't locked into any no compete clauses, and I got to stay in Miami. I told Bill I was definitely leaning on accepting the job, but asked him to give me a few days. "No problem," he said. Maybe two days went by, and I just couldn't pull the trigger. It was nothing against Tanner or the station, I was just having a very hard time crossing the street and competing against Kid, Lee, Eric, and the other folks on the staff at 96-X that I had drawn close to. While it all made sense on paper to make the move, it just didn't 'sit right' with me down in my gut. A part-time engineer at The X named Paul was living at my apartment in Hallandale, so I decided to drive up to Orlando to spend a week with Mom and Dad. The next few days would prove to be monumental.

WLOF in Orlando was the station that I grew up with, and it just so happened that they needed a morning guy. My old friend from Jacksonville, Dave Edwards, hooked me up with the Program Director, Tom West. Since there was now a big 'hit music' FM in Orlando called BJ-105, WLOF was on the decline, but they still had quite a few listeners. There was a certain magic and fascination about the possibility of working there, since growing up listening to it and hanging out there as a teenager got me interested in the business. I flashed back to my meeting with Pat O'Day, who told me I had no future in the business. How ironic if I was to get his old morning shift.

Tom and I had a good meeting, and I could tell he was impressed that I had been involved in the Miami radio wars. I made it clear to him that I didn't know how long I could commit for. If I got an offer from a bigger market, he understood that my stay could be short-lived. That was okay by him, all he had to do was get my hire approved by his general manager. I had one air check (a taped sample of my on-air work) that I left with him since he wanted to play it for his boss. It was Thursday, and he would call me to confirm the deal probably by Monday. I could be working as early as Tuesday. It was practically a done deal. I was looking forward to getting back on the radio, and I was genuinely excited it was going to be WLOF in my hometown of Orlando.

Jim Dunaway was another radio friend from the Daytona days. He was now working and living in Melbourne over on the Space Coast. Since he lived close to the ocean, I decided to head over to the coast and hang out with him and his wife Dianne for a few days. After an afternoon at the beach, we were just relaxing on his front porch when the phone rang. Since my last known phone number was my Miami apartment, somebody had to make quite a few phone calls to find me. First the call to Miami, where Paul passed on that he thought Frank was in Sarasota, so try calling him at Jim's. Jim got a call and said, "No, Frank is not here, try his parents in Orlando, here is the number." Mom got a call and said, "No, he is not here, try him in Melbourne, here is the number." I was kind of blown away that somebody would go to so much trouble to track me down!

Dianne came out to tell me the call was for me. "Person to person call for Frank, from somebody named Bob Pittman in New York," she said.

The call was brief, and the first thing I noticed was the slight southern accent. "Frank I'm the new Program Director at WNBC in New York, and I have two openings left; a weekend shift, and the overnight shift, was wonderin' if you'd be interested in flying up here and talkin' about it."

At the time of the call, I already had quite a few beers with Jim, but thankfully I seemed to have my act together on the phone. I told him absolutely, and was told somebody would get in touch with me about arrangements, and I would probably see him Monday or Tuesday. I headed back to Orlando to tell Mom and Dad, then back to Miami to pick up some clothes. My travel itinerary: Miami International flying non-stop on National Airlines to Laguardia Airport in Queens, New York. I had one thought in mind: Frank, whatever you do, don't blow this!

TWELVE

30 Rock

------- ·⌒∂ -------

I needed to bring an air check with me on the trip to New York, and the only copy I had was in the hands of Tom West. Of course, Tom thought as soon as he played the tape for his boss I would probably start working for him the next day. I called Tom and told him I needed my tape, and that I had an interview at WNBC in New York. He paused for a moment, but understood completely, and didn't even begin to try to talk me out of it. He had been in the business long enough to know this was a big deal. I told him I would let him know how it went and if New York fell through, I would still be happy to come work for him.

I had another conversation with Pittman before I made the trip, and asked him how we should work it out, as far as him picking me up at the airport. He told me don't worry about a thing, just get on the plane, everything was taken care of. I followed orders, and got the non-stop from Miami to LaGuardia. When I got off the plane, everything made sense. As soon as I arrived at the gate, there was a guy holding a big sign that said FRANK REED, and my name was surrounded on the sign by stars! I approached the guy in the suit with the cap, and introduced myself.

His name was Ted Peck, and he was my limousine driver from Fugazy Limousine. I was shocked, excited, and nervous all at the same time. I was trying to remain cool and calm, but inside I was absolutely flipping out.

"A limo, are you kidding me?" Ted proceeded to tell me on the trip into Manhattan that he was Bob Hope's only driver when Bob was in New York. "Yes sir, I am Mr. Hope's guy," he was telling me. Ted, I found out quickly, was a chatterer, and that was fine because he was explaining all of the landmarks on the way into Midtown. The only things I remember him mentioning are the 59th Street Bridge, which Simon and Garfunkel sang about, and The United Nations. He told me a lot more, but I was oblivious. The next thing I knew, he dropped me off on the 49th Street entrance to the RCA Building, Rockefeller Plaza.

"What do I do now?" I asked. Ted told me they were waiting for me on the 2nd floor, "Just go to the center of the building, NBC security, and tell them you have an appointment." Ted wished me luck and was on his way. Nice guy.

I checked into security, which was very impressive. The building was obviously old, but very classy. A lot of marble and it seemed like everything was black and white. There were a bunch of elevators in the NBC security foyer area and I grabbed the first one going up. Getting off at the 2nd floor, the first thing I noticed were the WNBC radio studios. They had big windows, obviously for observation for the famous NBC Guided Tours.

The first person I laid my eyes on when I headed toward the offices was, incredibly, Walt 'Baby' Love, who was on the air at the time. We briefly saw each other through the glass, and he gave me a gesture similar to a tip of a hat, if he had been wearing one. Ironically, this wonderful guy who predicted one day I would work in New York was part of the staff that was on its way out. I would be the last hire of an all-new on-air team, replacing Walt, and even the famous Don Imus. I introduced myself to Bob's secretary, Brenda, and she told me to have a seat.

Bob Pittman had just completed an amazing turnaround at NBC-owned WMAQ in Chicago. He flipped the format to Country, and it was a big success. Now he and his General Manager, Charlie Warner, were given the task of turning around the NBC Radio Flagship, WNBC. Bob put me at ease right from the start. He came off to me as cool, calm, and confident. He asked me if I had brought a tape, but I don't even think we listened to it. Hearing him comment that, "I can't find anybody that has anything bad to say about you," I was feeling pretty confident I would get offered a job. It came about that Bob had called Bill Tanner at Y-100 and told Bill he was looking for one more good talent, and did Tanner know anybody? Bill passed on my name, and that was how I ended up getting approached about the job. It was definitely one of those 'right place, right time, and who you know' situations.

Bob and I connected pretty easily and I spent most of the day just hanging out in the office. After dinner, we headed back to his apartment, which was a brand new high-rise at the corner of 38th Street and 3rd Avenue. It was very cool, modern and contemporary. I wondered in my mind how much the rent was. We also hooked up with Lee Masters, who was going to be our new afternoon guy. I knew that I was booked on a flight back to Miami about 10pm, and just before my cab came, Bob took me aside and had a small piece of brown paper cupped in his hand. On it was written a number. It was big. "I can pay you this much to do the 2-6am shift, I need you here a week from today."

I told him, "Great, see you in a week." I grabbed my cab to the airport, and broke a five dollar bill for a bunch of quarters. I found a pay phone and called Mom and Dad, my friend Jim, and a few other radio friends in Florida. I was ecstatic. One thing I'll never forget is while I was on the phone, an announcement came across the intercom at LaGuardia that the police had just nabbed the infamous 'Son of Sam' murderer. The date was August 10, 1977. I had just landed the biggest job of my life. I celebrated on the flight back to Miami with scotch and water on the rocks. Make that two.

I called Tom West when I got back to Florida and told him thanks for the offer, but I was on my way to New York. Tom was excited for me, as was everybody I knew. New York was the biggest market in America, and I was on my way to the Big Apple at the age of twenty-six, after about seven years in the business. The words of Jerry echoed in my mind, "No lateral moves, only New York, Chicago, or Los Angeles."

When I look back on landing the job, I can see God's sovereign hand in the situation, even though my life at the time was totally devoid of anything spiritual. There were so many other people in the business who were as qualified for this job, if not more so. I think having a decent reputation probably played a part. It was just being out of work and available at the right time, with the right person passing on my name to the right guy. Had I been working I would have dropped what I was doing to take the job, but who knows if Tanner would have mentioned me if I was working for him, or even somewhere else? Everything just fell into place perfectly. Even landing the overnight graveyard shift. This would make me the low guy on the depth chart, but there was something even exciting about that. I would be the guy talking on the air at WNBC in New York, New York at 3 o'clock in the morning, in the city that never sleeps.

Paul the engineer agreed to sub-lease my apartment, so I left behind the little furniture that I owned. I would have it shipped up in a few weeks after I got settled and figured out where I was living. Everything else I owned, I crammed into my VW, and I hopped on I-95 northbound. I gave myself plenty of time to get there, and thought I would stop and see friends on the Space Coast on the way up, as well as a visit to my sister in Baltimore.

Somewhere in Brevard County, I got pulled over by the Florida Highway Patrol and I thought it was all over. I was going to stop and see my friend Gabe, but I missed the exit and was going about 15 mph over the speed limit. I had a cold Miller Lite in my hand, and five other cold ones from the six-pack on the floor of the passenger side. I also had about an ounce of pot in the glove compartment. I pulled over and got out my license and proof of insurance. My heart was about to explode out of my chest. I tried to remain calm. When I handed the officer my license, he peeked in and saw the beers on the floor.

"Drinkin' that lite beer, huh? Don't wanna get fat?" he said.

"No sir," I calmly replied.

He checked my license, told me to slow down a little, and sent me on my way. Talk about dodging a bullet. I could just envision my call to Pittman: "Uh, hello Bob, I think I'm going to be delayed a few days, I'm in the Brevard County Jail!"

Thank goodness it never happened. It's almost like getting the job, and getting there without getting busted, was pre-ordained.

The station put me up at a great hotel, The Americana (it is now The Sheraton), at the corner of 7th Avenue and 52nd Street, right in the heart of Midtown Manhattan. NBC and Rockefeller Plaza was less than a ten-minute walk. Since the cost to park my car in Manhattan was about the same as my rent in Miami (about $170 per month), I quickly concluded if I was going to be living in Manhattan, the car would have to go. If you live and work in Manhattan, you walk, take the subway or bus, or catch a cab.

Walking into Rockefeller Plaza to work was almost surreal. Our building was right next to the world famous Radio City Music Hall. I kept waiting to run into somebody like Bryant Gumbel, Tom Brokaw or Jane Pauley. Limousines were commonplace at the entrance by the skating rink. I often wondered who they were for. I knew one probably belonged to Imus, but he was on the way out.

We began to have meetings every day, with the goal of launching The All New WNBC on Labor Day. The new team was now in place. Ellie

Dylan, from WMAQ, Chicago, would be doing mornings. Ellie also happened to be Bob's girlfriend at the time. Johnny Dark, from WRKO, Boston would be doing middays. Lee Masters, from WLRS, Louisville, was our afternoon guy. Allen Beebe from KMJC, San Diego, would be on from 6-10pm. Batt Johnson, from KCMO in Kansas City was on from 10-2, and Frank Reed from WMJX, Miami, 2-6am. It was a kick to see our names printed in *The New York Times*. An article had been written about the impending format change. Rounding out the programming team was Assistant Program Director Jay Stone (who would eventually be replaced by Ron 'Buzz' Brindle), and our Music Director was a really neat lady named Roz Frank.

It seemed like everything that was being done for 'the new guys' was first class. I remember there was a concern about all of us knowing the market, since everybody was from out of town. Our General Manager, Charlie Warner, spared no expense in making us feel special. Limos took us on tours of the five different boroughs, Queens, The Bronx, Brooklyn, Staten Island, and of course Manhattan. I remember us circling The City on The Circle Line, which was a big boat that gave you a tour of Manhattan via the water. We passed under a bridge in Harlem, and a young kid was relieving himself off the side of the bridge, announcing, "Welcome to New York!" Our first promo publicity headshots were taken on board The Circle Line. Pretty heady stuff for a young kid from Florida.

The final 'get to know New York' trip landed us in Westchester County, where the station leased a couple of twin engine Cessnas to give us a tour by air. Since I've been fascinated by planes since I was a kid, sitting right next to our pilot with all of the controls and instruments was just the best. Ellie Dylan and I shared the same flight, and when the pilot had a hard time starting the second engine, Ellie gave me one of those looks that said, "Uh, are we sure we want to do this?" We got the engine started, took off, and headed straight down the Hudson River headed toward the Statue of Liberty. Banking around the landmark, I felt like I was on top of the world.

Charlie even pulled some strings and got us all into the famous Studio 54 Disco. As the overnight guy, I may have been the low guy on the depth chart, but nonetheless I felt special, wanted, and appreciated. And I hadn't even been on the air yet.

Johnny Dark and I became friends. Maybe it was the Florida connection. Before landing at the highly rated WRKO, Boston, Johnny had worked quite a bit in the Sunshine State. I remember him stopping in for a visit when I was at 96-X. Since we were both staying at the Americana, we would have drinks at The Blarney Stone, which was right next to the hotel on 52nd Street. New York is famous for its Irish bars, and The Blarney Stone was very typical. They served cheap drinks, with the actual prices plastered like a menu on the wall above the bar, the whole length of it. Plus they had a carving station with great stacked sandwiches. It was just a comfortable place to hang out.

Johnny would remind me about WNBC's nighttime signal. At 50,000 watts and a clear channel signal at 660, I would be getting calls from listeners all over the northeast and beyond. Shortly after we had arrived in New York, he and I were in what was called 'the jock lounge.' This consisted of a couch, some desks, places to keep our personal stuff, and a stereo. This was our private space where the on-air staff could go and relax before or after their air shift. Johnny and I had been listening to Clifton's former station, 99-X, when they broke the news on the air that Elvis Presley had just died. Since WNBC had a huge local news department at the time, I was certain that they would have the information, but I thought what if they didn't? I ran out of the jock lounge and sprinted down the hall to the newsroom. I threw open the large glass door, and loudly pronounced, "Elvis is dead!"

Allow me to explain the awkwardness of this situation. First, all of the people working in the WNBC newsroom had been working there for a very long time. Second, I'm one of the new guys that nobody knows. All they know is their friends that have been on the air for years are all getting fired, and I'm one of the young punk replacements. And oh, by the way, this wise guy is screaming Elvis is dead! Is he nuts? If looks could kill, I was six feet under about one hundred times over. After I yelled my announcement, it seems like time stood still for a few moments, and immediately all of the news teletype machines began ringing like crazy, meaning there was an urgent bulletin coming across the newswires. Well, what do ya know? The new kid was right; Elvis WAS dead!

My comp time at the Americana was going to run out after two weeks, which meant I was going to have to find a place to live. My friend who helped me out in 1972, Bill Donovan, still lived in White Plains. Bill agreed to let me sleep on his couch until I figured out what I was going to do. I kept my VW and began commuting between Manhattan and White Plains. Since I would be doing the graveyard shift, I would be going to work about 1 in the morning, and I would be leaving against the incoming NY traffic at 6.

We launched the station at noon on Labor Day, with Bob announcing the new format, and Lee Masters playing the first song, which was 'Star Wars' by Meco. The station bought quite a bit of TV time to announce the change, with Bob sitting with a bunch of record albums explaining about 'The All New WNBC.' The station was noticeably different. Since the goal was to go after WABC, which was the dominant music station for what seemed like forever, we wanted to differentiate ourselves from them in a big way. And we did. Since we didn't have a lot of business on the air at the time, we played noticeably fewer commercials. Also since most Top 40 stations had high energy jocks talking over the beginning of the songs, we were more conversational, and made it a point of not talking over the music. One of the easy ways we positioned it that everyone could understand, was to say that, "It sounds like FM on AM!"

One of the more comical 'inside the business' things that we did was to make fun of WABC's famous reverb that they had on their microphones. It actually made them sound distinctive, but we wanted to turn it into a negative. We would often remind people that on The All New WNBC, "it sounds like FM on AM, and with no echo!" I think we all got the biggest kick out of saying that. Bob had staff meetings with us regularly to tweak the sound, which was inconvenient for me, being the overnight guy, but I eagerly threw myself into the job, the mission, and the city.

It paid off. I hadn't been working there but a few months when I got moved up to the 10pm-2am shift. Bob liked the way I sounded. From there, it was only going to get better.

Getting moved up to the 10pm shift coincided nicely with my move to Manhattan. I considered some high rises in New Jersey overlooking the Hudson River, but I really wanted to be close to the radio station. After checking over by Ellie's apartment building in Turtle Bay, and another building up around 56th street, I settled on a newly renovated building at the corner of 38th Street and Madison Avenue. This building used to be a printing company, but was now brand new luxury apartments. Batt Johnson and Allen Beebe were already living there, and the location was great. Pittman lived right down the street a few blocks at 38th and 3rd, and the station was about a twenty-minute brisk walk. I had the choice between a studio apartment on the 6th floor, or for a few dollars more, they had the same floor plan available on the top floor, also known as PH, or Penthouse. I opted for the fancy address: 244 Madison Avenue, Penthouse G, New York, New York 10016. Since I had a corner unit, one entire twenty-foot wall of the apartment was a giant window looking north up Madison Avenue. I was on the 16th floor, and the view was the best. A spiral staircase went up to a loft that had just enough room for a bed and dresser. For a single guy living in the Big Apple, it was perfect.

Living in Manhattan was completely different. I lived in a doorman building, where a guy in a hat opened the door for you and hailed your cab with a whistle. I quickly learned the absolute fastest way to get from point A to point B in the city was the subway. Cabs were fun but cost a little bit, and of course traffic could completely stop your trip. If you got within a few blocks of your destination, and the traffic held you up, you just paid the cabbie and got out and walked the rest of the way. It seemed like in New York there was a bar or a restaurant on every corner, and you could spend your life visiting a few new ones each week, and probably not hit them all.

I adjusted fine, and honestly, was having the time of my life. The station initially got a nice bump in the ratings, and things were going well. I kept getting promoted. Soon I was doing the 6-10pm shift. The station sounded great, and I was getting lots of compliments for the way I sounded on the air. I remember doing my air shift with a news guy named Marc Gibson the night that Reggie Jackson hit his three home runs at Yankee Stadium in the 1977 World Series. I was on the air that night at one of the biggest radio stations in America, in the media center of the world. Welcome to the big time.

I began to date a girl who answered the request lines at the station, and since she was drop-dead gorgeous, it was another boost to my growing ego. Michelle was born and raised in Manhattan, and lived with her parents and sister in a nice apartment at the corner of 82nd and Lexington. I found it comical and odd that she didn't know how to drive! Living in New York all of her life, there was really no need. Michelle had an agent, and had gotten some jobs for some print advertising, and was even getting some extra parts in movies that were being shot in the city. She was always sending out her promo photos to different people, looking for that big break. She really had the looks for it. She looked amazing. She also loved to dance, and was always going to a dance class somewhere. I could easily imagine her on Broadway or in the movies. She was also a singer, but for whatever reason, she kept that private. She was talented, sweet, supportive, and for my part I was self-centered and self-absorbed. She deserved better. I'm certain she was seeking a solid, secure relationship with a decent guy, and I was selfishly content with the fact that she made me look good. It was wrong, and I have huge regrets when I reflect back on that season in my life.

It's painful to remember how selfish I was. Rather than being honest and transparent in the relationship, I faked it and would just drink if the phoniness made me uncomfortable. Not dealing with feelings and drinking or drugging instead became a pattern. Over time it would become a real problem. But at the time I had a beautiful girl on my arm, a penthouse apartment overlooking Madison Avenue, a bunch of money in the bank, and I was on the air at 660 WNBC in New York, New York. By just about anybody's standards, I was doing very, very well.

In 1978 we went through our first shake-up at the station, when Ellie Dylan exited. We had positioned her as the first woman to take over a morning drive shift in a market the size of New York. Of course she was replacing the legendary Imus in the Morning, and for whatever reason, it didn't work out. Lee Masters, the afternoon guy, got moved to the morning slot. I had already been moved up to 6-10pm by this time, and the decision was made to put me into the coveted afternoon drive shift. I liked Ellie a lot, and was sorry to see her leave. She always had an encouraging word for me, was very kind, and even cared enough to politely mention to me that maybe I should take it easy on the drinking.

Whenever I would visit Bob's apartment and Ellie was there, it seemed like I always had a drink in my hand. She was never judgmental, just politely concerned, like a caring friend would be. People like that tend to stick in your memory. You don't forget them. At the time I always figured I could drink, or not drink whenever I wanted. For the time being it didn't seem to be a problem, and I always felt I was in total control.

Fast forward a few more months and Lee left the morning show, replaced by a seasoned professional who had worked at some really big stations like WLS Chicago, and KHJ Los Angeles, named Scotty Brink. Bob seemed to go through a season where he was into the comedy scene at places like Catch a Rising Star, and he teamed up Scotty with a then very young and talented comedian, Richard Belzer. (This is the same 'Belz' who would go on to play Sgt. John Mulnch on 'Law and Order.') The team came to be known as 'Brink and Belzer,' and the station promoted them heavily with a big TV campaign. Whenever Scotty would miss work, I was the one who would get the phone call to come in and fill in. Working with the Belz was kind of crazy and unpredictable, as we basically just flew by the seat of our pants. He had certain bits that he and Scotty had been working on, and I tried my best to be a good straight man. I always dreaded getting the call, which seemed to happen often, but my attitude was if I could become the 'go to' guy in situations like that, it would just add to my job security with Pittman. Despite being heavily promoted, the show did not do well in the ratings, and that paved the way for the return of a man who is arguably one of the best radio personalities to ever sit behind a microphone. Making his way back to New York and WNBC would be none other than John Donald Imus.

THIRTEEN

The I Man

D on Imus had made his mark in New York at WNBC starting in December 1971. His outrageous antics and over the line innuendo had made him the talk of New York, and the talk of the radio industry. If there is somebody on the radio today being over the line and pushing the envelope, Imus paved the way. He was the first, the original 'shock jock.' Charlie Warner had left as our GM, and the new Manager, Bob Sherman, along with Pittman, orchestrated the return of the I-Man. When Don was let go with the rest of the staff in the summer of '77, he ended up going to WHK, Cleveland. Or as Don would describe the city, "The mistake on the lake!" Upon his return, the station launched a big advertising push, touting 66 WNBC as 'The Next ONE!' Don seemed totally engaged and was (at least for me anyway) easy to work with.

The morning show had an amazing cast of characters that were concocted by Imus and a true genius, his sidekick and newsman, Charles McCord. Characters like Imus General Manager, Geraldo Santana Banana (played by The Earls lead singer Larry Chance), Hollywood reporter Rhoda Ruder (played by our music director and soon-to-be traffic lady, Roz Frank), and of course the infamous Right Reverend Doctor Billy Sol Hargus became regulars on the show. A very nice guy named Al Rosenberg became part of the team, along with Producer Lyndon Abell. A very talented Larry Kinney rounded out the group with his amazing repertoire of character voices. I even had my own bit part on occasion, becoming known as Captain Frank Reed, leader of the Moby Worm Observation Corps, on "66 WNBC your official Moby Worm observation designation station"! Moby Worm was a fictitious character that was something like ten city blocks long, and five stories high, that would roam the Tri-State area of New York, New Jersey and Connecticut and terrorize school children by attacking their school! (I've been told there is a Moby Worm bit in the Imus audio exhibit at the Museum of Television and Radio in New York. My friend Bob Lepine informed me that the worm and I are immortalized at the museum!)

My involvement with the worm and the show was a pretty simple deal. Charles would write the script, and we would voice the bit in the production studio after Don's show. Then the recording engineer would add in the sound effects that made it sound like I was reporting from a helicopter. It was my job to describe the carnage and destruction, and then at the end of the bit, I would always get eaten by the worm. A song or two would play after it aired, and then Don would announce that I somehow miraculously survived, and would be on the air at 66 WNBC that afternoon. Pretty soon school kids started writing in, requesting certain teachers to be eaten by the worm! It was all pretty innocent and fun stuff.

Meanwhile, down at 77 WABC they were responding to the current disco craze, and radically shifted their music away from playing the hits and leaning more toward disco music. The combination of that change, the return of Imus, plus our 'Next ONE!' marketing campaign worked. Soon we became the most listened to station in New York in the ratings, and for a season my afternoon shift was #1, even besting the legendary Dan Ingram at WABC. Frank Sinatra had released the song, 'New York,

New York.' For a while anyway, I really was "king of the hill, and top of the heap."

I've had the privilege of working for some really smart people, and Bob Pittman has to be included in a group at the top of the list. The whole New York experience, especially those early days, were very memorable, and Bob and the original group that was hired in '77 played a big part in that. I think we all realized we were a part of something very special. I can remember a bunch of us hanging out at Bob's on Saturday nights, watching the original cast of 'Saturday Night Live.' Before the VHS craze he had a Betamax, and I remember being blown away that you could actually videotape a show, and watch it at a later time!

Bob became a fan and encourager to me early on, and would remind me often that I was his 'Star.' For a young kid from Florida, his encouragement fueled my passion to continue to grow and mature as a personality. I also had a desire to get into programming someday, and he told me that I would probably have to make a choice: either get into programming, or continue as an air talent. I enjoyed the nuts and bolts and creative side of the business, and he probably sensed that in me, as I would ask a lot of questions, and at times even questioned why we did things a certain way. He was very research-driven, and very focused. I felt that I had gained some favor with Bob since I started out as the lowly overnight guy, and had worked my way up to afternoons with his mentoring and coaching. It was a good position to be in. I was grateful for his influence.

When Bob announced his resignation, I was shocked, and thought to myself, "Where in the world do you go after you've programmed one of the biggest radio stations in America?" Bob and Lee Masters had hosted a late night weekend TV show on the NBC-owned and operated television stations called 'Album Tracks.' I had the privilege of auditioning for the show, but Lee ended up getting the job. So it didn't come as a total surprise when Bob said he was going to be getting involved in television. What he said next, though, did not compute with me. He said, "We are going to take music videos, and play them on cable TV."

"Excuse me?" I said in shock. "You are going to do what?" I'll never forget taking Pittman aside, like a concerned friend, and saying something like, "Uh Bob, are you sure about this?"

He assured me that yes, this was a good move for him, and that he knew exactly what he was doing. Honestly, I had my doubts. What he was talking about at the time was completely off the wall and unheard of.

My routine at vacation time became heading home to Florida for a few days, and quite a few months after Bob left I was visiting an old high school friend, Stuart, who had a lakefront place in Winter Haven. It was a great place to visit, just chill out and enjoy the water. It just so happens that Stuart was one of the first on his block to have cable TV. I began to click the remote from channel to channel, and once I saw it, I immediately 'got it.' Mick Jagger was screaming at me on the TV screen that he wanted it and had to have it. My friend and former boss Bob was going to do just fine. He had started MTV! (Bob Pittman would go on to become one of the most successful business executives in America, and is now President and CEO of Clear Channel Communications.)

Since I determined that the Long Island beaches were the closest thing to finding Florida in New York, I ended up buying a home in Merrick, Long Island. Merrick was on the south shore of the Island, and I could literally be at the Atlantic Ocean at Jones Beach in about ten minutes. The house itself was a typical three-bedroom, two-story Colonial, built in the 1930s, and it really had some character to it. Hardwood floors, a big fireplace, and an awesome wooded back yard that was very private. The price tag was $67,000, and I remember applying for my first mortgage ever from The Dime Savings Bank in Brooklyn. The interest rate was 9.75 percent, and I remember people commenting to me that I got a great rate! Economically, the country was in a time of very high inflation, but I was making big money, I was single with no debt, and I absolutely loved the house. I remember after the closing just walking in it from room to room for hours. I bought a house! I couldn't believe I was a property owner.

Moving from the city was another one of those stories that could only happen in New York. Since I didn't have that much to move, I rented my own truck and just asked Allen Beebe, who lived in my building, to give me a hand with the bigger stuff. It was a Saturday morning, and everything was going well, but I had this one very unusual piece of furniture that got stuck in the elevator. When I worked in Miami, we ran a contest where we had a custom phone booth built, which was called the 'X Phone.' We took the booth to different shopping malls, and if you dialed the right telephone number (this was before touch tones), an alarm went off, and you won $10,000 cash! When the contest was over, they were going to trash the booth, but I thought it was unusual and looked really cool, so I took it home with me and wired it to work like a regular phone. It made for a great conversation piece. Allen and I were trying to get it into the elevator at my building, but it got jammed in the door opening, and we couldn't get it to budge.

About thirty minutes went by, and the supervisor of the building threw open the stairway door, having trudged up sixteen floors, and was cussing up a storm. Not knowing proper New York high-rise living protocol, I had not reserved the elevator for my move. Evidently somebody else was moving that morning also, and had the other elevator tied up. Only having two elevators in the building, people were stranded on all of the floors! It was safe to say that building super was very happy to see me move.

Like thousands of others, I was now a New York commuter. The train ride from Merrick into Penn Station on the Long Island Railroad was anywhere from forty-five minutes to an hour, depending on if I caught an express train, or a local train. Then I could either catch the #1 train on the Broadway line subway, get off at 50th Street and Broadway, and walk over to Rockefeller Plaza, or leave Penn and walk over to the 34th Street station below Macys, and take the B, D, or F train directly to the lower level of Rockefeller Plaza. Either way, it was anywhere from seventy-five to ninety minutes door to door. The great thing about the commute was I would usually find an empty seat on the train, and could enjoy some coffee, a bran muffin, and the newspaper. On the way home, it was the bar car. You could either purchase miniatures, or a beer.

My drinking would usually start at Lindy's at Rockefeller Plaza when I got off the air, then the bar car, and before I got home I would stop at a place called the Rhineskellar, which was right by the Long Island Railroad station. At the time I did not consider the fact that I was drinking a lot a big deal. I was performing at a very high level on the air and just concluded big time radio was stressful. I did feel under constant pressure to perform well daily, so the alcohol did help me to relax and take the edge off.

I began to hang out with some Long Island radio folks, Gary and his friend Dave, who I would play racquetball with pretty regularly. I got hooked on racquetball. I loved the workout and loved the competitiveness of it. A typical day would be work, hit the bar, then bar car on the way home, racquetball, and then maybe a bunch of us meet at the Rhineskellar later. Michelle would occasionally visit, but moving away from her and the city was a convenient way for me to start to put some distance in our relationship. In my heart I knew my relationship with her was not genuine, so I was hoping when I moved she might begin to pull away.

It was a regular Monday night of racquetball and then the Rhineskellar with Dave when Howard Cosell broke in on Monday night football to announce that John Lennon had been shot at The Dakota, which was his residence, up around 72nd Street and Central Park. Tributes began to pour out on the radio, and Imus in particular did a tribute that to this day, was one of the most memorable moments I ever heard on WNBC. When Don wanted to be serious (which was not very often), he could move you to tears.

Kevin Metheny became our Program Director at WNBC in 1980. We met the first time when Bob and a bunch of us took the Metroliner to Philadelphia, where Kevin programmed Wizzard 100, which was very similar to what we were doing in New York. He had dropped me a complimentary note on my air-work when he was in Philly, so it was always a good thing if the new guy coming in already liked your work. The business has a reputation of being volatile, and I've been fortunate down through the years of having pretty good longevity at most of the stations I've worked at. One of the things I've learned is if you are working for a decent guy, loyalty is a good thing. There are so many egos in the business, I always figured if you could stay out of trouble, keep somewhat of an even keel with the ego, and do everything within your power to help the boss win, in the long run it will pay off. Forty some years into the business, I've still found that to be true. Be low-maintenance, and provided the guy you are working for is decent, be loyal to him. In other words, don't undermine his authority. Let him know you are on his side. Be his advocate and supporter. If you don't agree with something, close the door and tell him personally, don't go whining to somebody else. I had that kind of relationship with Kevin, and we are still friends to this day.

Since heading out on vacation usually meant going home to Florida for a few days, I would always make it a point to stop in and see Mom and Dad. I had a crazy habit of circling my vacation days on my calendar, and then telling Metheny what the starting date was for vacation. Then, I would go to the calendar and circle the date two weeks prior to my vacation. This was the date that I would stop drinking, and pick up my workout regimen, so when I got home to Florida, I appeared to be healthy and (for lack of a better term) appeared to have my act together.

For many years my relationship with my parents was just a sham. Just like all of my other 'close' relationships, it was very much on the surface, and honestly, just fake. I wasn't a jerk or obnoxious, or rude, and I think most would agree I was a decent guy. There was just no depth with people, and at that time in my life, that was what I preferred. Especially since my parents were now pretty plugged in with their faith, that was definitely something I did not want to deal with. If I appeared to be 'okay' with them, I figured I could avoid any uncomfortable conversations.

Then in early 1982, somewhere a line got crossed. I had a dilemma. I had to go to Kevin not once, but twice, and ask him to change my vacation date. I kept circling the two-week mark prior to vacation, but it kept moving. I couldn't stop drinking. I couldn't put together two or three days, much less two weeks of abstaining. At the time I was functioning very well, and nobody had a clue I had a problem. I never drank in the morning or prior to work. It was always after work that I had the problem. I would drink and drive on numerous occasions, and I'm forever grateful I never hit anybody or had any wrecks. I would occasionally have blackouts, where I had no recollection of the crazy things I did the night before. I can remember taking joy rides in my classic MGA with the top down on the back streets of Merrick at 2 o'clock in the morning. Looking back, this kind of behavior was dangerous and insane. Things were definitely getting out of control. And every day, standing on the platform waiting for the train to work was just like out of the movie 'Groundhog Day.' I would be standing in my usual spot, with a bit of a hangover, saying,

"Well, I'm not going to drink today," and then the next day, there I was again, saying, "Well, I'm *for sure* not going to drink today!" and so on it went. Until one night, in the spring of 1982.

FOURTEEN

The Crisis

———— ∽ ————

Heart attack. That was the first thought that popped into my head to explain what had to be going on with my body. This was the day that I determined that no matter what, I wasn't going to drink. Dave and I had actually played some racquetball earlier that evening, and I felt fine. I had a healthy dinner of some roast chicken, some broccoli, and some wheat toast. My usual game plan of doing everything I could to feel healthy before I went home was once again on its first day, but I had no reason not to be hopeful that I could string some 'straight' days together, and pull it off. Everything seemed fine and normal till about 11pm. I was just about ready to doze off when it hit.

In a matter of seconds, my chest felt like it was going to explode. My heart felt about twice its size, and was pounding uncontrollably. It felt like it was actually going to burst through my chest. Something was very wrong with me physically, and I hadn't a clue of what it was. I got up in a panic and thought to drive myself to a hospital, but my car just happened to be in the shop that day. My next door neighbor, Mae, was a sweet widow lady who was always very motherly toward me, so I thought maybe she could help. I banged on her door and a window, but got no response.

My only option was to dial 911. It was just a few minutes and two officers from the Merrick Police Department were at my door. I opened the door and as soon as they looked at me they had me lie down on the couch in the living room. The first question caught me completely off guard:

"Do you do cocaine?" an officer asked.

I was thinking, "Oh great, I'm dying here, and this guy is looking for a drug bust!" I told him "no sir," and he asked if I had a history of drug or alcohol abuse. My response was, "Well, I drink a little bit, but it's not a problem."

About this time, one of the officers said an ambulance was on the way, just try to remain calm and relaxed. Fat chance. I was scared out of my wits. My heart continued to pound, and it seemed to come and go in waves of intensity. The ambulance showed up, lights flashing, and the next thing I knew, I was on the stretcher, we were rolling, sirens and all, and they were phoning my vital signs into the emergency room. It was just like out of one those medical emergency shows on TV. *Will he make it, or will he die right there in the ambulance? Find out right after this commercial!*

In all honesty, I thought it was all over. Whatever was going on, I felt like I could check out at any moment, and not wake up. Talk about a reality check. There I was, thirty-one years old, successful, at the top of my game (which was really about all I cared about at that point in my life), and I was thinking that any second, it could all be over.

I immediately began to take stock of my life, and began to think through the question of life after death: Is heaven real? Am I going there? And every other thought in between. My mind was working overtime. There's a saying that you're not ready to live until you're ready to die. For sure, ready was not me. I wasn't ready to die, and without a doubt

I did not want to die. I was wondering if the folks at the hospital had different thoughts.

The closest hospital to my house was in Freeport, Long Island. If there is a hospital from hell, that's where they took me. Rude, insensitive and unprofessional pretty much sums it up. Some admission guy kept asking me questions that I didn't have an answer for, and basically told me they couldn't treat me till I answered all of his questions.

I told him, "If I die lying here, you are for sure not going to get your questions answered, right?"

I still had the waves of the heart pounding, and I also felt like I was coming out of my skin. I told the guy I felt like I was dying, and he seemed like he couldn't care less. This was definitely the worst. I finally got treated by the doctor on call that night, and his diagnosis was that I was suffering from 'anxiety neurosis.' He shot me up with a heavy sedative, told me to make an appointment with my family doctor, and sent me on my way. I asked him if he was sure that was all that was wrong. He gave me a dirty look, and told me to "have a nice day." It was as if they were playing a joke on me, and I wasn't in on it. I was confused, to say the least. The hospital called me a cab, and I got home about 3am. About an hour later, I began to experience the same symptoms, and I called my attorney, Bob, who lived about ten minutes away in North Merrick. Luckily, he picked up the phone, and I explained to him that something was really wrong with me physically, my car was in the shop, and could he please drive me to the emergency room at Mercy Hospital in Mineola? He said he would be right there.

The difference between the hospital in Freeport and Mercy was night and day. After giving me another injection to relieve my symptoms, I got a complete checkup from another doctor. He was very thorough, and very professional. I finally felt like medically I was in good hands. He politely excused himself, and after about a twenty-minute wait, a very grandmotherly looking lady in nurse pinstripes came in to talk to me. Her manner was very calm, but she was very sure of her words, as if she had had this talk before with others.

I recall it went something like this: "Frank, what you are experiencing is alcohol withdrawals. Your body, after being used to having alcohol in its system day after day, is reacting to not having it. You've also been experiencing very severe and intense anxiety attacks. That is what is going on with your heart. According to your EKG and all of the tests, your heart is fine. However, it's obvious you have an issue with alcohol, and you should consider admitting yourself immediately to the hospital and go through a detoxification program."

What? You're kidding, right? I was in immediate denial. I thought, "Okay, maybe I have a bit of a problem, but admit myself into the hospital? No way, lady." I was polite and told her thanks for the advice, but I could handle this on my own. If somebody could just write me a prescription to deal with the anxiety, I would be on my way. They did, and I was. You see, I had some important things to do. Like maybe straighten up the house a little bit. Because would you believe, my Mom and Dad were flying in from Florida for a visit, the very... next... day. No kidding. YJCMTSU!

I stumbled through the visit with Mom and Dad with no major problems. Being self-sufficient as I was, I completely and successfully hid what was going on. Initially, nobody knew, with the exception of my attorney, Bob. I continued to function okay at work, and my life became manageable to a certain extent, using the tranquilizer, Valium.

Deep inside, though, I knew I had issues that needed to be addressed. The night in the ambulance and the hospitals was a wakeup call. For all of my adult life, I had been in total control. Now I had come across something that had turned the tables on me. I began to ponder if spiritual things were at the root of the issues, and I made two phone calls to finally talk to somebody.

One was to Wanda, my friend whom I had known since the 7th grade and who I visited in 1972 during my first trip to New York. The other was to David Loveless, whose dad pastored the church where I met Pam. David was now married and pastoring his first church in Vancouver, British Columbia. Wanda had become a Christian, and encouraged me to move toward that direction. David was a great listener, and very non-judgmental. There were many nights we would burn the long distance lines between coasts, I in Long Island, and he in Vancouver. I began to entertain the thought of pursuing my faith again, but was very leery of where that could lead me.

My concept of Christianity was not very deep. My theology consisted of this: being a Christian means you believe Jesus died for your sins, and then you try to do good. Doing good meant you don't do a lot of the stuff I'd been doing. Well, what if I actually enjoy doing the stuff I've been doing? *Uh Houston, we have a problem.* At least with all that had happened, I was now in a position to be slightly open-minded to possibly move in a spiritual direction. Maybe I could take some baby steps. I dug out an old Bible and began to read a little. I also started secretly attending a little church in Merrick. I knew the verse that says, "faith comes from hearing," so I thought, "Okay, I'll go on Sunday morning and listen."

However, I didn't really want to deal with anybody. I sat way in the back, alone and hidden away as best as possible. I arranged it so I could make an early exit when the service was over. I even gave a donation in the offering plate a few times, but I would white out my name and address on my check so nobody from the church would come visit me! As much as I tried to visit this church unnoticed, there was one guy in particular who it seems would always search me out, shake my hand, and tell me thanks for coming. At the time I didn't know his name, but

I knew I had seen him somewhere around Merrick before, somewhere besides the church.

Weeks went by, and I continued to function quite well on the tranquilizers. I was careful not to abuse them. My performance on the air was never affected. Amazingly, I had little desire to drink. I guess you could say the night in the ambulance and the hospitals had sort of scared me straight. If drinking could get you that much out of whack, I wasn't in a hurry to get that way again. The anxiety issues seemed to subside with the medication, and I began to try to taper off of it. I was still very unsettled with the spiritual issues.

Out of the blue, I got a call from my old friend Jim, the drywall guy from Sarasota. He had relocated from Florida to the eastern end of Long Island, where he was now working with a prosthetics company. I told him it would be great to see him and that I would head out Friday night after work. I always loved driving east out on the Island, because you could pick up Connecticut radio stations from across Long Island Sound. I was about three-quarters of the way to Jim's house, probably a good fifty miles from Merrick, when I realized I didn't have any medication with me. After weeks of not having anxiety issues, I had a full-blown anxiety attack while driving eastbound on the Long Island Expressway. I was out in the middle of nowhere and began to scream at the top of my lungs, "Jesus help me, Jesus help me!" I had nothing else to do but scream for help. I was terrified. I had no idea if Jesus could help, if Jesus was the answer, or if I would make it back to Merrick without crashing my car. All I knew was I was hurting. I was scared. And I was in desperate need of help.

I made it back to the house and took triple Valium to relieve the anxiety. I was devastated, tired, confused, and just flat worn out. I looked like hell. I felt even worse. I began to replay the events of the last few weeks, trying to figure things out. It was frustrating to not be in control of the situation. To this day, I still have some control issues, but back then it was an obsession. I didn't get any sleep, and around sunrise I wandered over to the Merrick train station, thinking I might get some breakfast at a diner I frequented. Parking at the almost empty station, I got out and began to walk to the diner, when surprisingly I ran into the friendly guy from the church. His name was Rich, he was a cabbie, and his home base was the Long Island Railroad Station at Merrick. That was why I recognized him when I visited the church. I had obviously seen his face before at the railroad station when I would catch the train to New York. He recognized me, offered his hand, and tried to begin a conversation.

"Whatcha doing up so early on a Saturday morning?" he asked.

I was so burned out, tired and frustrated, I just sort of opened up to this guy I barely knew. I told him about the alcohol problem, that I was now doing tranquilizers, the anxiety issues, searching spiritually, the whole bit. I was expecting to hear the typical, "You should give your life to Jesus and all your problems will go away," mini-sermon, but was about to be completely surprised. What he said next was so simple, but profound at the same time.

"Have you ever thought you have an addiction problem, and you just replaced one drug with another? I go to AA, have you ever thought of giving that a try?"

Rich Havemeyer still lives in Long Island, but no longer drives a cab. He now drives a school bus. To this day, I still count him as one of my dearest friends. Rich only worked one Saturday morning his entire life during his many years of driving a cab. That was the one morning.

FIFTEEN

The Program

ill Donovan. That was the first person who came to mind when Rich mentioned AA. When I visited Wanda in New York in 1972 and couldn't track her down, I remember staying with Bill and sitting in the back of his AA meeting. After crashing on the couch for a few hours, I got Bill on the phone Saturday afternoon, and he asked for directions to my house.

"I'll be right there, hang tight," he said.

We went out to dinner and I filled him in on the past few weeks. After dinner, he took me to my first AA meeting, in Bethpage, Long Island.

The first thing I noticed at the meeting was the acceptance. People openly shared their experiences and struggles, and the honesty was shocking, yet refreshing at the same time. As I listened, there was a lot that I heard that I related to, which made me realize I was not alone in my struggles. When they got around to Bill and me, Bill of course started with the traditional, "Hi, my name is Bill and I'm an alcoholic," and proceeded to talk for about five minutes. He obviously had years of experience at this stuff.

When it was my turn to talk, I think I said something like, "Hi, my name is Frank, this is my first meeting, and it's good to be here." The leader of the group welcomed me, told me I could find answers here, told me to "keep coming," and then moved on to the next person.

Nobody tried to fix me. No quick answers. Just keep coming. I liked it. The meeting lasted a few hours and we headed back to Merrick. I was still kind of reeling from the anxiety attack from the night before, and I asked Bill if he could spend the night because I was just simply afraid to be alone. He crashed on the couch. Bill has now been clean and sober for forty-three years. He still speaks at AA meetings and now lives outside of Richmond, Virginia. Four years ago, he found the love of his life and got married at the ripe young age of sixty-one. We connect by phone or email quite a few times a year. I'm grateful for a friend like Bill.

If you want to get plugged into Alcoholics Anonymous in Long Island, or anywhere in the New York City area, there are meetings going on all the time, everywhere. Most people get plugged into a local group. My new friend Rich introduced me to meetings that were held at Cure of Ars Catholic Church on Merrick Avenue. Though I visited other meetings, Cure of Ars became my home base. We met in the basement of the rectory, and since many attendees smoked, it wasn't the healthiest room to hang out in, but I was determined to find out all I could about sobriety, addiction, and basically try to find some answers, so the atmosphere didn't bother me. I even showed up at my first meeting with a notebook to take notes! My thought was, "Just tell me what to do to feel better and get a handle on this anxiety thing, and I'll do it."

Most people recommend you get a sponsor, somebody who has been in the program for a while to sort of guide you, especially at the beginning. I really shied away from that, and since Rich and I were quickly becoming friends, I concluded that my relationship with him would have to do. That was another thing I really liked about AA. Nobody made you do anything. Everything was suggested, but your involvement and 'working the program' was all up to you. I soon began hanging out with AA folks after meetings at places like The Merrick Diner, and Rich preferred a place called Byer's in Freeport. People in the program consisted of all types. Charlie was loud and obnoxious, but was totally accepted in 'the rooms.' Danny worked at the Post Office, was friendly and outgoing. We ended up jogging together quite often. Marilyn was always mad and had issues with men. William was more or less a street person who had a hard time holding a job. It didn't matter. We became friends. It eventually became known that I was the guy on the radio, but nobody seemed to make any kind of big deal about it. That was fine with me. I just wanted to feel better, and if AA could help me achieve that, then count me in.

After doing some research on the program, I concluded correctly that Christianity and the Bible were the foundation for the twelve steps of Alcoholics Anonymous. When you think about it, it's pretty basic stuff. Some of the steps that immediately jumped out at me: Admit you have a problem (be humble). Admit you are powerless (I can't do this on my own). Ask for help (God, or as they say in the program, your 'higher power,' can help). Make amends (forgive, and ask for forgiveness). Take inventory (search your heart for bitterness, wrong motives, etc) and pass it on (evangelism). Whenever people talked about their 'higher power,' I always equated that with Jesus.

I knew that my faith was seemingly real at times in my past, I just did not have a clue of how it related to me now. All of the things I may have thought were true at one time seemed so outdated, and so traditional, boring, and religious. But since AA had a spiritual component to it, that kept me moving in that direction. I continued to quietly visit the church in Merrick, and the conversations continued with Wanda and David. Wanda was more matter of fact, imploring me by saying, "You know the truth, what are you going to do with it?" I had a feeling that maybe everything that happened up until this time had some purpose to it, but I was nervous and scared about moving forward, quite frankly fearing that I would become some sort of goody-goody, smiling all the time, Bible-thumping religious wacko!

I continued to half-heartedly pray for guidance, but felt any prayers were bouncing off the ceiling. I would even stop by St. Patrick's Cathedral on 5th Avenue. It was only a few blocks from Rockefeller Plaza, and I would often stop in before work, find a quiet corner, and try to say a prayer. I began to wrestle with what is truth, what is not, and how it relates to me. In the black and white, it didn't. The only way anything made sense even remotely was to look at it from a faith perspective. I did know the Bible well enough that if I made a decision to once again pursue a relationship with God through Jesus, it was not exactly something that you kept to yourself. Not that I saw myself broadcasting to the world any decision I might make, but I determined early on if I was going to follow Christ, I would not, I could not deny him. If I was asked, I would tell. I went back and forth in my mind. *No way, I can't do it. Too much risk of rejection. Let me get this straight: afternoon radio personality at one of America's biggest radio stations makes a decision to do what? I don't think so.*

SIXTEEN

The Decision

Dr. Joseph LaFlare was an older doctor in Massapequa, Long Island. Dr. Joe was known in AA circles as being a 'program' doc. In other words, he was familiar with alcoholism issues, and had a sympathetic side for those who struggled with drinking and drug abuse. I liked Dr. Joe a lot. He had gray hair, and was very laid back. He could easily be your grandfather.

My blood pressure was elevated again, probably not unlike how it was when I went through the draft scare in 1970. Dr. Joe encouraged me to give myself time in letting my body adjust to life without alcohol. It seemed like I was always tense and wound up. Over the course of a few weeks, I went through some things that were out of the ordinary, if not downright bizarre, in what I was going through physically. Looking back, I suspect it could have been because I didn't properly detox. I also realize now that anxiety can manifest itself in many different ways in your body, physically. It seemed like over the course of a month I was always hurting. One week I had a headache that refused to go away. Then it was chest pains. Next, abdominal pains. It seemed to be non-stop. Dr. Joe was trying to encourage me to just let time pass, but I was impatient. I called my attorney, Bob again, and he recommended his personal physician in

New Hyde Park, Dr. Blum. I went to see him a few times, and the last time I was there, he looked me over and sat me down. What he said next startled me.

He said something like, "Look, I have no doubt you have been going through the physical symptoms you described, but I've run every test imaginable, and you are really very healthy. I really think what is going on is all up here," as he pointed to his head. He continued, "I have a friend who has an office down the hall, let me see if I can get you in to see him."

As I waited, I was thinking to myself, "Oh great, psychosomatic stuff. I am totally fine, I'm just a nut job!"

Dr. Blum came out, I thanked him, and I was on my way down the hall to see a psychologist, Dr. Polumbo.

Dr. Polumbo was pleasant enough but got right to the point. "Tell me what's going on, and how can I help?"

I laid out the drinking history, the transfer to tranquilizers, AA, how important my work was to me, and I briefly touched on the spiritual issues, but tried to keep the whole conversation more on the surface. I probably didn't talk for more than five or ten minutes. I suspected the whole conversation was merely a setup to work me in as a regular patient. What he said next was like a laser aimed straight at my heart.

"Look," he said, "I don't know specifically what it is you are going through, but it seems you are struggling with something. Maybe you're wresting with some kind of decision? I'll tell you what, whatever it is, deal with it, make a decision, and if you are still having problems, call my office and I'll work you into my schedule." He stood up, I shook his hand and thanked him, and I was off to catch the train to Manhattan.

The ride from New Hyde Park to Penn Station was about thirty-five minutes. I began to ponder the words, "make a decision." *What do I do with this moment, and what do I do with this information? Do I blow it off?*

I began to replay all that had happened the past few months. What did it all mean, if anything? Was this a God thing? Was God trying to lead me into something that I wasn't even sure I wanted to do? There were two things in my life that I held onto very tightly: my career, and my relationships with women. I wanted to be in total control and I wanted to call the shots. Sure, I had been slightly involved with the church in the past, but how was that relevant now?

Let's face it, if you are going to be serious about your faith, don't Christians lead boring lives? "Hey, let's all go sit in some old church on Wednesday night and sing a whole bunch of old hymns. That sounds like fun!" Not!

But, what if it's all true? If following Christ really was the answer, wouldn't it just make sense to follow? What about my fear of rejection, and what about the job? How do I continue to work at one of America's biggest radio stations, and pursue a faith journey? I just didn't see how that was going to work. I still didn't feel right physically. I wanted more than anything to just feel better. I came to the conclusion I was going to take a risk. I had no expectations. I do remember this: I was very sincere in what I was about to do.

As the train headed west into Manhattan, I bowed my head, and said a prayer that went something like this: "Dear God, if this is all about you, I've got to know. I know that I've taken things into my own hands, and done my own thing for a very long time. If you really are the way and the truth, I forsake it all to know you, and to know the truth. You know I've held onto things like my job and relationships very tightly. I give them up if that's what you want. If the job goes, so be it. I know the relationship I have been in is not honest, and I know it is wrong. I release these areas of my life and everything as best I can to you. Please show me the truth, and guide me in the days ahead. I surrender all, every bit of it, just for the sake of knowing you. Amen."

I also remember ending almost jokingly as an afterthought, "And oh yeah, dear God, if at all possible, please don't let the rest of my life be boring."

Little did I know. My life was about to be completely, undeniably, radically changed.

SEVENTEEN

Howard

———— ✎ ————

S ince my afternoon drive shift at WNBC was from 2-6pm, I usually headed into The City around noon. This was great because I didn't have to deal with the rush hour crowds on the train. Less than forty-eight hours after the prayer on the train, I got a phone call about 8 in the morning. Nothing had changed as a result of my little devotional time on my ride into work. I had no earth-shattering revelations. I still felt the same. On the phone was Metheny. It was odd to get a call at 8. I was more used to getting a call in the middle of the night whenever he needed me to come in and fill in for Imus.

"I need you in the office this morning at 10, an important meeting with Fioravanti," he said. I asked him, "What's up?" He told me he would tell me when I got in.

I caught the 8:30 train and made it into the office with about fifteen minutes to spare. I waited for Kevin to come out of his office, and I could tell as soon as I saw him he was stressed. It was all over his face. We headed down the hall to the boss' office and all I remember him saying was, "Look, Frank, whatever you do, don't freak out, everything will be okay."

As we entered the office to have a seat, I had a feeling that maybe this wasn't going to go too well. Dom Fioravanti, our General Manager, got promoted to the position after being our Sales Manager. I genuinely liked him. His body language and manner was fairly positive and upbeat as we greeted, but Kevin's demeanor tipped me off that maybe I was either in deep trouble over something, or heaven forbid, for whatever reason maybe I was being let go. After a few pleasantries, Dom jumped right into the issue at hand.

"Frank, you are one of the best in the country at what you do. We like you a lot. But we're making changes." I was feeling okay until the, "we're making changes" part. At this time, my mind started going into overtime, big time. To me, making changes meant one thing: You are fired! You are getting blown out!

Great. I've "given my life to Jesus," I surrendered my job in that stupid prayer, and now I'm history. God is going to send me to Africa to do missionary radio! Honestly, I thought it was all over. Less than forty-eight hours. I'm thinking, "Wow, God works fast, huh?" I was braced for him to say, "Sorry, we're letting you go."

And then, just seconds later, Dom continued talking, and things completely turned around. He said, "Frank we need to let somebody go, but it's not going to be you. However, we are taking you off afternoon drive. We are not quite sure yet, but we think we want to put you on the midday shift after Imus. We'll keep your salary and everything else the same. We hope you will stay. We want you to stay. But we've hired somebody who does something completely different to do the afternoon drive shift. He's on his way from Washington, DC, and his name is Howard Stern."

I sat there trying to not appear stunned. For a quick moment I thought, "Howard who?" My mind was going a mile a minute in overtime, trying to process everything. It was all happening so fast. And then my next thought was one of relief. Talk about a 180. One moment I think I'm out, the next moment, I'm thinking, "Okay, uh, let me think through this; I'm still making big bucks, and the midday shift is still a prime time. I'm still employed by the National Broadcasting Company, and when you think about it, the pressure is going to be on the new guy coming in, and less on me." I had gone from the overnight guy, to afternoon drive, now moved to middays. This was a pretty big change, but it was not the end of the world.

Looking back, this was a pivotal moment in my journey. My whole idea of Christianity up until this time was so narrow, rigid, and legalistic. I thought for sure I was on my way out, and I initially thought it was because of the prayer I said on the train. If God and all of this talk of faith were real, was he really going to be okay with me working at a big time secular radio station? I was certain at the beginning of the meeting I was gone. Things were upside down from what I expected.

The result of that meeting was the beginning of me looking at things differently, and the beginning glimpse of realizing that following Christ was not going to be anything like I thought it would be. It was like looking at my faith and life with a new set of glasses. Everything that had happened felt so *personal*. I actually considered the thought that God was taking a personal interest in what happened to *me*. When I said the prayer on the train, I thought my life as I knew it could come to an end. I didn't realize it at the time, but in reality, my life was actually just beginning.

I sent the new guy, Howard Stern, a congratulatory telegram. I found out we hired him from DC 101 in Washington, so I just sent it to him in care of the radio station. I didn't get a reply, but didn't think anything of it. I was so relieved that I dodged a bullet with the job, and was grateful to still have a prime daytime shift. After I found out a little more about Howard's reputation in Washington, I understood the move that management was making. Imus was outrageous in the morning, and Stern would make a good complement for the afternoon shift. I got that, so it made it easier to accept my new position.

I've always been a team player, and while all of us have some sort of ego, I didn't consider the step down to a less important time slot to be that big of a deal. I looked at it this way: I was a good, basic air personality who was good at following a format. I could probably be described as likable and friendly on the air, but certainly not outrageous. I continued to reflect on the meeting and the change. It was as if God was saying to me, "Walk this way, trust me, just keep moving forward. I've heard you. You don't have to figure everything out. Just take it one step at a time."

I began to consume the Bible, and one of the verses I held on to closely was Romans 8:14, which says, "those who are led by the spirit of God are sons of God." I knew without a doubt I was being led, so that verse was a great comfort to me. It was like I was heading into a season of entirely new beginnings. I started to view everything in my life with the possibility that God can be intimately involved with every aspect of it. It was exciting and scary all at the same time.

I continued to get involved with AA, and Rich and I became good friends. I finally had somebody I could bounce things off of, and somebody who would listen and offer counsel. He was an AA guy but also a solid Christian. He lived in a dumpy rooming house in Freeport, but I put my ego aside and was often knocking on his door. We made a lot of AA meetings together, and would often drive to a rehab hospital to get B-12 shots. Word was that could help with my anxiety. The anxiety was intermittent, and continued to be an issue, but I was slowly learning how to live with it and accept it. If the Apostle Paul had some sort of thorn in the flesh to keep him humble and dependent on God, who was I to demand immediate relief?

Back in the early '70s when I was semi-involved with the church, it seemed like the message was, "God loves you, come to him, and your troubles go away." What I've found in my own experience is that God is more real to me in the difficult times, rather than when life is going smoothly. Let me be clear: my personality is such that I would just as well like to avoid pain, disappointment, heartache, and conflict. I don't go out of my way to look for those things, and frankly, sometimes I probably go out of my way to avoid them. But I can't deny the fact that the hard times draw you closer to God. It's bitter sweet. The physical anxiety issues I was dealing with definitely kept me on my knees in prayer, so in retrospect, that was a good thing.

I felt that I should let Kevin know what was going on, so I laid it all out for him, but didn't share that much about the spiritual issues. Amazingly, with everything that was going on, I don't think I missed one day of work. Since I never really went to a rehab when I got clean, I found out about a place in upstate New York where you could voluntarily go and check yourself in. The name of the place was Veritas Villa, and Kevin gave me a week off so I could go there. I didn't have to lobby for the time, he just said, "No problem," and told me to do whatever I had to do to take care of myself. Upstate New York is night and day from Manhattan. I took a week off to focus on myself and my sobriety. It was a good decision.

The Stern era at WNBC began a little shaky, but once Robin Quivers arrived, the show began to really take off. From my perspective, the Stern movie 'Private Parts' seemed to define those times pretty well. It was a real kick to hear Captain Frank get a mention in the film. My interaction with Howard was pretty limited to running into him in the hall, and me coming off the air while he was coming on. A few times he did mention to me that management was "messing with him," and I tried to occasionally offer him a word of encouragement. It wasn't much more than me saying, "Well, hang in there," but I figured that was better than not saying anything at all. My feelings toward him were mixed. As part of the team, I wanted him to succeed.

He mocked Christianity, so of course I was a natural target. I had no animosity or jealousy toward him; it was just kind of awkward. He did say some things at times that were genuinely funny; things like, "Captain Frank walked to work today across the East River," and at Christmas time, "That Frank is a real Christian, I drove by his house and he's got a live nativity scene, live donkeys, camels, even a live baby Jesus!" Often his barbs were rather personal, but I refused to let it bother me.

I look back on that time, and am amazed at how God provided just the right counsel, at just the right time. We went thru a pastor change at the church in Merrick, and the new guy, Clyde Michener, took a personal interest in me and was aware of what was happening on the air. He encouraged me to not take the insults personally, and pointed me to some great verses in the Bible that put things in perspective. He also offered the single best piece of advice that I would hold onto for the next three years. Something to the effect of this: "Frank, it's no coincidence you are where you are. You are working at living out your faith, while being employed by one of the biggest radio stations in America. Whatever you do, don't leave because it gets a little uncomfortable. When it's time to go, you will not have any doubt. God will make it perfectly clear." Once again, God had used somebody to bring me just the right advice, at just the right time. Since I was now looking at everything from a "Yes, God really is involved!" perspective, I knew it was no coincidence.

EIGHTEEN

Jennifer

M y AA friends encouraged me to take it slow with any personal relationships, but now believing things in my life didn't just happen by chance, I began seeing a girl named Jennifer, who went to my church. She was a fashion designer in the city, and I vaguely remember seeing her before at the train station catching the LIRR into Manhattan. Her father, Ken, led an adult Bible study at my church, and was just an awesome Bible teacher. Jen played guitar and would lead worship in the class, and it was great to be dating someone who I could connect with on a spiritual level. Amazingly, Metheny let me have a 5:30 am slot on Sunday mornings at WNBC for a Christian music show, so we spent a lot of time listening to music. I can remember getting Michael W. Smith's second album, and telling Jen, "Hey, wait till you hear this!"

Little did I know there was an AM station on Long Island that actually played Christian music. Lloyd Parker was the program director of WLIX, and I can remember it like yesterday, driving out to his home, where he and his wife Ellen gave me a crash course in one night on Contemporary Christian Music, or CCM as they called it. There was a little Christian bookstore in Wantaugh, Long Island called 'The Rock,' and I was there often to check on the latest music that was coming out of Nashville, which is where the majority of Christian music was being produced.

The thirty-minute show on WNBC consisted mostly of me just playing the songs, so with only thirty minutes, I determined to play 'the best of the best.' I played a lot of Michael W. Smith, Amy Grant, DeGarmo and Key, the hipper Sandi Patti stuff and the like. Lloyd would eventually invite me to the Gospel Music Association convention in Nashville, and Jen and I went and attended the Dove Awards in 1985. I wondered if Christian radio might be in my future someday. I also needed to know about the music because I ended up going into the restaurant business with two other guys that I had met at a Christian singles group. The Mustard Seed in Manhassett, Long Island, had sort of a health food theme, and I had put together Christian music tracks for our background music at the restaurant. The business failed after about a year, but it was cool to go in there on a Saturday night and see the place packed out. The concept was good, the food was great, but being off the beaten path in downtown Manhassett, the location just didn't work. Imus would occasionally joke about us and give us a plug on the radio when he would say things like, "Of course since Frank is a Christian, all of the waiters have to wear sandals!"

Jen and I really connected, and without talking about it, I think we both might have had thoughts of, 'Is this the one?' I liked her a lot. I thought it was very neat she was a designer. She was very talented and really good at what she did. Since I lived alone, she made the suggestion that perhaps I get a dog. That ended up being an excellent idea. I contacted a breeder on Eastern Long Island, and got a very cute golden retriever puppy. I named him Josh, and he would become a loyal friend for about the next twelve years.

I only had one big run-in with Imus on the air while we were working together, and my new girlfriend was right smack dab in the middle of it. Jen had custom bathing suits made for all of the guys on the air staff, and had them delivered by courier to the radio station. She worked for a company owned by Joanna Carson (of Johnny Carson fame), and they had the rights to use prints by a very famous (unnamed) artist. The prints were rather loud and colorful, and I thought they made a great bathing suit! The morning after Don got his suit, he went on this verbal rampage on the air on how disgusting it looked. If I recall correctly, he said it looked like somebody threw up! Now of course I know that this is what Don does, but I took it very personally and blew a gasket. As soon as I got to the station that morning I confronted him in his office and let him have it. I'm screaming at him, he's screaming at me, and we are getting nowhere. I think the last thing I shouted was, "Look, I like this girl a lot, you went over the line, and I am really ticked off!" I stormed out of his office. Since this is way, way out of character for me, I'm wondering who heard, what are they thinking, what am I thinking, and am I stupid, in love, or both.

The next morning, Don was talking to Charles, his longtime sidekick on the air, and said something like, "Captain Frank's girlfriend made me a bathing suit and I said some unkind things about it, and, uh, I'm sorry, and that will never, ever happen again." I was shocked. It was totally unexpected and out of character. We never discussed it again.

My WNBC journey continued for about three more years after the arrival of Stern. My on-air time there totaled, amazingly, just under eight years. The station wanted more personality between Imus and Stern, and ended up hiring the famous TV personality, Soupy Sales, to take my place. When I got called into the office by then Program Director Dale Parsons to be told my contract wasn't going to be renewed, I was at total peace. Pastor Clyde told me when it was time to leave it would be crystal clear, and it was.

WNBC was a once-in-a-lifetime ride I will never forget. I got to meet some big time celebrities, like Barry Manilow, Meatloaf, and my personal musical favorite at the time, Billy Joel. It was a kick to run into people like Bill Murray in the elevator during his run with Saturday Night Live. We added Wolfman Jack to the on-air lineup, and it was neat to be on the same radio station with another one of the icons in my business. But the biggest take-away from my time in New York is that is where I truly found God. It was now the real deal, and I couldn't deny it.

My last week on the air, I filled in for Imus per his request since he was on vacation, and my last show on WNBC was a blast. My friend Elliot, the guy who got me the meeting with Clifton in Miami, now had his own video production company in New York, and he came in and videotaped the whole show. I had lots of on-air calls from old friends all morning, and a special recorded farewell from Imus, who wished me well, and "hoped that I would get a lot of sex in Florida!" which was typical Don.

I decided rather than try to get another job as soon as possible, I was going to head home to Florida and take a break. I had some money in the bank, and for the first time in my working career, I determined to just decompress for a few months. Before I hit the road, I had emceed a high school prom for a Christian high school in Long Island. During one of the breaks, I was tracked down by a young female Christian artist who I went to see perform many times on the Island. I was definitely a fan and even tried to pursue her once for a date. She heard that I was moving and was seeking my advice. She explained to me she had the opportunity to move to Nashville and write for Sparrow Records. I told her absolutely, I thought she had the talent to do a lot more than just write, and that she should go. (About a year later, I would be in a Christian bookstore in Orlando, and was overjoyed to come across Margaret Becker's debut album!)

With the house sold, and a long goodbye to Jennifer, I loaded my stuff and the classic MG into a big Ryder truck, and attached my car to the back with a tow bar. With Josh riding shotgun, we said goodbye to New York and headed south to Florida.

NINETEEN

Homeward Bound

The Clermont Chain of Lakes is about thirty to forty-five minutes west of Orlando, depending on the traffic. I had always dreamed of living on The Butler Chain, which is closer to Orlando in a little town called Windermere. (This was the chain of lakes where I had hoped we would have lived when we moved from Baltimore, but my mom had vetoed the idea.) Lakefront prices there were out of reach for me, so the Clermont Chain was a little farther out, but more affordable. I had purchased a lakefront lot on Lake Louisa on the chain of lakes in 1982 for $45,000. Heading home, one of my first thoughts was to build my dream home there. I netted over $100K on the sale of the Merrick property, so I was in good shape to pretty much build what I wanted, with a decent down payment and a reasonable mortgage.

When I got home, I stayed with Mom and Dad for a while. Dad was even kind enough to fence in the backyard for my golden retriever, Josh. Dad always did like dogs, and he genuinely liked having Josh around. I filed for unemployment, but wasn't in any real hurry to find work. Most days were spent out at the lake lot, clearing the beach from vegetation, and huddling with a few different builders on a house design. Josh loved being in the water, so it was relaxing just driving to Clermont, do a little manual work, work up a sweat and then just jump in and go swimming in the lake at my vacant lot.

Clermont was surrounded by orange groves, and when the orange blossoms would bloom, the aroma in the air was intoxicating. I felt incredibly blessed that I had my own little spot on the water. The Clermont Chain had a special designation by the state, categorizing it as an 'Outstanding Florida Water.' The water was so pristine, and my little personal beach was perfect sand. It really is a special place.

An old high school friend, Philip, had a boat moored across the lake at a lot owned by his parents, and I really got into hyrdrosliding, or kneeboarding. My thought at the time was to get moving on the house, find a job on the radio somewhere, enjoy living on the water, get plugged into a good church, and hopefully figure out what was going on with my personal life.

Driving back to Mom and Dad's house in Pine Hills always gave me time to scan the radio in Central Florida to see what was going on. Jon Hull, who Lloyd introduced me to when Jen and I were in Nashville, was programming a 100,000 watt Christian music noncommercial FM out of Lakeland called WCIE. It really was a very good sounding radio station, and I got to keep up with all of the Christian music coming out of Nashville. I visited Jon, but there weren't any openings. One of my old places on the dial, 1440 on AM (which used to be WABR) was now a Christian teaching and talk station. During the daytime, I could pick them up pretty good in Clermont, and I began listening to a program on the way home out of Dallas called 'People to People.' It was a call-in counseling show, and the host, Bob George, had a very casual, relaxed style on the air. He was very easy to listen to, very normal sounding, not your typical radio preacher. I began to listen on a regular basis, and just like other times in my life of being in the right place at the right time, I went though a season of emotional and spiritual healing through listening to this program. I began to truly understand the unconditional love and grace of God. It sank deep into my spirit, and it began to revolutionize my way of thinking. Daily listening to the radio was almost like this healing balm that was being poured over my soul. I continue to be amazed to this day, how it seems God gives you just what you need, when you need it.

The first few years of my sobriety, I dealt with a lot of remorse and regret. It was as if feelings and emotions that had been suppressed for so long began to rise to the surface. Listening to the program and cross-referencing everything I heard with scripture helped me to release my past and let it go. Though I knew in my head what the Bible said was done on our behalf at the cross of Christ, it was now translating down deep into my heart. I came to the conclusion that I was totally, 100 percent forgiven. I was totally accepted. I was being set free from the guilt and shame of my past actions. It was incredibly liberating and life-changing. I took to heart a verse in Romans chapter 8, verse 1. There was no condemnation for me. None. It was as if those months of not working were custom designed to help me stabilize even more emotionally and spiritually.

After a few months of kicking back, I was ready to look for work. Star 101 was the hot new station in town, and the General Manager personally knew Randy Bongarten, who was one of my station managers at WNBC, so through that connection I got an interview. They had an afternoon opening, but I tried to convince the program director he should hire me for mornings (After all I explained, I was Imus' choice when he was away!), but that idea that didn't go over too well. I never got a call back. I read that the owner of WALK-FM in Long Island was buying WELE-FM just outside of Orlando and would probably change the format from Country to Adult Contemporary, which was a hot format at the time. I wrote the owner, Alan Beck directly, told him I used to be at WNBC (hoping he had been a listener), that I was now in Orlando, and would love the opportunity to work for him. A few weeks went by and the new Program Director for the station, Bill Gable, called and asked me to lunch with him and the new general manager. We set a date to meet, and I began to pray about what could be my next career move.

Growing up in Orlando as a kid was great if you were into rockets and the space program, which I was, since Dad worked for Martin-Marietta. I remember being let out of class for a few minutes on a clear day so we could look east toward Cape Canaveral, and we could see the flume from the rockets during the Mercury and Gemini missions.

January 28, 1986 I had lunch scheduled with Bill and the new GM of the station, George Toulas. I had played racquetball that morning in College Park, and as I was leaving the building, I noticed people in the street looking east. It must be a space shot, I thought, probably the space shuttle. I got over to The Hilton Hotel for lunch, and noticed everybody huddled around the TV in the lounge. The space shuttle Challenger had exploded, and folks were noticeably shaken, myself included. I thought of my Dad since he had worked on the external tank for the shuttle, and wondered if he knew the news. It dampened the beginning of our meeting, but we moved on and worked out a deal for me to do the afternoon shift.

Both Bill and George seemed like good guys, and it was exciting to be building a new station on the air from scratch in my home town. WOCL (formerly WELE-FM) was at 105.9 on the dial and we would brand it as CLASS-FM. They were building brand new studios in Longwood, just north of Orlando off of Interstate 4, and I was part of a brand new staff. We would be advised by an up-and-coming consultant in the industry whose expertise was AC, or Adult Contemporary, Mike McVay.

I told Mom and Dad thanks for the free rent, but I was going to get an apartment five minutes away from the station. After a few months of me being at home, I think they were probably ready to see me go! Since I didn't have a place for a dog, they agreed to keep Josh for me, and I think Dad preferred that anyway. They had become buds.

We had dinner one night before my move, and Mom announced that she had some tests done, and told me not to worry, but it looked like she might have cancer. I tried to give the appearance of calm, and I think for the most part I pulled it off. I told Mom I'd be praying for her, told both her and Dad, "I'm here if you need anything," and that I would just be thirty minutes away. I settled into my new place, and began working with Bill and the new staff getting ready for the on-air launch of CLASS-FM.

I hadn't been in my new apartment more than a week when I got a call from a guy named David Pierce in Dallas. He was programming a brand new full-power FM station in Dallas that was playing Contemporary Christian Music twenty-four hours a day. The frequency was 94.9, the call letters: KLTY. This was the first time I had heard of a full-time commercial radio station programming that music 24/7, and I was genuinely intrigued. A big signal, in a major market, playing Christian music. I wondered to myself if there was enough good music to program a station like that full-time. While I was flattered that he was interested in hiring me, and even though it sounded exciting, I knew immediately the timing was not right. Mom just announced she was sick, I was in the middle of having a custom home built on a beautiful lakefront lot, and I was genuinely excited about helping build a new station from scratch in the town I grew up in. I told him thanks for thinking about me, but this was definitely not the right time for me to make a move.

I ended up working with a great builder named Rick Weber. Rick grew up in Clermont, and had made quite a name for himself as a custom homebuilder. He and his wife Linda and their kids lived in a real show-case of a home on Lake Mineola, which was on the Clermont Chain, but on the opposite end of where my place was on Lake Louisa. We broke ground and framed out where the foundation would be poured, and after he had it all laid out, I told him I thought the house should be back another ten to fifteen feet away from the road.

"Well Frank, that ten or fifteen feet is going to cost you an extra hundred fifty dollars!" he said.

I just laughed and told him, "No problem, let's move it," and that was really about the only problem we had in the whole process.

I had always been told that having a home built can be a nightmare, but if you've got the right guy, it can be super fun and exciting. Rick and his crew were the right guys. From Longwood to Clermont was a good forty-five minute drive, but I was out there often to check on the progress. We were building a custom two-story cedar home, three bedrooms, two baths, two living and two dining areas. I had 100 feet of lake frontage, so we designed it so just about all of the living areas and bedrooms faced the water. I particularly liked the design of the master bedroom suite, which took up most of the 2nd floor, and had a covered balcony overlooking the water. Rick told me to expect completion in six to eight months.

My childhood dream of living in a waterfront property someday was within sight.

TWENTY

You've got Class!

C LASS-FM was a fun place to work, and Bill had assembled a
good team. I began to hang out over at the Gable's often, and
have developed a close friendship with them down through the years.
They had a pool area that was screened in, and it was very welcoming,
just a really great place to hang out. Bill's wife, Patty, told me that she
and Bill had prayed for the right people for the staff, which led me to
conclude that could have been one of the reasons I didn't get the call
back from STAR 101. I was more than qualified for a job there, but
after the interview couldn't even get my calls returned. George Toulas,
my General Manager at CLASS, would prove to be instrumental in the
future with me getting into Christian radio, so this was one of those
instances where you feel that things happened, or didn't happen, for
a reason.

That has been one of the best discoveries down through the years.
When you give control of your life to Christ, and believe the creator of
all things can truly guide you and direct you, it makes for an incredibly
exciting journey. Since he made me, he knows me better than I know
myself, and he alone knows what's best, even if I can't see it at the time.

Steven Curtis Chapman had a great song from one his earlier albums called 'Higher Ways.' It's a reminder that God sees the big, total picture, while our vision for the future is limited.

I got the word from Mom that she had lung cancer, and it hit me pretty hard. Mom had smoked probably all of her life, and even though she tried to give me the impression while I was living at home that she had quit, she obviously had not. The good news was Dad had just retired from Martin-Marietta after working forty-four years, and he could devote all of his time to helping Mom battle the disease. They told her surgery was out of the question, so they were going to try to target the tumor with radiation. She began treatments immediately. I stayed in close touch with both of them, and Dad and I attended some therapy groups especially for families dealing with cancer.

Mom was very independent, and for whatever reason didn't want to go to the sessions. I knew my Mom was a Christian, no doubt about it, and I knew she prayed for me often, if not daily. That was why it was hard to accept the fact that she couldn't get a handle on this addiction or even if she wanted to. Having an addictive personality myself, I've never judged others who struggle with various dependencies, no matter what they are. I think many of us will have issues with one thing or another until our earthly bodies are replaced. We've all got our weaknesses. The good news is, as you grow in your relationship with Christ, it may take time, but there are many things that can be overcome. I just wish earlier in her life my Mom could have overcome this killer.

I got involved with a great church that met in the auditorium at Loch Haven Park in Orlando. Orlando Community Church was an off-shoot of Northland Church in Longwood. OCC had quite a few professional singles who attended there, and it was a great fit. The teaching was solid, and it was a very laid back and relaxed atmosphere. I developed a friendship with Curt Heffelfinger, who was the Associate Pastor. I've always felt it was just a good idea to hang out with people who were more mature than me spiritually, and I've always been keen on soliciting sound advice from others. It's scriptural that the counsel of many is a good thing. Curt was a great person to run ideas by, and just a great person to have lunch and share life with.

I still had feelings for Jennifer, and I really hadn't met anybody in Florida I was interested in, so I invited her down for a visit. It went well. I didn't really want to press the issue if the timing wasn't right, but I began to think about what our life would look like together. I took her over to the house to meet Mom and Dad, and as we were leaving, Jen said something to Mom like, "Take good care of him," and my Mom, never at a loss for words and speaking her mind, replied right back, "Well I wish ya'll would just take care of each other!" I just had to laugh. I knew that Mom would love to see me married, but for whatever reason, God would delay that for a few years yet. Even though I was now thirty-six, I was content with letting God dictate that part of my life, as well as everything else.

Things seemed to be going pretty well at CLASS-FM, but we did have a lot of competition. BJ-105 was right down the dial from us, and was the FM station that played the Top 40 hits. STAR 101 was also in the top tier of stations, and we were having a hard time breaking through, even though in my opinion we sounded great. For whatever reason, George decided to demote Bill from the Program Director position, and he paid me well to fill in as interim PD. I pitched for the job, but he had his eye on somebody else.

I had everything caught up at the station on a Thursday night, and was in good enough shape at the office to take a few days off. It was as if the next few days were all planned out in advance. It was Friday, September 26, 1986, about noon when I got the call.

From as early as I can remember, I loved being in the water. This is probably from Holly Beach on the Chesapeake.

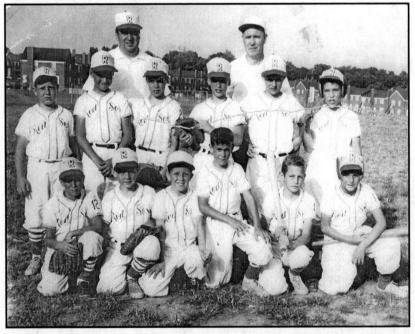

I lived for Little League. Of course my favorite team was the Orioles. That's me on the back row all the way on the right.

Dad and me, at the house on Hornet
Drive. Around '65.

Around 1969 all of a sudden I got
tall! With Mom and Dad.

Larry Shannon and I with a promo piece for Disney's first Grad Nite. The first few years of Disney World in Orlando was an exciting thing to be a part of.

On the air at WIVY Jacksonville. I lived a block away from the ocean and loved my time there.

On the air at WMJX, 96-X Miami. My business attire consisted of jeans, shorts, t-shirts, and sneakers.

WNBC "Next One!" launch party. Don Imus, Charles McCord, Chief Engineer Bill Krause, me and Allen Beebe.

Afternoons at WNBC, Studio 2-A, 30 Rockefeller Plaza.

WNBC promo piece for the on-air lineup, around 1984.

With Mom, Dad, and Kit in the mid 80's. Celebrating their 40th wedding anniversary.

Josh and me at my home on Long Island.

My spot at Lake Louisa, Clermont, Florida.

Promo piece with Sharon Davis, at my first Christian station, WWDJ. Sharon is now heard on Star 99.1 New York.

Our wedding day, October 5, 1991.

Our son Ryan Christopher arrived in September 1994.

Patti with baby Hope, 1999.

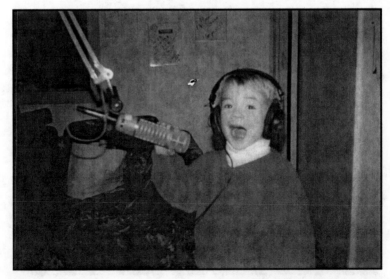

My son Ryan, future broadcaster, KLTY studios at Christmas time 1998.

My good friend and amazing co-host and news anchor, Starlene Stringer. She is definitely a "party in a person!"

One of my best decisions as Program Director of KLTY; hiring Andi Jaxson! Andrea is now heard nationwide as host of "Nightlight".

When Patti ran The Shepherd's Guide, I was often her delivery guy. Hope was helping Dad on this day.

I have always been a big fan of 4Him. This was backstage at Gateway Church during their final tour.

If I'm not listening to KLTY, I am probably listening to our sister station, 660AM The Answer. I've always been a Mark Davis fan, and I'm delighted he is on the air down the hall from me every morning from 7-10am. This pic was shot as we shared the sideline at a Grapevine Faith football game.

I always dreamed of having a lake place where I could share my love of the water with the kids. Ryan and Hope at Lake Cypress Springs.

After being separated for 75 years, we celebrated the reunion of Uncle Dave and Barbara (Nanny) at our home in Colleyville. That's Uncle Dave on the left, and Nanny seated. Cousin Paula, who had a life change during her visit here, is standing next to Patti.

One of the neatest things for me as a Dad has been to introduce my kids to some of the artists. Ryan with Toby Mac.

On the air with Amy Grant. She sent a very touching on air message when I celebrated 20 years at KLTY.

Patti and I made a trip back to New York in 2008 for our 17th wedding anniversary, and it coincided with the timing of a big WNBC reunion. It was the 20th year anniversary of the sign off of WNBC. It is now 660 WFAN.

My sister Kitty and brother in law John came down for Celebrate Freedom a few years ago. Kit wanted to meet Mac Powell. No problem Sis!

My amazing team. If it sounds like we're having fun, it's because we are! Cowboy Chris Chamberlain, Perri Reavis, and Starlene Stringer.

My rising star, Hope, in the lead role as Annie for The Acting Studio, Grapevine, Texas.

Steven Curtis Chapman and I share a long history. I'm honored to call him my friend. He stopped in on the air with Starlene and I during his "Glorious Unfolding" tour.

Receiving an award at the National Religious
Broadcasters Convention, 2009.

My family. A wonderful gift from my Heavenly Father. At Ryan's high
school graduation, Spring 2013.

TWENTY-ONE

A Farewell

I answered the phone in my office and it was Dad. "Son, I'm at the hospital, I think you should get down here as soon as you can."

I knew that Mom had been weak and losing weight from all of the treatments, but evidently something happened and Dad had to call an ambulance. I drove as soon as I could downtown to the hospital, and rushed up to the room on the 6th floor. Dad was alone in the room with Mom, and it was eerie, almost spooky, but not in a necessarily bad way. He was holding Mom's hand, and he was a man at total peace. It was as if he was surrounded by some sort of supernatural presence, something I could sense, but could not see. It was comforting, but a little uncomfortable and scary at the same time. Mom was looking straight ahead, eyes wide open but not moving or blinking, and she seemed to take a loud breath every two to three seconds. That scared me.

Then my Dad said something like this: "Son, your mom has had a stroke. She is dying. Our pastor just left, he prayed with us, and told your mom it's okay, it's time for her to go home. I've had her for forty-three years, and I'm prepared to let her go."

I couldn't get over his calm demeanor; it was as if he wasn't real. I told Dad "okay," and that I would be right back. I left the room and headed down to my car as soon as possible to get my Bible, which I just happened to have with me. For some reason, I just felt like I needed to have it close to me. I headed back up to the room and ran into the doctor in the elevator.

"Are you Thelma's son?"

I answered, "Yes sir, is she, uh..."

"Yes," he said. "I'm sorry."

When I got back to the room, Dad was waiting for me outside, and we shared a long hug. I thought of going in to say my goodbyes, but I knew she was gone. I told Dad I had a few days off, and that I would come stay at the house with him for a few days, and left to head up to my apartment to get some clothes. For some reason, I had this fear of being overcome with grief, and I didn't want to be alone. My old friend that I've known since junior high, Wanda, was now back home in Orlando. I called her, told her about Mom, and asked if she could meet me at my apartment. We met there within the hour.

I kept on waiting for it to hit, and it never happened.

"What are you talking about?" Wanda wanted to know.

I told her I was afraid to be alone because I expected this wave of overcoming grief to overtake me, and it never arrived. That was why I didn't want to be alone. Then it dawned on me, I really believed what I believed! Since I had never experienced a loss like this before, I didn't know what to expect. For some reason, I had this preconceived notion that this had to be a terrible experience. The reality was, it was not. I was sad that Mom was gone, I felt bad for my Dad, but if the gospel was true, and I believed that it was, Mom was in a better place, I would see her again, and I had nothing to fear! I was so overwhelmed with this revelation, I asked Wanda if we could just stop and pray. We got on our knees just inside my apartment's open front door, and just began praising God for who he was, for Mom's life, and for victory over death. It was a neat moment.

As a believer, you just have those times when you sense God's presence. Little did I know that an old bachelor friend, Bill, who lived right across from me, had his front door open, and was witnessing the whole thing. It was kind of funny and embarrassing at the same time. As we were leaving, Wanda felt our behavior needed some sort of explanation and said to him, "Frank's mom, Thelma just passed away, and we are happy and rejoicing because we know that Thelma is with Jesus and the angels right at this very moment, and isn't that something! Bye-bye now!"

I headed home, and one of the pastors from Mom and Dad's church was already there to visit with Dad and talk about the funeral. He asked me how I was doing, I told him much better than I ever imagined, and made the point that as believers we really needed to pass on the fact that this is different for us because of the cross! He suggested that maybe I would like to make that point myself during the service. I told him and Dad if that was what they wanted, I was fine with that.

We contacted my sister, and everybody we knew. Mom was the oldest in her family, so we had lots of relatives we had to reach. We planned the funeral for Tuesday, which would give everybody ample time to get to Florida.

People started pouring into town, and of course this was a special time for me and Dad and my sister, Kitty. I had grown closer to my sister as we got older, and I had so much respect for her and my brother-in-law, John. They've also raised some amazing kids, and Johnny, Jeff and Lena all made the trip. Aunt Helen came down from Virginia, and I think she cried the most at the first visit to the funeral home. Since she was just a year younger than Mom, she said through her tears that, "Sissy had always been there." I distinctly remember my sister doing her best to comfort and console her. Everybody gathered at Mom and Dad's before we all drove to the funeral. It was quite a long procession heading over there.

The church was filled with old friends I hadn't seen for years, and all of Mom's surviving family were there: Uncle Bill, Uncle Larry, Aunt Libby, and of course Aunt Helen. Mom wanted the gospel preached at her funeral, and if she had any wish, it would be that all of her siblings came to faith in Christ. An old friend of the family, Clarence Walters sang the solo, and Reverend Hicks from her church talked fondly about Mom and presented the gospel. When it was my turn to speak, I had my brother-in-law John standing by and sitting next to me if I couldn't pull it off, but for the most part I held it together pretty good. Before I got up to talk, I reflected on the fact that I got to share the last fifteen months home in Orlando close to Mom and Dad after being away for so many years, and what a gift that time was. I shared one of Mom's favorite scripture passages before I offered my thoughts. From the book of John chapter 14, Jesus said: "Do not let your hearts be troubled, trust in God, trust also in me. In my Father's house are many rooms; if it were not so, I would have told you. I am going there to prepare a place for you, And if I go and prepare a place for you, I will come back and take you to be with me that you also may be where I am."

I don't remember my exact words from that morning, but I know I wanted people to know that there is a difference when a loved one dies and your faith is rooted in the foundation of the gospel of Jesus. We grieve, but not as those who have no hope. I do remember the last thing I said, which was: "Mom wanted her service to be a celebration, and she wanted everybody to stand and sing loudly one of her favorite hymns, 'Victory in Jesus'!"

And just like Mom would have wanted it, we all stood, and we all sang loudly:

I heard an old, old story, how a Savior came from glory. How he gave his life on Calvary, to save a wretch like me; I heard about his groaning, of his precious blood's atoning, then I repented from my sins, and won the victory.

O victory in Jesus, my savior, forever. He sought me and bought me, with his redeeming blood; He loved me ere I knew him, and all my love is due him. He plunged me to victory, beneath the cleansing flood. (Eugene Monroe Bartlett, Sr. composer)

We laid Mom to rest at Woodland Memorial Park, in Winter Garden, in a beautiful plot overlooking a pond. It was a beautiful day. It was bittersweet. Sorrow and joy intertwined. I'll never forget it.

TWENTY-TWO

Lake Louisa

I stayed with Dad for a few days because it just seemed like the right thing to do. Dad had always been a hard worker, and now he was retired, and Mom was gone. As fate would have it (or should I say, as God planned it), I worked out a deal with Rick the builder to save a few dollars by doing all of the interior painting and exterior staining on the cedar siding at the lake house myself. The thing was, they were on a schedule and I didn't know how I was going to pull this off since I was putting in some long hours at the station, because I was now programming the station as well as pulling an air shift. I asked Dad if he'd like to help me out, and he agreed. It was almost like for a few weeks he had a reason to get up in the morning. While I went to the station, he packed a sack lunch and went out to Clermont and worked all day painting my new house. I joined him on the weekends and we knocked it out just in time.

I got occupancy to the house New Year's Eve, 1986. It was perfect. The place was a real showcase. I gained a new friend I met at church, Peter, who had a boat, and I ended up buying it. Nothing super special, a 17-ft. inboard outboard bowrider, 140 horsepower; a decent little boat for hydrosliding, water skiing, or just cruising around the chain of lakes. An old high school buddy named Tom had moved back into town and rented a bedroom from me for a while. We spent a lot of nights grilling out, and I loved being on the lake on the kneeboard kissing off the wakes as the sun was going down, especially if the water was calm and glassy. I know this sounds crazy, but being on the water alone behind the boat was just a great place to experience God and his creation. It was kind of worshipful. I was at total peace with myself and my life. I thought to myself, "I could enjoy doing this for a very, very long time!"

I ended up shooting a video of the new house and sent it to Jen. She had seen the lot during her previous visit, but I wanted to share the excitement of the new place with her. I invited her down for another visit, thinking maybe we could move things to the next level. She came down, but for whatever reason I couldn't move the needle with her. I got a little frustrated and began to question God: "What in the world is the deal with this relationship?" I had a great home, a great job, was having a blast right in my hometown, and was feeling like I was ready to settle down. That obviously wasn't happening.

My GM at CLASS George Toulas ended up hiring his new PD, Scott Sherwood, from Jacksonville. Scott and I got along fine, and my contract was going to be up soon, and my assumption was we would work it out with no problems. Since I helped George out in the interim period, he assured me when the time was right, that he would take care of me and we'd work out a deal. I was making okay money for the market, but I felt under-compensated. I was performing well for the station, and always had the thought that everything would work itself out in the long run.

In the meantime, I heard from Brad Burkhart, who had his own consultancy, and was consulting Lloyd Parker's station in Long Island, WLIX, as well as WWDJ in New Jersey just outside of New York City, KSLR in San Antonio, and WZZD in Philadelphia. Brad approached me about the possibility of coming back to New York and being a part of WWDJ. Since my career was no longer in my hands but God's, I told him I'd pray about it. I had only been gone from New York for a couple of years, but I was intrigued at the thought of going back to New York, but this time to work in a Christian format. However, I was loving the lifestyle of living on the lake and being on the air in my hometown, so I wasn't holding my breath.

Maybe a month went by and I heard from Brad that a group of Christian broadcasters would be meeting at Disney World for a convention. John Mueller, the CEO of Communicom (the company that owned WWDJ), along with the General Manager Joe Battaglia would be there. He suggested we all get together for breakfast. We talked again about the possibility of me returning to the market, and I told him I would type up some thoughts on what I would do if I was given the opportunity to program WWDJ.

We had breakfast at a hotel at Disney, and it did not go well at all. Before we even started discussing things, John asked me how much money I would have to have to make a move, I threw out a number, and he announced flatly, "Well, that's not going to happen!" My only thought was maybe Brad was trying to push me on these guys, and John made the determination to blow the meeting up before we could discuss anything. I left a little disappointed, but since I was content doing what I was doing, I just attributed it to more confirmation I was where I was supposed to be. At least for the time being.

It didn't take long till my sixty-three-year-old Dad started dating. This was kind of charming and fun to watch. I stopped in one night at the house and he had a lovely lady over for a candlelight dinner. He eventually starting seeing a lady from his home church, and Dad married "Grandma Bev," as we call her, in June 1987. This was kind of funny to me, because I hadn't even been married once! I even took Dad aside and said something like, "Uh, this is kind of quick don't you think?" as if I had all of this wisdom. He assured me she was the one, he was absolutely sure, and would I go with him and Beverly to their pastor's office where they would do the official ceremony. I told him of course. Though I couldn't imagine my Dad without my Mom, I was very happy for him.

I continued to approach Sherwood and George about a new deal and I kept hearing that an offer was coming, but the whole process was taking unusually long. I bided my time and did my best to be patient. I was enjoying life, and especially loved living on the lake. I was having dinner on a regular basis with two other guys and three single ladies, all professionals from church, but it was more fun and fellowship rather than romance. They were just good solid folks to hang with.

Since the Jennifer situation was up in the air, I reconnected with another neat lady I had dated from Long Island. I had met Judy at a singles group in Long Island, and she was now studying to be a counselor and lived in Chicago, but her mom and dad had relocated to Boca Raton and had a high-rise apartment at the ocean. I went down for a visit while Judy was visiting her folks and had a great time, but was unsure if there was anything going on there for the future. I mentioned to her that maybe she would like to come spend a few days at the lake some time, but for whatever reason didn't feel led to press it or follow up with her.

All of a sudden, things changed dramatically almost overnight. Jerry Clifton and Bill Tanner, former rivals in Miami, were now jointly consulting a contemporary urban station together in Orlando called 102 JAMZ. Interestingly, their studios were right down the street from CLASS. They had an opening for a morning personality, and I got a call. I knew immediately I really wasn't interested in doing that format, but because it was Clifton, I didn't decline at first, and told them I would get back to them. I would love working with Jerry again but wasn't crazy about the JAMZ format.

Then probably two days later, I got a call from Joe Battaglia at WWDJ, who said Mueller had reconsidered and they would pay me what I needed, and could offer me the Program Director job and the morning drive air shift back in New York. Brad Burkhart called and asked me to seriously consider it, and even said he'd be come down for a visit from Atlanta to talk about it with me.

This really forced the issue with Scott and George, and I told them we really needed to figure out what we were going to do. I met with Scott again, and gave him a ballpark figure of what I would have to have. It wasn't out of line for the better personalities in the market, and I figured he would just go to George and get it done. Since I had two other options on the hook, I told him I needed a final offer in writing by a week from Friday. He agreed.

Since God had so radically changed my life a few years earlier, I now prayed about everything. I was confident God would make things clear. I got my pastor friend at OCC, Curt, up to speed and in the loop. He assured me he'd be praying. I was loving being back home in Orlando, but if God wanted me to relocate again, there was really nothing holding me back except that I loved the new lake home and the Florida lifestyle.

They say the best negotiations are the ones where both parties feel like they had to give a little more than they wanted to. I've always looked at it this way: Do I feel terribly taken advantage of making the wage I'm making? I'm not one to bust the bank or hold somebody up. I'm just looking for a fair deal. If the other party has a bit of an edge, I can live with that, provided I enjoy the job and have a certain amount of security and some benefits on the side. There is something to be said for enjoying your work and being able to say you love what you do. Not everybody can say that. So that is worth something to me, and if I concede a few dollars because I feel good about what I'm doing, I'm okay with that.

Amazingly, Brad came down and spent a few days with me at the lake. I appreciated the fact he would take the time to do that. I was touched that he took that much interest in the situation. We spent a lot of time in the boat, and talked about the future of Contemporary Christian Music, Christian radio, and the crazy thought of me possibly moving back to New York. We discussed me bringing my talents to WWDJ and being back in the number one market, but this time on a Christian station. Brad's dad, Kent, had made a name for himself as a famous consultant, and now Brad was following suit, but doing it with Christian stations. I knew working with him would be rewarding professionally, but even more importantly, we connected personally. We were becoming good friends. The thought of working with Brad definitely had me interested if things didn't work out at CLASS.

I got the offer midday Friday at the station, and it was ridiculously low. I had already told Scott and George I wasn't into playing any negotiation games, that I had played this completely straight with them, and to please give me their best offer. I went to Scott just to double check.

"Are you sure this is the best you guys can do?" I asked. "Yes," he said. I asked one more time. "Absolutely sure?" Yes, that was the offer.

I thought to go straight to George at this point, but he was out of pocket because he and his wife Carol were expecting their first child any minute. And since Scott told me he was absolutely sure, I had no reason to doubt him. I hopped in the car and drove around for a while in Longwood. I revisited in my mind everything leading up to this time. If I stayed, I would feel like I would be taken advantage of. Not good.

102 JAMZ, though I would love working with Tanner and Clifton, was not an option. I felt like with my new God-led perspective on music and culture, this would be a terrible fit. At WWDJ the money was what

I wanted, it was actually an excellent offer financially, so that was not an issue. It was the New York market, and I knew it like the back of my hand, so that was a positive. I believed Christian music was in its infancy and would just continue to grow. Christian radio was a much smaller job market, so perhaps with my mainstream radio experience I could quickly make a name for myself, which could lead to future job security.

Dad was now remarried and happy, so there were no worries there. Really, the only thing holding me back was enjoying the lifestyle of living in my new home on Lake Louisa. I called my pastor friend Curt, and ran things by him one by one. He listened closely with an occasional, "um hum" or "right." After talking for about five minutes, I took a breath and said something that I'm sure many would think to be totally absurd:

"Curt, I think God wants me to leave here and move to Hackensack, New Jersey!"

There was silence on the other end for what seemed like an eternity. Then he confirmed what I already knew in my heart, when he said, "Brother, you're out of here."

TWENTY-THREE

New Jersey

———— ⸎ ————

I immediately called Brad and then got Joe Battaglia on the phone
and told him I was coming.

"What?" he screamed. I think he might have thought it was some
kind of joke.

I explained, "I'm coming, Joe, no kidding, I'm supposed to make
this move. Let me take care of some things here and I'll see you in a few
weeks." After I got off the phone with Joe, I walked out into my front
yard and walked down by the lakefront that I loved so much. I had lived
in the new house just over a year, and I was moving yet again. I took a
moment to thank God for the time here, and that I trusted this move was
his leading.

My mind started to go through some doubts. WWDJ was on the AM
band, 970 on the dial, with 5,000 watts of power. Not exactly a blowtorch.
They played Christian music in the morning (that I would be hosting),
Christian music in the afternoon, and the rest of the time was filled with
paid religious programs. Had I lost my mind? As my thoughts ran back
and forth, one thing got me genuinely excited. What if a Christian music
radio station could actually compete on a level playing field someday
with the big mainstream stations? What if the music and programming

improved to the point where it could actually make a big difference in the lives of people? I knew that KLTY in Dallas was a commercial music station trying to make a go of it. I didn't know how far we could take a hybrid project like WWDJ, but I knew myself well enough that I would give it my best effort.

I called Dad and asked if he'd like to drive up with me, and I could drop him off in Baltimore to visit my sister. He said that sounded like a great idea, that I could plan on it. I called Judy in Chicago to tell her even though I thought we had a great visit, I didn't really sense that from my standpoint, there was any leading from God as far as our relationship went. I felt it important to be completely transparent and honest with her. She was a good friend and an amazing lady. Though part of me wanted to 'make things happen' with her, I knew in my heart it wasn't God-led.

After a pause, she told me quietly, "I've met somebody." I wished her well. She would eventually marry.

In my personal life that was another door that was now closed. And knowing that with normal traffic I could go from Hackensack to Jen's house in Long Island in a little over an hour, I wondered if this had anything to do with her. The decision I made was for business reasons, not personal. Still, I couldn't help but wonder if she was somewhere in my future.

Dad and Bev agreed to lease my house from me for a while, which was a great blessing. Since I had so much personal input in the house, I had a lot of emotions tied up in the place, so it was good to know that people I was close to would be staying there. Of course Dad loved Josh, so until I got settled and figured out what I was going to do, he agreed to keep Josh for a while also. That dog absolutely loved being in the water, I knew he wouldn't mind. My friend, Peter, even bought his boat back from me. Everything was falling into place. Dad and I hooked up a trailer I rented from Hertz, loaded it up with all my stuff, and headed north. We hadn't gotten about thirty miles up I-4, right around Sanford, when the transmission went out on my Chevy Blazer. The transmission shop told me it would be at least a week, and I couldn't wait, so I ended up renting a truck. I concluded when I got to New Jersey, I could just rent a car till I figured out what to do. Dad and I got to South Carolina, and the truck went! It was almost as if there was this unseen force trying to prevent me from getting to New Jersey! It seemed like it was one hassle after another. Ryder hooked us up with another truck, and I dropped off Dad in Baltimore.

Growing up as a kid, I have fond memories of us taking road trips everywhere, and my Dad was always the one behind the wheel. Just us traveling alone together on a long road trip was therapeutic, I think, for both of us. We got to talk quite a bit about Mom, and genuinely enjoyed each other's company as just father and son for a few days.

When I arrived into Hackensack, it was a Sunday afternoon, and there were a few inches of old snow on the ground. It was February 1988, and it was cold. If towns had a color, Hackensack would definitely be gray. It was very typical suburban New Jersey. Jerry Clifton's former girlfriend, Rosemary, lived in New Jersey and had connected me with a friend who did maintenance for a guy who owned some apartments. They hooked me up and I pulled up to my one-bedroom basement apartment on Vreeland Avenue. I had agreed to rent it sight unseen. Rosemary assured me the place was not a dump, the rent was $500 a month, and while it wasn't fancy, it was clean and adequate. I unloaded, crashed on my queen-size mattress lying on the floor, and went to work the next morning.

Hackensack is the county seat of Bergen County, New Jersey, just a few miles west of the George Washington Bridge that connects Jersey to

New York. The cool thing was, with the exception of rush hour traffic, I could make it into midtown Manhattan in about thirty minutes.

The radio station was downtown on Main Street, and could just as easily have been a store or shop like all of the other businesses downtown. WWDJ was once a Top 40 station competing with the legendary WABC, but with only 5,000 watts of power at 970 on the AM dial, it was not likely they could match up with the 50,000 watt signal that WABC had at 770 on the dial. The station flipped to a Christian format in 1974 and was family owned by a guy named Ken Palmer. He passed away, and his wife, Lee inherited the company, which was named Communicom. Lee ended up hiring a banker, John Mueller, to be CEO and run the company, which also owned WZZD in Philadelphia, and KSLR in San Antonio.

Usually when a station gets a new Program Director who is also going to be the morning air personality, somebody would be losing their job. That wasn't the case at WWDJ. George Flores, who had been doing the morning show, would move to part-time on the air, and would put all of his efforts into the Public Affairs department of the station. Joe LaZizza, who had been Program Director, would now be the Operations Manager. Because WWDJ was the only outlet in the New York market that carried Christian teaching programs, it was very profitable. We ran all of the major ministries that were popular at the time; 'Focus on the Family' with Dr. James Dobson, 'Insight for Living' with Chuck Swindoll, 'Grace to You' with John McArthur, and 'The Word for Today' with Chuck Smith. If it was a major ministry and they had a program, they were probably paying WWDJ very well during those days to be on the air.

We also had some local talk programming at night, and one program in particular was really very entertaining. 'Two Nice Jewish Boys' was a call-in show hosted by a Messianic pastor, Jonathan Kahn, and a guy named Gary Selman. Gary owned a forklift company and was a converted Jew. Naturally with a huge Jewish population in the New York metro, these guys were a lightning rod for controversy. But they were very honest and genuine on the air, and I really liked the show. (At the time of this writing, Jonathan has a book on the New York Times bestseller list, called 'The Harbinger'). So the format at 970 WWDJ was Contemporary Christian music from 6:30 to 9am (hosted by me), music from 3-6pm, and the remainder of the time was filled with paid programs. I found it comical, and felt that God must have a great sense of humor to think that when I left WNBC I was on the air between Don Imus and Howard Stern. Now with my return to the New York City market, I was on the air between Chuck Swindoll and Dr. James Dobson!

Joe Battaglia (or Joe B., as he is affectionately called) was our General Manager, and was very plugged into the Christian music scene, which was based out of Nashville. We had easy access to all of the artists, and we sponsored a concert series in Manhattan at a little Off Broadway theatre called The Lamb's Club. This place was great. It was small and intimate, so selling the place out was the norm. I had a lot of memorable nights there, introducing people like Twila Paris, David Meece, Phil Keaggy, and one of my early favorites, Steve Camp.

One of my best memories, though, was emceeing a concert in the gymnasium of Mahwah High School in Mahwah, New Jersey. At the most it might have been a hundred people attending, and I knew the artist's music from some of his songs we played on the radio, like 'Weak Days' and 'Hiding Place,' but I was impressed from day one with this young man's ability to connect with an audience, his sense of humor, and his transparency. Twenty-four years later, after countless awards, thousands of concerts, and numerous gold records, he remains humble, genuine, and real. I became an early fan of Steven Curtis Chapman.

I hadn't been at WWDJ for a few months when I got a call from Steve Kingston, who was programming WHTZ, Z-100 New York. They had a midday opening, and I suspect Clifton dropped my name to him as Jerry was really making a name for himself as a consultant, and Z was now one of his clients. Since they were now the #1 station in New York (and I suspect probably in the country), I thought about it for a brief moment, and told him I was flattered to be considered, but no thanks. I also heard from my former boss Kevin Metheny who was now programming KFRC-FM in San Francisco. I felt certain the Jersey move was the right one, and the big time glamour of both stations just didn't have the appeal that they would have had ten years earlier. Until I heard from God that I should be doing something different, I was determined do my best to grow the audience at WWDJ and put all of my energy into learning the ins and outs of Christian radio.

I had a few other surprises the first year. The Jimmy Swaggert and Jim Bakker scandals broke in the news, which felt very awkward because I was now officially in 'Christian Broadcasting.'

Plus I got a call from Boy Gary, producer of the Stern Show. Howard had been fired from WNBC, and was now doing mornings on an FM station in New York called K-Rock. He had an anniversary show coming up, and Gary was calling to see if he could set me up to be a surprise guest during the show. Since I knew I could probably mention WWDJ on K-Rock during the call, I told him sure and he made the arrangements. I was on the air a few days later and it went surprisingly well. Howard was cordial, and shocked me by telling me he had gone to management about me when we had worked together. My NBC contract had me available to do voiceover work for the station, (on things like WNBC promotional announcements) and also for Imus and Stern if I was available. I did the Moby Worm bit for Imus and other things for Don on occasion, and I was also the announcer on the Stern Show for 'The Gay Lone Ranger.'

But occasionally Howard would bring me a script that I found objectionable. If I came across a line I felt was inappropriate for me, I would just hand it back to him and say, "Uh, sorry, not reading that." He would try to persuade me to just disguise my voice, but I was adamant. I felt if it wasn't something I wouldn't do while I was on the air during my own shift, I wasn't going to record the part for him. What I didn't know was he told me he had been complaining to management about me not doing his scripts, and that NBC management didn't mess with it for fear I would file a suit based on religious discrimination! I was totally clueless of anything like that going on behind the scenes. During those days I was just trying to navigate my way through sobriety, and getting spiritually grounded in what I believed. I also shared with Howard about walking with my Mom and Dad through the cancer, her funeral, and how it was different because of my faith, but he quickly moved away from wanting to discuss it, explaining I was "bumming him out!" All in all though, I felt the whole thing was a positive, and was a good decision. Just getting to mention the fact that I was now back in the market on WWDJ made it a win from my perspective.

Howard would mention me on the air occasionally in subsequent years, especially if he and Robin (Quivers) got on the subject of religion or Christianity. I would get a call from an old radio friend somewhere around the country and be told, "Howard mentioned you again this morning." I'd like to think that somehow, some way, I made some kind of impact on him. In God's economy, you never know how you could impact a person, even years later. The one thing I do remember, is as abusive and crude as some of the verbal attacks were, somehow God gave me the grace not to react. I just kept my cool, went about my business, did radio as best as I possibly could, and continued to move forward in growing mature in my faith.

One of the neat things we decided we wanted to do early on at WWDJ was to have a presence at the Gospel Music Association Convention and Dove Awards, held every year in Nashville. This also coincided with the NCRS, or National Christian Radio Seminar. Basically this is one time during the year where everybody having anything to do with Christian music gathers. Concert promoters, record companies, artists, radio, everybody is there. Joe was the new president of the NCRS, so we made the trip together, along with Wendy Bucceri, our Promotions Director.

Wendy had a connection with Rich Mullins, and told me she could hook me up for an interview. We played a few of Rich's songs on the air, and musically I really liked the song 'Pictures in the Sky,' but I was also impressed with the fact that he had written 'Sing Your Praise to the Lord' for Amy Grant. I remember when Amy first played the famed Radio City Music Hall (which was right next door to where I worked at WNBC), and Rich was on the marquis. It read, 'IN CONCERT, AMY GRANT,' and then right underneath it, 'WITH SPECIAL GUEST, RICH MULLINS.' At the time of our trip to Nashville, Rich was recording tracks for 'Winds of Heaven, Stuff of Earth.' Little did I know at the time he was in the process of recording what would become a classic, 'Awesome God.'

Wendy had developed a reputation as quite a cook, and rather than meet at the hotel, I was told we would be driving out to Rich's house, where Wendy would prepare a meal, and then I could get my interview. So that Tuesday afternoon we hopped in our rental car and drove. And drove. And drove some more! We must have been an hour out of Nashville when we pulled up to Rich's very modest little house in the country. I remember he had one roommate, and his dog named Bear, who was also prominently featured on the album cover of 'Winds of Heaven.' I had heard later about how frugal Rich was, how he was not materialistic at all, and that was evident as I remember his house. It felt more like a worn out college dorm that desperately needed to be cleaned. The only thing that would give you any sort of clue that this guy was even an artist, he had a framed picture of that Radio City Music Hall marquis when he played there with Amy.

The interview went fine, I don't remember anything special about it, just that he was kind of different. I couldn't put my finger on it. While most artists in an interview setting seemed kind of polished, that was not Rich. Raw and real might be a better description. That night before we left, at about ten o'clock, he insisted that we hop in his very used Ford Bronco and drive to 'the river.' I was dead tired since I had been up early to do the morning show, but I agreed. At the time, I didn't know what the big deal was. It was, well, a river! We stayed for a few minutes by the river, with our headlights focused on the water. It was actually kind of bizarre, but it was obviously a big enough deal to him that he wanted to share it with us! I don't recall anybody saying much, we drove back to the house where I picked up the rental car, and that was it. It was really kind of odd, but Rich was anything but conventional. Rich wrote a song a few years later called 'The River,' but I never had the chance to ask him if THAT river that we visited had any connection to the song.

While I was in New Jersey, I began to see Jennifer on and off a little bit, but she was semi-involved with some other guy, so I just continued to pray about my personal life and keep an open mind to whatever God wanted to do. I was very involved with my work, but still felt that maybe moving north was not a coincidence. I just felt confident that somehow, someday, God would lead one way or the other.

In the meantime, I wanted to find a good church to go to, so I started saying on the air that I was looking for a church, and people began calling and writing to me with their suggestions. Maranatha Church of the Nazarene in Paramus was pretty cool. I really liked the pastor, Charlie Rizzo. He had a Saturday program on WWDJ, and their worship band was very contemporary. It actually had a rock n roll feel to it. Plus I had a connection with Mike Lupica, the sportswriter who wrote at the time for the *New York Daily News*, who was also a regular on the Imus show. Charlie had an influence on Mike spiritually and he would occasionally speak at Maranatha. Since I knew Lupica from my days at WNBC, I always wanted to get there to hear him speak.

The church I ended up getting plugged into was Pascack Bible Church in Hillsdale, in upper Bergen County, which was about a twenty-minute drive from my apartment on Sunday morning. The senior pastor, Fred Beveridge, was, in a word, awesome. The worship was more spontaneous, it had a little bit of a charismatic feel to it, and it just felt like a good fit. They also had a pretty good-sized singles group. The first time I visited the place it was packed out, as they had Ravi Zacharias as a guest speaker during a missions conference. I got there late so I was actually sitting in the center aisle. The place was so full that they had to set up chairs wherever they had a little room. When the service was over, with me being a normal, un-attached single guy, I noticed the most beautiful blonde girl a few pews ahead of me down on the left. I tried to make a little eye contact, but she was oblivious to me. I didn't think much of it and headed home.

The first summer I was back in the New York metro, I made it to the beach whenever I could. Even though Jones Beach was a bit of a trip, I preferred going there, probably because I'm so nostalgic. I would drive by my old house, drive through Merrick, try to see if Jen was around, or would look up my old AA buddy, Rich. I really loved jogging or walking the Jones Beach boardwalk. It was really long, two or three miles one way. Of course Jersey had beaches, but I still preferred Long Island.

WWDJ at one time had a summer concert down on the Jersey Shore in a town called Ocean Grove, and the first summer I was back we decided to bring back the event. It was appropriately named Big

Splash. Ocean Grove had this very old, open air auditorium that held about 7,000 people. The original structure dated back to the 1800s. We planned to broadcast live there all day with various fun family events, and then we had the ticketed concert that night. One of my favorites, Steve Camp, was scheduled, and BeBe and CeCe Winans were the headliners. The concert sold out, and it turned into an amazing day.

A local Bible teacher, Wayne Monbleau, did his show live from a covered pavilion overlooking the ocean, with a big crowd looking on. We had a 5k run, youth group volleyball tournaments, food, the beach, the ocean, everything just came together. Before I introduced BeBe and CeCe, I did have one pressing matter that I needed to share with the sold out audience. We got word that Chuck Swindoll's program, 'Insight for Living,' was not getting enough financial support from the WWDJ listening audience, and if the support did not pick up, we might lose the program. Since the teaching was rock solid and Chuck was a great communicator, I really did not want to see the station lose it. I made a pitch to the audience, and asked them to please make a gift to the ministry, because I really felt like Chuck Swindoll needed to stay on the air in New York. With that, I introduced BeBe and CeCe and they absolutely rocked the house. They also had a little help that night from a friend of the family who was in the background, singing backup. It was none other than Whitney Houston!

A few weeks went by when we got word that Insight for Living was canceling. One of the things I did on the morning show was to play short clips of some of our better programs so I could promote them. As a programmer, I felt since these programs were part of what we did, I might as well try to turn it into a positive, and Swindoll was one of my favorites. So besides losing the program, I was also losing one of the better guys I played clips from on the morning show. I was upset by it, but what happened next had me livid.

WMCA at 570 on the AM dial had been sold, and the format was flipping to Christian teaching and talk, which was exactly what we did when we weren't playing music. We got word that Insight was leaving us and moving to the other station! I was beside myself. I typed a letter to Chuck Swindoll personally, explaining the long relationship WWDJ had with the program, my pitch at Big Splash, and my disappointment with the decision. To their credit, one of his right hand guys who handled radio stopped in for a visit a few weeks later to try to smooth things over, but the decision had been made. 'Insight' wasn't the only program to leave. We began to get other cancellation notices. The new company that owned WMCA obviously had influence with many of the programs we had on the air. The name of the company was Salem Communications.

Salem owned a very big station in Los Angeles, KKLA, and I suspect they were building strong relationships with the major on-air radio ministries. While I knew Christian radio was going to be different for me in a lot of ways, I was naïve to think that it wasn't still in many ways all about business. Salem and Communicom both owned commercial stations, in business to make money. Just like in my mainstream radio days, we now had a competitor. Once I knew the rules, I knew how to play the game. We still had a lot of great programs on WWDJ, we knew the popularity of the music we played was growing, and WMCA was basically an outlet for the programs and nothing more. They did a good job of contacting the local churches to increase awareness, but besides that, I didn't hear anything on the air that made me think we were in serious trouble.

The financial impact of losing some programs was felt, but we quickly replaced those with others. I moved Sharon Davis, who had been doing afternoons, to mornings with me to do the news. Keith Stevens, who had been 'Bubba the Love Sponge' on the Z-100 Z Morning Zoo with

Scott Shannon was a Christian, and I hired him to do afternoons. Brad Burkhart, my friend and our consultant, started doing music testing and research for us so our music was on target. We hired an ad agency, and had print ads featuring Sharon and me with placement in places like the subway cars and Path Train. Want to compete with us? Game on.

(Ironically, Salem Communications would eventually purchase WWDJ, and become my long-time employer when they acquired KLTY in 2000. They also own the company that published this book. They are, without a doubt, one of the best-run media companies in America today.)

Competition is good. It makes you better. This is great for business, but I had no interest in competing in my personal life. Since Jen seemed to be seeing somebody else, I just bided my time. I got to the point where I concluded this was totally God's territory. Funny though, as you get older, and you're still single, not divorced, and not gay, people wonder what's the problem with you? I knew I wasn't going to settle for second best in this part of my life, and just decided to wait on God.

Sadly, I got the word that Jen's mom died of breast cancer. We had conversations before about how our lives had mirrored each other's in various ways. This was another example. We both lost our moms way too early. I made it to the funeral service, which was at my old church in Merrick, and was asked to help move the coffin to the hearse. Wendy was an amazing lady, and I could tell that Jen's dad, Ken, loved her dearly. He spoke at the service, and I was reminded again, just like when Mom died, how different it is for those whose faith is rooted in Christ. We grieve, but not as those with no hope.

I had a thought in the back of my mind that after the grieving process, maybe things would change with Jen and our relationship would move forward. Believing that God had it all under control, I gave her a hug and headed back to Jersey.

Back at Pascack Bible, I was getting a little involved with the singles group, and a listener named Rosey introduced me to a bunch of people, including the cute blonde I had seen during my first visit. Her name was Patti, and I immediately thought well, yep, she sure is gorgeous, but she is way too young for me. I was thirty-eight at the time, she looked like she was in her early twenties, maybe twenty-five at the most. Again, I didn't think that much of it, and went about being totally focused on work.

The GMA event and Dove Awards were coming up again soon. We broadcast live this time from the Stouffer Hotel (which is now the Renaissance Nashville Hotel) and we had a plexiglas broadcast studio on the mezzanine floor, overlooking the lobby. Our setup looked awesome. This was before the days of ISDN lines, which allow you to send high quality audio back to your studio over telephone lines. To broadcast our show, we had to have an equalized telephone line send our signal to a satellite uplink, the satellite picked up the signal, and sent it back down to another equalized line that was connected to our studios in New Jersey. This whole arrangement was rather pricey, but in 1990 if you wanted to broadcast live from somewhere and you wanted it done right, that was the way to do it. I secured a sponsorship from one of our commercial sponsors to help pick up the cost.

I was now making a name for myself with the record companies, so we easily secured a lot of guests while we were there. I had a great relationship with Jenny Lockwald, who was the promo lady for Sparrow Records, so we easily got Steven Curtis Chapman, Margaret Becker, Steve Camp, and BeBe and CeCe. I invited Jennifer to join me and she flew in for a few days. We went to the Dove Awards together and had a great time. I was confident and optimistic our relationship would finally move forward.

TWENTY-FOUR

Moving on

We had another successful Big Splash that summer, and I started to like Ocean Grove. It was directly next to Asbury Park, of Bruce Springsteen fame, and the Jersey Shore was actually starting to compete with my devotion for Long Island. Jennifer also came down for Big Splash, but it took some coaxing. She was not always the best at getting back to me, or sometimes we would make plans and something would come up. I just wrote it off to the fact that she was busy or maybe sometimes forgetful. Since we had been seeing each other on and off for so many years, I started praying about exactly what the deal was. I knew we had a love for each other, but I didn't know exactly where it was going. I came to the conclusion it was time for me to try to move us along one way or the other.

I had scored second row seats at Radio City Music Hall for The Brooklyn Tabernacle Choir in concert, featuring Michael English as guest vocalist. I knew this would be a killer show, so I asked Jen to join me. She said that sounded great, I would drive in from Jersey, and she would take the Long Island Rail Road into the city and meet me there. I began to pray about the conversation I would have with her after the show.

I had been to Radio City before, but never had seats this good! I was really psyched for this show. Pastor Jim Cymbala came out before the concert, and I had a great respect for him. We actually had Pastor Jim on a short five-minute daily feature on WWDJ, and the whole Brooklyn Tabernacle story is just amazing. You can read all about it in his book, 'Fresh Wind, Fresh Fire.' His wife, Carolyn, led the choir in a great show, but the highlight for me was watching Michael English join them for 'Bowed on my Knees and Cried Holy.' To this day, I think that has to be one of my favorite Christian concert moments. It was incredible.

Jen enjoyed the show too, and I suggested we get something to drink (of course, for me that meant a Coke!) at a midtown bar before I dropped her off to get her train home on the LIRR. I began to share my heart and make my case. I told her that we had been seeing each other off and on now for over six years, and I thought we should seek God together to see if we really had something there, or if it was time to move on. I had the utmost respect for her dad, Ken, and knew him to be a very godly man. I made the suggestion I spend a weekend with her and her dad on Long Island, to just hang out, have fun and begin to pray together about all of this. She agreed, and we set it up for the weekend two weeks away. I gave her a kiss goodnight and dropped her off at the LIRR.

I was anxiously looking forward to the weekend. It felt like the right thing to do. Neither one of us was getting any younger, and frankly, Jen had seen me at my worst, back when I was first getting sober and still dealing with a lot of anxiety issues. Getting healthy emotionally and spiritually takes time, but I knew I had come a long way and was getting better. I was optimistic as the weekend drew closer. Plus, I genuinely enjoyed her dad a lot, so getting to spend some quality time with Ken (out of respect, I insisted that I call him Mr. Mills, after all he was Jen's dad) would be a bonus. As the day got closer I got more excited. Finally, we are going to figure this thing out.

The radio guy and the fashion designer. Will they or won't they? Is he the one? Is she the one? Sounded like a daytime soap opera. Stay tuned!

Of course, in the days before cell phones, most of us had answering machines for our home phones. My particular machine had a blinking light, and each blink meant the number of messages you had on your machine. The Thursday before the big weekend, I had a late day at the station, and came home to one blink on the machine. It was Jen. Something had come up. She said she couldn't make it that weekend. No explanation. I know from experience it's not wise to make big decisions when you're emotionally upset. But for some reason, this instance was different. I had a definite direction and resolve inside of me. I picked up the phone and called her. I was calm, but crystal clear: "Sorry, I'm done," I said. It was time for me to move on.

TWENTY-FIVE

A Prayer and The Pew

I went through a season of disappointment after my decision, and began to question God about what in the world was going on with my personal life? Jen had so many good qualities, and we had so much history and great moments together, I couldn't get a handle on why it never came together. I was really done with the uncertainty, though, and felt good about making the decision. I got a nice raise at the radio station, and was very pleased with the way the station was sounding. I was running quite a bit, and felt as good as ever physically. There was a great tree-lined trail in Rochelle Park that went along the Saddle River, and it became one of my favorite spots to go walk or jog. I liked to walk and pray, and would just imagine Jesus being by my side, and I would have these one-way conversations. I've never been one for fancy rhetoric when praying. I just talk like I'm talking to a friend. Sometimes I would walk and forget that I was praying audibly while going around the trail, and I'm sure that many people who saw me while they were walking probably thought I had issues! I ran into the young blonde, Patti, again at a singles event at church, but thought nothing of it. I was doing my prayer thing at the park one day and she came to mind, so I just threw it out there.

"Hey Lord, what about that younger girl at church?" I sort of ran this game plan by God: "Here's what I'm thinking, if I see her at church this Sunday, I think I will ask her out. If she's not there, then that will be my answer."

Let me make it clear, this was not a pour your heart out, "Oh Dear God, I must have an answer from you about this!" kind of prayer. However, I didn't take the thought lightly, and was confident that God could make these kinds of things clear to me, one way or the other. One thing I knew I did not want to do was 'do my own thing' when it came to dating or relationships. I wanted God to be in control.

Sunday came and I made it to church at the normal time. I knew from being observant before that Patti usually sat on the right hand side of the church closer to the front. I preferred to sit closer to the back, on the left hand side. Pascack was pretty full this particular Sunday, and from what I could tell she wasn't there.

"Okay, that makes sense," I thought. "She's much too young for me anyway."

We were about fifteen minutes into worship, and there was a little bit of space between me and the end of the pew. As worship was ending, I noticed out of the corner of my left eye somebody coming to sit at the end of the pew, which would put them right next to me; obviously it was somebody arriving late. I turned to the left and it was her! I quietly said hello and acted like everything was normal. Inside, though, I was absolutely freaking out. *Are you kidding me? I pray about this and the next Sunday she comes in and sits down right next to me?* I was so dumbfounded, the service ended and I didn't even ask her out! That would have to wait for another time. But I knew it was coming.

As I reflect back on the years, I've concluded that the word 'coincidence' should not be in my vocabulary. While some people may look upon certain circumstances as luck or a twist of fate, I'm certain it's a loving God orchestrating those circumstances in my life. I liken it to a giant tapestry that can only be woven by a creator. The people, the events, and the timing are all intertwined. It's way beyond my comprehension. That's where faith comes in. I choose to believe. The cool thing is, over time God develops a track record with you. You realize that in the good times and even the bad times, his ways can be trusted. Frankly speaking, it's the only way to live.

I saw Patti a few weeks later at church and asked her out to lunch. She said no. I saw her a few weeks later and asked her out again. Again she said no! Knowing that rejection and I don't co-exist very well, I was thinking I didn't want to ask her a third time!

Joe B. and his wife LuAnn had begun attending Pascack, and about a month after my second 'no,' we were hanging out in back of the church at the end of the service. Patti came up to us and handed me her business card. "Call me sometime," she said. I thought it would be funny to turn the tables and tell her "no!" but I resisted. I called her the next week.

Patti Pilkington was a Jersey girl. She grew up in Leonia, which was right next to Ft. Lee, just a few minutes from the George Washington Bridge. I was close on the age. There was twelve years difference between us. She ran the men's department at Macy's in Paramus, and considering the way I dressed, she probably saw me as a project! She had left a few years earlier and moved to California, and it was there that her older brother shared the gospel with her. She felt that God wanted her to move back home to share her newfound faith with family and friends. What's bizarre is she told me her family used to listen to WNBC in their car. That means that some of her teen years she was probably listening to me on the radio. I gave her a call and decided I would take her to lunch at Houlihan's.

Well, honestly, lunch didn't go too well! I did most of the talking, and it seemed like the only things we had in common were Bruce Springsteen and our faith. Since many of our programs ending up going to WMCA, I was thrilled we had added Bob George and the 'People to People' program from Dallas, so I shared with her about my thoughts on grace and how the program had made an impact on me. I couldn't tell if she didn't want to engage, was nervous, didn't like me, or any and all of the above. One thing I did notice is she didn't seem to smile much. As dates go, I don't think you could term it as a success.

We had lunch after church one Sunday at a diner in Westwood, which was right next to Hillsdale, but I really couldn't sense if there was anything there for us. Then she invited me to a Phil Keaggy concert to benefit a ministry called Mercy Corps. We got a bite to eat afterwards and were joined by at least six of her friends. I was not exactly Mr. Social Butterfly, and I had a terrible time. The whole thing was terribly awkward. I was beginning to think that maybe this whole Patti experiment was just a waste of time.

Meanwhile, back at the radio station everything was going smoothly. I now had some personal endorsements for some clients on the air, so I was making some extra money, which was always fun. One of the things I was always promoting to Joe and the sales staff was if we were going to add programs to our on-air schedule, let's try to do things that made sense. The more mass appeal we can make the programs, as well as the music, the bigger the potential to reach more listeners. I was ecstatic when our sales manager, Ed Abels, told me that Billy Graham would be coming to Central Park, and that the Billy Graham Evangelistic Association would be purchasing time from us so we could broadcast it live. Yes! Now that was what I was talking about! I could hear the promotional announcement in my head: "Can't make it to Central Park to hear Billy Graham?

Be listening right here and hear it live on New York's Christian Radio, 970 WWDJ!"

I hadn't seen or heard from Patti for over a month, and I was pulling a shift on the air Thanksgiving morning. It was cold early that year, and we even had some snow on the ground that day. I heard a knock at the back door, and she had brought me some Dunkin Donuts. I had some coffee on, so she stayed for a while and we had a good visit talking between the songs. I was doing a remote broadcast the next afternoon at a Toyota dealership, but would be done about six, and asked her if she wanted to have dinner. She said sure, and said she would meet me at the dealership.

After my remote we headed to Friday's for dinner, and this time it was different. She was engaging, she was fun, we laughed, and I felt like we connected. On the way back to the car, I kissed her for the first time. I knew I wanted to see her again.

I found out that the reason Patti didn't go out with me earlier was because she was getting over a previous relationship. They had been engaged, and she broke it off because she felt that God made it clear he was not the one. It sounded to me like Luke was a great guy, and it was obviously a difficult time for her emotionally after she made the decision.

I totally get that; everything looks great on paper, but if you're in tune with the Spirit, you know that something is not right and you are conflicted if you keep moving forward. It's like an undeniable gut check. I've found that following Christ is like having a new internal guidance system, which is the Holy Spirit. Of course you have the option to do your own thing, but deep down in your heart you know you'll be miserable.

Christmas was coming up, and our church was having a pretty big Christmas party. It was sort of our 'coming out' event as a couple at church, with a great dinner and music. Patti was dressed in a cream-colored lace dress and looked absolutely stunning. We had a great night. Even with the age difference, I began to entertain the possibility that we might have something special.

The next year, Patti and I began to see each other exclusively. We were investing the time to see if we had a future together. She came from an alcoholic household growing up and had been involved in Al-Anon, so having open discussions about alcohol, drugs and addiction was easy, and we were on the same page. If she wanted to occasionally have a glass of wine with dinner, that wasn't an issue for me. I just kept with my AA commitment to abstain. I think my non-judgmental, non-legalistic nature rubbed off on her. After studying the scriptures through the lens of God's grace, and focusing more on the new covenant in the New Testament, life for me became more of an adventure to be experienced, rather than a list of rules you had to keep. The guidelines in the Bible are there to protect you, not make you miserable. I think she had spent a lot of time beating herself up over past mistakes, and my influence helped to free her up.

That's something that has been a pet peeve of mine, I guess, down through the years; legalism has kept so many people unhappy and miserable in doing their best to try to live the Christian life. In and of itself, without the power of the Holy Spirit, that is an impossible task. It can frustrate a person to the point of tears. Only with the revelation that one is totally forgiven and accepted because of Christ's sacrifice can one find peace for their soul. Jesus bridges the gap between us and God, so we can have access to the Father. God's entire wrath was poured out on his son, there is absolutely none left for you and me.

Once you get that, it will revolutionize your life. It's like the pressure to perform a certain way is turned off. It's incredibly liberating to know, deep down inside, that you are loved and accepted just the way you are. Following Christ becomes an adventure you 'get to do,' rather than a bunch of religious stuff you 'have to do.' A few of my favorite verses that remind me of this are from Paul writing in Titus: "For the grace of God that brings salvation has appeared to all men. It (grace) teaches us to say 'No' to ungodliness and worldly passions, and to live self-controlled, upright and godly lives." And, "when the kindness and love of God our Savior appeared, he saved us, not because of righteous things we have done, but because of his mercy." When the truth of God's grace, love and mercy gets deep down inside of you, frankly speaking, it will change your entire outlook on life.

I continued to be consumed with the radio station, and it became an issue for Patti. Radio people are notorious for having broken marriages and relationships. We tend to get very wrapped up in what we are doing. Add the fact that my business was now also a ministry, and it's easy for things in life to get out of balance. It's very easy to justify spending all of your time on work; after all, it's for the sake of the ministry, don't you get that?

No, she didn't get that! In hindsight, this was one of the best things about the amazing lady who would eventually become my wife. She wouldn't put up with me being totally consumed in my time commitment to work. We split up over it right before Christmas 1990. I didn't realize it at the time, but this was a good thing.

I ended up spending some time with a friend of her family, Pete Scazerro. Pete was pastoring a big church in Queens, and was the one who led Patti's brother, Chris to Christ. Chris passed on his faith to Patti. So Pete had a special connection with the Pilkingtons. He counseled me about being a workaholic, and I knew if I had any chance of things working out with Patti, I would have to make some changes. I prayed about it, and also began to pray about her, and was seeking God on what to do.

Pascack Bible Church always had a great nighttime Christmas Eve service. I did some serious walking and praying over by Teterboro Airport for part of the day, and I determined that I needed to send Patti a message.

I knew she would probably be at the service that night, and I laid out my plan. I began to work on a script, and write down exactly the way I felt, and what I was going to say to her.

I headed to church, and since it was Christmas Eve, the only thing I found open on the way was a 7-11. I paid $1.99 for one single long stem rose, put it in a small brown paper bag, stuck it in my Bible, and headed to the service. I sat with my friends, Glenn and Liz, way up front that night, and when the service was over, I noticed Patti way in the back. I moved quickly through the people to reach her before she left. I asked her if she had a minute, and we headed downstairs to the kitchen area where we had some privacy. I began to read her what I had written. I even had a spot in the script that said, "hand her the rose here," which I did, and continued to share my thoughts.

Bottom line: I loved her, and she could make this the happiest Christmas of my life. I got to the end of the script. "Will you marry me?" I asked. She didn't even take a moment to think about it.

Rather nonchalantly and coldly she simply said, "I can't marry you." We didn't discuss it, and I didn't argue. We went our separate ways without a word.

TWENTY-SIX

Patti Forever

—⟶ ⟍⟋⟍ ⟵—

Since I was single, whenever possible I tried to work on holidays and give somebody with family the day off. I worked that Christmas morning, and I was completely miserable. On Monday, I went to Ed Abels, who was now our General Manager, and told him I needed to take a few days off. For the first time ever I scheduled two weeks away from a radio station and made plans to spend a few days at the beach in Ocean Grove. Dad and Grandma Bev had gotten their own place, so my lake home in Florida was vacant, so I thought I would also head down there for a week. I stayed at a rooming house at the beach and they had one black and white TV in the parlor area. CNN had wall-to-wall coverage of the Gulf War, so I got caught up in that for a few days, and also did some serious walks and prayer on the boardwalk. It was relatively mild that winter, and I knocked out a lot of miles.

I came to the conclusion I had done everything I could to restore my relationship with Patti. So the only thing left to do was to give it to God. If God wanted me with her, he was going to have to somehow do it. I had basically washed my hands of the whole deal. Since I'm very tenacious, this was hard to do. It's not my nature to give up, on anything. But I knew this was the right decision. If somehow things got reconciled, I would know it would be God's doing, not mine.

After a few weeks off, I got back to Jersey, but when Sunday came around I didn't go to Pascack. I thought it would be awkward to run into Patti, so I opted to spend a few Sundays at Charlie Rizzo's church in Paramus. The third Sunday back from my time away was Superbowl Sunday, and I missed my other friends at church, so I headed back. I ran into Patti after the service. I wasn't looking for her, it just happened. I asked her how she was, she said fine, and I asked her if she'd like to go to lunch. She agreed and we hopped into my car and drove to the diner in Westwood. I don't even think we said anything on the drive there. When we got to the diner I came around to open her door, and when she stepped out I just had to kiss her. We had lunch, and got invited to a Super Bowl party at a friend's house.

The Giants beat the Bills when they missed a last second field goal, but we were both on another planet. We went back to Patti's apartment but barely spoke. We knew this was it. It was as if God had parted the skies, and said to both of us, "This is the one," and we didn't even have to speak. It had been supernaturally revealed it to us simultaneously. God's presence was so real I felt like I could reach out and touch it. It was one of the most significant and amazing moments in my life. It was as if lightening had struck.

She's the one.

Valentine's Day was coming up and I'm a romantic at heart, so I was determined to go over the top. I was doing commercials for a jeweler in Manhattan, so I immediately called him and told him I was looking for a diamond in the range of $3,000. He was plugged into the diamond district and began the search. I saw a story in the newspaper about a spot in Lambertville, New Jersey, called The Stockton Inn. The place was over 200 years old, and the dining room had a lot of fireplaces, and the spot was known for it's romantic atmosphere and ambiance. It sounded perfect, so I reserved a table for the night of February 14th. I knew it was going to be at least ninety minutes getting out there, as it was right on the Pennsylvania border. It was going to be a weeknight and I would have to get up the next morning, so I lined up a limo. I mixed some songs together on a cassette for our own private soundtrack on the way out. I set up some snacks and drinks and I was good to go. Joe B. gave me the contact for the limo, and our driver was Warren Keller, who used to be the chaplain for the New York Giants. He turned out to be a great guy. I picked up Patti and she knew this was going to be the night.

She said yes!

Patti and I picked October 5th for our wedding date, and Pastor Pete lined us up with a great lady named Sue for pre-marital counseling. Sue had an office in Manhattan, so Patti and I would commute into the city from Hoboken once a week where we would get the Path Train going under the Hudson River. There was a long street where you could parallel park for free close to the train station, but depending on where an open spot was on the street, you might have to walk a little bit.

I had just bought an almost new solid black Chevy Tahoe from Condemi Motor Company, which was another sponsor I endorsed on the air. One night we got back from the city and were walking to get my truck, and I thought, "Gee, I really don't remember parking this far away." I backtracked toward the station, and then walked even farther in the opposite direction. After about twenty minutes of walking back and forth, I came to the obvious conclusion, somebody stole my truck! After the shock wore off in a few days, I realized even this was an answer to prayer and God's provision in my life, and also Patti's. Patti had acquired a little bit of credit card debt, and since we were both footing the bill for the wedding and honeymoon ourselves, we were in need of cash. I got a check for $13,000 from the insurance company, which more than covered everything and then some. I always liked the Nissan Pathfinder, so rather than buy a new one I opted for a lease payment, which freed up the cash.

What was really funny was about a month after my truck was stolen, I got a ticket mailed to me because whoever stole it had illegally parked somewhere in Jersey City! I had to go through quite a bit of red tape to convince them I wasn't responsible.

We all go through embarrassing situations in life, and right after Patti and I got engaged, I had a doozy. The radio station was doing a promotion with Amy Grant and her record company, and Joe B. and I had the opportunity to fly to Virginia Beach for a taping of The 700 Club where Amy would be appearing. Sheila Walsh was co-hosting the show at this time, and she and Joe were old friends. She graciously invited us over to dinner at her place the evening after the show. We got a ride over to her place, and this particular day it was pouring rain outside. We pulled up to the beautiful townhouse, and since we didn't have an umbrella, we ran across the short front yard to the front door. Sheila greeted us with a smile, and was busy in the kitchen cooking, apron and all. The home was beautiful, and actually looked like it came out of *Better Homes and Gardens*.

Sheila told us to make ourselves at home, so Joe and I had a seat on the couch in the formal living room. Meeting somebody for the first time is always a little bit awkward, but I was a little anxious because of course I'm in the home of Sheila Walsh from The 700 Club! Ten years earlier, this would be a perfect opportunity for me to ask the host if they had something to drink!

Joe and I were making small talk while Sheila was cooking, and as I was sitting there I faintly began to smell something. I tried to ignore it, but yep, I smelled something, and it was not good. I glanced down at my shoes, and somewhere on the grass I had stepped in dog poop! And as I glanced at their beautiful white rug between the front door and the couch, I had left a nice brown track! Sheila was very kind and said don't worry about it as she went off to get some cleaning stuff to clean up my mess.

Of course the proper thing was to take off my shoes, clean them up, and put them by the door. Patti had given me some socks for Valentines Day, and wouldn't you know I had them on. They were, shall we say, unusual? Bright red, with white hearts and sayings written all over them; screaming things like 'I love you,' 'You're the one,' and 'I think you're hot!' So now I'm sitting on the couch with my bright red Valentines socks planted on their perfect white rug. Well, it was perfect till I walked in! In spite of it all, we had a great evening, but wow, that was embarrassing.

Sheila now lives in the Metroplex and is ministering to countless women through her many books and speaking engagements with Women of Faith. It's cool to know she is a regular listener of our show.

Since Patti lived in a two-family home, and I lived in an apartment, we needed to find a place to live. I found us a really neat three-bedroom home in Waldwick, which was up Highway 17, and right next to a beautiful town called Saddle River. I loved this area in upper Bergen County. The oak trees were huge, and the area had a lot of character. If we had the resources to buy a home, we would have definitely searched for one around this part of Jersey. Josh and I moved immediately, and Patti would move in after we got married.

We were determined to keep our relationship pure, and especially since I was a public person, I didn't want to have any appearances of anything inappropriate. Everything seemed to be proceeding pretty normally and uneventfully as we looked forward to the day and our honeymoon. But that was about to change, and in a major way.

TWENTY-SEVEN

The Call

B rother Jon Rivers was heard on hundreds of mainstream radio stations nationwide as host of the syndicated radio program, Powerline. We had sat on a radio panel together at the Gospel Music Association Convention when I went there the first time in 1985. He was now Vice President of Programming at KLTY in Dallas. David Pierce, who had contacted me in '86 about going to work there, was moving to the K-Love Network, which created an opening at KLTY in the afternoon drive. Marc Rodriguez, who owned the station, asked Jon if he could hire anybody in America, who would it be? I'm honored that Jon mentioned my name and gave me a call. I knew that KLTY was the premiere commercial Christian music station in the country, and I was very excited they programmed Christian music 24/7. But I really did love working and being in New York, plus with our wedding a few months away, it didn't seem feasible. I told him thanks for thinking about me, but it didn't seem like the timing was right.

I ended the conversation, and stepped out of my office for a minute. Coming through the back door at that very moment was a group of people from our corporate office in Denver, including Richard Kylberg, who was now going to be running Communicom. Richard was Lee's son, and I was informed that John Mueller was out as running the company, and Richard was in. We were introduced, I shook his hand, and exchanged pleasantries. Call it a gut feel, a nudge from the Holy Spirit, or whatever. I had one thought: *Call Jon Rivers back. And do it right now!*

I actually waited a day and got Jon on the phone. I told him maybe we should talk, and he suggested I fly down for a few days. I told him I would get back to him and just began to pray about it. Brad Burkhart also consulted KLTY as well as WWDJ, and I wanted to get his thoughts. Patti and I continued to fix up the new house and finalize the wedding plans. I really wanted to go to Hawaii for our honeymoon, and she agreed. I told her I was thinking about flying to Dallas for a few days, sensed that she might be upset about it, but I couldn't understand what the big deal was. I had been on my own for so long, I didn't even consider if she wanted to go. I just assumed if something came together, and we had to move, well, we would just move! Even though she wasn't crazy about the idea, I called Jon and booked the trip. If it went well, I could continue with the process and see where it led. If it didn't, well then of course we would just stay in New Jersey.

KLTY flew me down first class on Delta and everything was impressive from the start. My visit coincided with Brad flying in to conduct a focus group, which I always found interesting and fascinating. Brad picked me up at the airport and we headed to the station. KLTY was in a brand new high-rise in Las Colinas, and as soon as I entered the lobby I was impressed. It was classy and professional, to say the least. The on-air studio had a wall of glass that overlooked a lake sixteen stories below, and Jon's office was on the corner with an amazing view. One of the first persons I saw besides Jon was Larry Thompson, who was the Production Director, and was also building his own company on the side called Thompson Creative.

"How soon can ya get here?" he jokingly said.

The atmosphere was relaxed and fun, and it felt good. Brad and I hung out with Jon, talked radio, and I made it clear I was in no position to make any kind of decision, that I was just visiting to check things out. He was fine with that, and the whole trip was easy, enjoyable, and relaxed. Brad directed a great focus group, and I was on the other side of the glass that night (focus groups allow you to observe the participants and facilitator through a one-way window) with Jon, KLTY Program Director Scott Wilder, Marc, the station owner and his fiancée, Sonya. Marc and Jon made it clear they were interested in having me, but I felt under no pressure at all. I came away from the visit open to making a move. I stayed another day and headed back to New Jersey.

As soon as I got back it was the week of Big Splash '91, and I was really pumped about the lineup. Steven Curtis Chapman was our headliner, so I knew we would sell out again and it would be a great show. SCC was staying in the same little beachside rooming house I was in, and since we also had listeners staying there, I was impressed at how accommodating, friendly, and accessible he was to his fans. It really made an impression on me, and was a reminder to be grateful for the folks who listen to me on the radio. They have a choice, and when they choose me and the station, I want to never take that for granted.

I could tell that something was up with Patti, and since we weren't really experienced yet at dealing with conflict, I just encouraged her to just get it out. Bottom line: she was really upset that I flew to Dallas without her, but was even more upset that I would consider making a move without taking into account the way that she felt about it.

I got that, and I went ahead and just threw out the question, "Well, would you be interested in moving to Texas?"

She said emphatically, "Not really."

Well now. Imagine that!

One of the things that I love about this lady who would become my wife is she is her own person. From the moment we met, she seemed unfazed about what I did, and if she was impressed with the fact that I talked to thousands of people every morning on the radio, she didn't show it. I found that intriguing and attractive. I know that if I were to die tomorrow, she would grieve, but she would be fine. She is very independent, resourceful, and tough when she needs to be. While this could be intimidating to some men, honestly it just made her that much more attractive to me. It just made me want her as my wife and life partner that much more.

I told her I was sorry, and, "Hey, let's just pray about it." She was a Jersey girl, and had spent her whole life there, with the exception of a few years in California. Her friends and family were from Jersey, so I got that. Moving for me was no big deal; I had done it my whole life in this crazy business. I tried to sympathize with her, but Dallas was still in the back of my mind. I just concluded if we were to make a move, somehow God would make it clear.

I called Jon and told him thanks so much for the hospitality, that I had a great time, and that the whole thing seemed very attractive to me, but I just didn't think it was a good time. I was about to be married, we just rented a house, I was working in the biggest media market in America, and it just didn't seem like a fit. I told him if he had a plan B that he should probably move on to his next option. What he told me next caused me to pause.

He said, "Well, I don't have a plan B, out of all the people in the country you're the guy I want, and I'm not going to even think about anybody else until you tell me absolutely, positively, no!"

Wow. I took a few seconds to process what he said and left the door open. "Let me get back to you," I said.

We touched base a few days later and I was just very open and honest with him. I explained: "Jon, I'm open to making a move, the issue is Patti. I really need for her to be on board with this. I don't want to start a marriage by telling her to start packing because I'm the head of the household. There is no way I'm going to pull off a heavy-handed move like that and tell her we are relocating halfway across the country. I really can't make any sort of change unless God gives us clear cut direction. If you want me in Texas, we need to pray that she would see it."

He suggested that we both fly down for a weekend. I thought that was an excellent idea.

I ran the idea by Patti, and she was cool at first.

"Look," I said, "they seem like nice people. Worst case scenario, we get a nice weekend getaway in Dallas."

She finally agreed. I called Jon with a short message: "We're coming, keep praying."

Big Splash was a hit as expected, and that Monday morning we had our usual department head meeting. Ed would start the meeting off, and we would go round robin around the room, sort of updating everything going on in our department, problems that need to be worked out, etc. We got to Stu, our engineer, and he reported that everything was worked out for the remote line the next Sunday for the interpreter. I had no idea what he was talking about.

"Interpreter?" I asked. "What interpreter?"

"The Taiwanese pastor," he said.

"What in the world are you talking about?" I said.

Ed chimed in next. "Don't you remember I told you we sold time to Billy Graham's organization? We have an interpreter who is going to translate his message into Taiwanese."

"What?" I screamed. "Are you kidding me?"

I was noticeably upset. When I talked about doing things that made sense, this was NOT what I had in mind. The thought that thousands of people would be tuning out the radio station made me crazy. The good news: I wouldn't be around to hear it. It's as if God knew I would be miserable being in town when the format of the radio station I programmed went unexpectedly Taiwanese! During the time Billy Graham was speaking in Central Park and the translator was on the air, I would be up 30,000 feet somewhere on a flight between Dallas and New York with my future bride.

Patti and I headed down when I got off the air that Friday. I opted to rent a car so we could explore the city a little bit on our own. KLTY had separate rooms reserved for us at the Homewood Suites in Las Colinas. Flowers greeted Patti when she arrived in her room. I was thinking, "Good move, Jon!" We relaxed that afternoon, and Jon and his wife, Sherry were going to pick us up and take us to dinner at a steak house on the east side of Dallas. I just remained cool and calm, and was determined I wasn't going to try to convince Patti of anything. Like everything else in my life over the past nine years, I was confident that if we were supposed to move, God would make it clear.

Jon and Sherry picked us up, and Patti and Sherry hit it off immediately. While they chatted away in the back seat, Jon and I attempted to take care of business while we headed to dinner.

"How much do you need?" he whispered.

"Jon, I need this much," I responded.

We countered back three or four times and came up with a number we could both live with, and agreed on a two-year deal. The girls were in their own world and were oblivious as to what was going on. I told Jon to continue to pray and that I would do my best to pull it off with Patti. But really, in my heart I knew if God wanted us to move, I needed for her to be on board with the idea.

Patti and I slept in the next morning and then hit the road to explore Dallas a little bit. She loved to shop, and was intent on finding a new pair of boots. There are boot outlets and western outlets in abundance in the area, and we hit two or three of them. One store greeted us with, "Welcome to Western Outlet, want a cold beer?" Now that's what I call hospitality. Free beer and I can't take them up on it!

Saturday night we got invited to Marc and Sonya's wedding reception, as they got married that afternoon, and they had it atop the very exclusive La Cima Club in the heart of Las Colinas. Everything was first class and elegant. Strolling violin players, delicious food, it was like out of a bridal magazine. Patti looked beautiful, and we got to meet just about everybody from the radio station. If KLTY was trying its best to make a good impression on my future bride, I don't think I could have written a better script. After a long night, we said goodbye to Jon and Sherry, and also to my friend Brad, who had flown in.

I had purposely not touched on the subject of us moving until I took Patti back to her hotel room that night. I went ahead and just laid it out there when I asked her, "So what do you think about all this?"

She whispered the answer I had been hoping for when she said, "Well, I think maybe God wants us to move to Texas!"

Wow. I was overjoyed. I gave her a kiss goodnight and headed off to my room, knowing once again God had come through. I was blown away.

I gave notice to my boss Ed as soon as I got back. He knew of KLTY's excellent reputation, so he understood completely and was very gracious. The Communicom home office wasn't quite as understanding. My game plan was to be grateful to the station and audience on the way out, promote the station like never before, and hand the morning show over to our very good afternoon guy, Keith Stevens. It would never be my intention to do anything to harm the station, and my mantra has always been "bless 'em on the way out," which is really the opposite of what many people expect in our business. The home office wanted me to be very limited in talking about any departure, and frankly, I was rather insulted. I had to send tapes daily to the home office in Denver, and the whole situation was rather ridiculous. Ed knew I would never do anything to damage the station and lobbied to let us do things our own way, but corporate was adamant. Bottom line: they were the ultimate authority, I needed the paycheck, so I did things exactly the way they wanted it.

TWENTY-EIGHT

Married and moving

S aturday, October 5, 1991, I got up early and worked out at the
Executive Health Club at the Hackensack YMCA. When I wasn't
walking or jogging, that was where I got my exercise in, and I had so
much adrenaline in my system on my wedding day a good workout was
in order.

Our wedding was at Pascack at 10:30 am, with lunch and reception
to follow at Pine Lake Inn in Washington Township. It was a great day.
Lots of friends and family were there. Pastor Fred from Pascack and
Pastor Pete handled the ceremony jointly, and probably the only change
I would have made was not to stand during Pete's message to us. It was
perfect, but rather long, and I thought we might faint! The reception had
some glitches, but all in all, it was a great day. Gary Selman, our Jewish
friend, did an amazing job doing the blessing in Hebrew.

A highlight was having Steven Curtis Chapman greet us on tape,
saying he checked with his wife Mary Beth, and for this special day it was
okay for their song to be our song. We did our first dance to 'I Will be
Here.' We were going to head to San Francisco and then Hawaii the next
day, so for our first night together I booked the Presidential Suite at an
oceanfront Marriott down at the Jersey Shore.

Patti was my wife. I was happy. And so was she. (In the future, whenever I was asked my wife's name, I would reply, "It's Patti Forever!")

I've heard of folks having nightmare honeymoons, but ours was great. We stayed over one night at a bed and breakfast in San Francisco, then headed to Kauai and Maui. Kauai was the highlight. It was very laid back, quiet and tropical. Hilton had just opened a resort there, and it was exceptional. We were going to fly non-stop back to New Jersey, changing planes in LA, but our plane was late and Delta put us up overnight. Even that was a blessing in disguise. We got an extra night's sleep in a nice hotel, and our flight back the next morning was practically empty, with Billy Crystal starring in 'City Slickers' for the in-flight movie. I had lots of rest followed by lots of laughs.

As soon as we got back, we packed and hit the road. It would take a few days to get to Dallas, and KLTY was running promos on the air in advance of my arrival, saying, "Where's Frank Reed?" I would call the station a few times over the next few days and let people know where we were on our road trip. I was off to another town, for another radio job, but this time I had my life partner by my side. Knowing that I still had a lakefront home back in Orlando, and I had committed to just a two-year deal, Orlando was remotely in the back of my mind. Would the Dallas job last? How would Christian music radio do in Dallas over the long haul? How long would my career last? Did I want to do this forever? Would I get back to the Florida lake house that I loved so much?

I didn't know it at the time, but I was in for a very long ride. One that continues to this day.

KLTY put us up at the same Homewood Suites for about a month till we found a place to live. Patti found us a really neat house to rent in Duncanville, which was south of Dallas, but it was a fairly easy commute to Las Colinas. The whole back of the house faced a greenbelt with a wall of windows, and it looked like a jungle. It was fine for our first place together. Patti had really gotten attached to Josh my golden retriever, and it was a perfect place if you had a dog. My newly married wife got a part-time job a few hours a week working over at Al Denson's office. Al did a big event for us at WWDJ on New Year's Eve 1990, and I took he and his wife Tracie on a New Year's Day sightseeing tour of New York City. (For a fun time, do *anything* with Al Denson!) The Denson's were very welcoming to us when we got to town. Since Patti had a successful background in retail, she easily moved on to a fulltime job at The Gap and was training to be a store manager. The only thing was the hours were crazy, and she was moving from store to store. After six months, our landlord wanted us to sign a long-term lease, or do a lease with an option to purchase deal. We wanted neither, so we began to look for a place to live in the Hurst, Euless, and Bedford area. It's hard to find an apartment that will take a ninety-pound golden retriever, but we found townhouses in Euless for rent that had a little fenced-in backyard. This was ideal, so we made the move. Patti was faithful to The Gap, but the crazy hours and moving from store to store was a hassle. I was making good money, so it wasn't like she had to work. I told her to give two weeks notice, and figured there had to be something more conducive for us being newlyweds.

I fit in well at the radio station and liked it a lot. We really sounded good, and the ratings, though not spectacular, were decent considering we were playing Christian music. When Patti and I first got to town, we stopped into a Joshua's Christian Store and asked for a copy of The Shepherd's Guide. We had The Guide in Jersey, and I did their radio commercials. It's a Christian business directory, and we needed everything when we came to town, like insurance, a dentist, doctor, etc. I always liked the idea of supporting Christian businesses whenever possible. The person at Joshua's had never heard of it, so I called the Shepherd's Guide home office in Baltimore, and explained I just moved to the Dallas area, right smack dab in the middle of the Bible belt, and asked them, "How come The Guide is not here?" My thought was if the franchise was available for Dallas-Ft. Worth, that would be a no-brainer for somebody. I was told a guy in Austin had bought the rights to the entire state, and that they would be moving in to develop the area that spring. I explained that I worked in Christian radio at a great station, and that whenever they got to town, to give me a call and I could fill them in on Christian media in the market. I left my name and number, not really expecting a call. I was just trying to be helpful and friendly, and hopefully plant a seed for some new business for the radio station.

Most marriage experts will tell you that your first year of marriage, you don't want to make any radical moves. We got married, went on our honeymoon, and literally moved over 1,500 miles! For us, though, this was a good thing. Since neither one of us really knew anybody, we didn't really have anybody or anywhere to escape to. We went through the typical stuff that newlyweds go through, but we had no options but to work it out.

One thing I learned early on is that a woman needs to feel secure. She can't be free to be herself if she feels like there's a possibility you could bail on her. On my side, men just need to be respected. That doesn't mean be my full-time waiter or be lower than me, it's just the way a guy is wired. You also have a better shot at a successful marriage if both parties are relatively healthy emotionally. One thing I love about Patti is that she challenges me to take care of myself, physically, emotionally, and spiritually. It's an ongoing process for both of us.

With both of us being 'program people,' me with a history in AA, and her in Al-Anon, we know the more we continue to work on ourselves personally, the better we can be for each other. We both brought some baggage to our marriage, but thankfully, I think our bags were rather small.

TWENTY-NINE

The Guide

———— ✍ ————

It was a typical day at the station when I got a call at my desk from a very energetic guy named Corky Butto. Corky was going to be the first publisher of The Shepherd's Guide in Dallas and Ft. Worth, and he got word from the home office that I knew something about Christian radio in the market. He invited me to lunch at a Chinese restaurant in Euless. Patti had nothing going on that day, so I asked her to come along. Also joining us was Doug Scheidt, who founded The Shepherd's Guide in Baltimore in 1980 and was also in charge of selling the franchises, Chip Winand, who had acquired the franchise rights for the whole state, and Sharon Sergeant, who was going to be a local sales rep. The lunch was great, and I could easily see they would have great success in a market like Dallas-Ft. Worth.

I filled them in on other Christian media in town, their competition, and also made a pitch for KLTY. Advertising with us would be a perfect fit. As lunch was winding down, they asked Patti what she did.

"Well, my background is in retail, but I just left The Gap. With us being newlyweds, the schedule and traveling all over the Metroplex to different stores was just a bit too much. So right now I'm not doing anything," she said.

Corky jumped right in. "You need to come work for us, you would be great! This is the perfect market for this, and I can train you. We'll have fun!"

Patti was very gracious and told him that maybe she would think about it, but I could tell she was just being polite. As we were leaving the restaurant, I asked Corky where The Shepherd's Guide office was.

"We are going to launch this business out of my three-bedroom apartment that I just leased," he said.

I asked him, "What town?"

"Euless!" he replied. The Shepherd's Guide office was going to be no more than five minutes from the townhouse we had just rented.

I immediately engaged Patti in a conversation about The Guide. "Why don't you just try it, you've got nothing to lose. They seem like nice people. We certainly believe in the concept," I said.

"But I've never sold anything," she replied.

Corky seemed like a combination of Zig Zigler and Tony Robbins on a heavy does of caffeine. But he was really very likable. If anybody could teach my wife how to sell yellow page advertising, he seemed like the guy. Sharon and Chip seemed solid, Doug was very impressive, and I could see Patti and her personality easily fitting in, even though there would be a learning curve.

"Let's just pray about it," I said. We did, and she started work two weeks later.

Both of us fell into getting involved with The Shepherd's Guide very easily. Corky and I became walking buddies, since there were some great trails right around where we lived in Euless. He was quite a character, and I liked him. Patti would come home and tell me about her latest sale and the sales tips she was learning from Corky. He really was a great salesman and teacher. In my spare time, I helped them out by helping deliver the printed books to the Christian bookstores. They had a deal with Joshua's Christian Stores, and I helped them get in with Family, a great store down by SMU called Logos, and Lifeway, though at the time they were called Baptist Christian Bookstores. I figured if I could do everything I could to help them succeed, it ultimately would help Patti succeed.

Corky invited us to his church, Abundant Life Assembly of God in Grapevine. I didn't really see us in an AOG church, but Patti and I really connected with the pastor, Eddy Brewer. We began attending regularly, and became friends with a few other couples in the church. One of the things I'm grateful to Pastor Eddy for is that every year, the first sermon of the year, he would do one message on giving. Patti and I had always been givers, but we made a decision after listening to Pastor Eddy that we would put God first in our giving. It's a decision I've never regretted. It was soon after we made this decision about giving that an amazing business opportunity came our way.

Things at the radio station continued to go well, and it was kind of fun that both Patti and I were now involved with Christian media. The Shepherd's Guide began to buy commercials on KLTY, and as I suspected, it was a good fit. It was profitable from the start and just continued to grow. We were shocked when we got word that Corky was leaving to purchase the Orlando Shepherd's Guide. Since he was in a partnership with Chip, who lived in Austin, the only thing I could figure was that he wanted to be his own boss. Left in the office was an office manager, and Sharon the other sales rep, who would soon be moving to Houston to launch the Houston Shepherd's Guide. That really only left one person in the office who knew anything about the business and how to sell ads, and that was my wife.

Chip Winand and his wife, Cathy owned and ran the Austin Shepherd's Guide, and his game plan was to develop the bigger markets in the whole state. Now that Dallas-Ft. Worth had launched, his next markets to develop were Houston and San Antonio. Since Patti was the only one left in the office, we went down for a visit. Chip floated the idea of a possible partnership, but our feeling was, "Let's try this out for a few months and see how it goes." He sent us off with some incentives that could put us in a position to own half of the business. With my involvement and contacts through the radio station, and Patti's growing confidence as a sales person, we began to pray about the prospect of becoming business partners. I knew that I would have to be careful not to do anything to compromise my position with KLTY, but it seemed like everything was falling into place. Just like everything else up until this time, we committed it to prayer, trusting that God would make things clear.

My two-year anniversary at KLTY was coming up, and since it seemed like they were pleased with my performance, I approached Brother Jon and Scott Wilder about a new deal. We were still renting the townhouse in Euless, but I've always loved the idea of owning property, so I thought if I could lock up another deal, Patti and I could start to look for a home. Plus the price of real estate in Dallas-Ft. Worth was a pittance compared to prices in suburban New Jersey. With our combined incomes, we could find a pretty decent place. I've always loved real estate. I now had a tenant in the Florida lake house, and I loved the fact that they were paying off my mortgage, plus every month I was making a few dollars.

I was disappointed when Scott informed me that the station didn't want to do a new contract. It wasn't that they wanted me to leave, they just didn't want to put any sort of commitment in writing. This really sort of ticked me off, but I liked the job and what I was doing, so I kept calm about it. Deep inside though, it kind of bugged me. I had moved my life halfway across the country, and now I felt a little slighted that they didn't want to make any sort of formal commitment to me.

A couple of days later, my former boss and now good friend, Joe B., was in town on business. He had started his own company, and he suggested we do lunch. The timing couldn't have been more perfect. It's a blessing to have a good friend who you can just be gut level honest with, and be totally yourself. I explained my frustration to Joe, and also shared the Shepherd's Guide opportunity that we had been praying about, and he was short and to the point.

He said something like, "Look, you like KLTY, they like you, they are paying you well, what's the problem? If you feel insecure about not having something in writing, why not build your own security along with Patti with the yellow page opportunity?"

I knew that made sense, but I still had to work it out in my own time, in my own way. I knew the potential for The Guide was really good, especially in a market like DFW, but I was having a hard time pulling the trigger. God was about to change that.

One of the things I've become certain of is this: if you really want God's answer on something, you can find it, but God's ways are not always predictable. While there may be some basics to follow on figuring something out as a believer, God is not always conventional. And, sometimes things at the moment may not make sense. Moving from a custom-built lakefront home in Central Florida to a basement apartment in Hackensack seemed crazy, but God led, and I went. It was a pivotal move, and the right one. Fast forward five years later, I now had an opportunity to help my wife build a business, in a market seemingly custom built for this particular enterprise, while working at a great radio station, and it seemed like a no-brainer. Still, I didn't want to make a mistake, so I continued to pray.

I had come across a great book by Pat Morley, called 'The Rest of your Life.' Interestingly, Pat was in my Boy Scout troop in Pine Hills, and was one of the cool kids who had a scooter! He was a few years older than me, and lived in my neighborhood, though I'm sure he doesn't remember me. He had a very successful commercial real estate business in Orlando, and then began doing men's ministry. This book was one of the follow-ups to a best seller he had for men, called 'Man in the Mirror.' I liked the book so much that I passed on a copy to Pastor Eddy at Abundant Life.

As the days went by and I continued to pray and work through the decision about The Guide, I felt led one night to go to a men's meeting they were having at the church. It was a typical men's gathering that they had regularly, and I slipped into the back of the sanctuary. I didn't know what the format of this particular meeting was, but I loved to hear Pastor Eddy teach, so when I saw that he was stepping up to the podium, I knew I hadn't wasted my time. Talk about an understatement. I was about to be overwhelmed.

Eddy got up and began to share about 'finding God's will in certain situations,' and while crediting Morley, began to teach from what he had learned from the book I passed on to him! I had been praying and wrestling with this decision, and I had been careful to go through steps that Morley had laid out, and now Pastor Eddy was speaking the same principles back to me. It was as if there was nobody else in the room, and God was speaking directly through him, going through the steps with me one by one, to confirm the fact that I had covered all my bases. I was awestruck! As Pastor Eddy concluded, I felt a flood of peace pour over my entire body. I was reminded of the verse in Philippians that says to present your requests to God, and the peace of God, which transcends all understanding, will guard your hearts and your minds. This moment felt even beyond that scripture. I sensed God's presence and peace in a powerful way. I broke down and began to weep over God's goodness to me. It was as if I was receiving marching orders for the next season of my life, however long that might be. Things were now crystal clear in my mind. *Continue to do your best for the radio station, and on the side help your wife build a business.* Patti and I called Chip the next day. We did the deal.

THIRTY

Down to business

———— ⟞⟋⟍ ————

Patti was now officially the publisher of The Shepherd's Guide for Dallas and Ft. Worth. I jokingly told people I was the full-time radio guy and official part-time wife helper! Chip put some sales incentives in place, and with our sweat equity, I figured we could become partners, amazingly, in about two years if we hustled. Patti negotiated a good salary for herself based on a percentage of sales. Since we had a big market, she sold half the year in Dallas County, and half the year in Tarrant County (which is Ft. Worth), so we had constant cash flow. She would eventually add the northern suburbs of Collin and Denton Counties. The timing was perfect. We had a few competing publications in town, but The Guide was definitely the better product. With my contacts, I helped her grow the distribution, and of course I did all of their radio commercials. Something else I found out early in our marriage is my wife is a great negotiator. I would listen to her do deals with people and realized she is gifted in that area. In the future if we needed a big purchase like buying a car, I would just say to the salesman, "Talk to my wife!"

Patti and I knew we could save money initially by operating the business out of a house, so we bought a three-bedroom Victorian home in Colleyville that had a huge living space over the garage with a separate staircase through the laundry room. It was perfect for The Guide office. We had a full-time office manager, and hired a few sales reps. I wanted to expand our awareness, so besides the presence on KLTY, we did some on-air announcements with KCBI, the inspirational station in DFW. I had also heard of a new Christian TV station in town that was right down the street from KLTY in Las Colinas. Channel 29 was the early beginnings of what would become The Daystar Network.

Patti and I wanted to run a business that was noticeably different from other media, and we knew it would be a benefit to the advertisers if we could have a big networking event where all the business owners could meet one another. I came up with the idea of having a client appreciation dinner, but of course that would be a big expense. If we could tie in the event with a TV station, we could sell sponsorships to help pay the cost, and we could even offer the first ticket to the advertiser at no charge. Any additional tickets, we would just charge the advertiser our cost. I ran the idea by the guy running Channel 29, and was excited when he called back a few days later and said they were interested! We got together and picked a date. We booked the ballroom at The Sheraton Grand Hotel in Irving, and began to make plans.

We found out quickly that Colleyville, Texas is a great place to live. It's just west of DFW International, so you have quick access equally to downtown Dallas or downtown Ft. Worth. Depending on traffic, you can make it to either downtown within thirty minutes or so. My commute to KLTY was only about twenty. We didn't realize it when we bought, but Colleyville is one of the safest places to live in the Metroplex, and the home values are on the high end for the area. Our Victorian needed to be completely remodeled, and since we had a lot of construction people in The Guide, that became one of our side projects. It was easy to barter with advertisers to get things done at the house.

My faithful golden retriever, Josh, who was now about twelve, came down with doggie cancer, and one of our advertisers, Gene Giggleman, was a very kind and compassionate veterinarian who made house calls. He came by a few times and gave Josh some shots to help give him some relief, but he told us we needed to get prepared to let him go. The day came just before Christmas 1993. The morning I couldn't get him up at all to take him out, I knew it was time. If you've ever been at this place with a faithful pet that you've had for many years, I don't need to explain the emotions to you. It's just plain sad and heart-wrenching. They become such a part of you. Patti had gotten very attached to Josh, and said that he was the only dog she had ever loved.

I got Gene on the phone and he said to meet him at Roanoke Animal Hospital. He met us there and carried Josh inside to a private examining room. Gene prayed as we held him and told him we loved him and said goodbye. Gene made the injection, saying he would feel no pain. He closed his eyes, and he was gone. I don't think I've ever cried as hard.

That Christmas was difficult. Patti and I both cried a lot. I would think to myself, "Get a grip, Frank, he was only a dog!" But rather than drink over the feelings I didn't like, I was learning to deal with life's ups and downs, and the feelings that came with them. I'm reminded of the song lyrics, "He gives and takes away, my heart will truly say, blessed be the name of the Lord." The deepest sadness lasted about a week. Brother Jon, who had recently lost a horse he was very attached to, left me a nice note one day at the station and said he knew exactly how I felt.

That verse in Corinthians that says, "we are comforted, so that we can comfort others," is so true. And once again, God's orchestration on the timing of events in my life was nothing short of miraculous. After a short season of mourning, it turned into a time of celebration. That New Year's Eve we went out with a few of the couples we had been hanging out with at church, but for the moment Patti wanted to keep this news just between us.

"Happy new year," she said. "We're having a baby!"

Unreal, I thought. Absolutely unreal.

Our son, Ryan Christopher (which means kingly Christ-bearer), would arrive in September 1994.

The day of the first annual Shepherd's Guide Client Appreciation Dinner was approaching, and I kept trying to get a meeting with Channel 29 to discuss a format for the show. When it comes to live broadcasts of any kind, I know there's a long list of things that can go wrong, so I'm a big planner when it comes to live events. I had my list of ideas on what we should do, and sent it over to the guy who was producing the show, but it was frustrating because we never could connect. Sure enough though, the day of the event I saw the TV remote trucks in the parking lot of the hotel, so I figured we would just have a big production meeting before we went on the air.

Since this was live TV, though, I had a healthy dose of nervousness and anxiety. It's one thing to mess up on the radio, it's another thing entirely to mess up on live TV! We were going to go on live that night from 7 till 9pm, two whole hours. My idea was to have Marcus and Joni Lamb (owners of the station and hosts of their own show, called Celebration) open the show, and then introduce me as the MC. I would then throw it back to them where they would be seated in the atrium. The idea was during the time the advertisers were eating dinner, Marcus and Joni would interview Patti, then Doug, the founder of The Shepherd's Guide who was our guest speaker that night, and then Dan Dean of Phillips, Craig and Dean, who would be doing a concert with his worship band from his church. After that, I would interview the clients who were sponsors on TV, then introduce Dan and his band, and then bring on Doug, who would close out with his personal testimony, how The Shepherd's Guide started, and then end with him encouraging all of the business owners in attendance.

Steve, the show's producer got there about 4, and I ran my ideas by him. Rather than have a big meeting, he agreed the format looked fine, and then he took me aside and tried his best to put my mind at ease. This is what he said: "See that door right there?" as he nodded to the ballroom entrance at The Sheraton. "Marcus and Joni will walk through that door about five minutes before air. I will meet with him for about two minutes, then Marcus will walk on the stage, step up to the podium, and everything will be just fine."

In my mind I was thinking, "Are you kidding me?? We are about to do a live TV broadcast for two solid hours and you're going to prep this guy in two minutes? And he walks in just minutes before?"

This was not what I had in mind. But what was I going to do? People began arriving around 6, and excitement was all over the place. Patti and her staff did a great job at decorating, Dan and the band sounded great during sound check, and everything seemed ready to go. The room filled up, and sure enough, just like Steve said, Marcus and Joni arrived just past 6:50, they met with Steve for a couple of minutes, then Marcus nodded at me as I took my place just off to the side of the stage. In just a few minutes we were live on the air, and Marcus had the place fired up and cheering. It was electric. Next Marcus gave me a gracious introduction and said, "And now please welcome your host for the evening, from KLTY radio, Mr. Frank Reed!"

The applause was still going strong when I took the mic as Marcus and Joni made their way off the stage to head to the atrium to get set up for the next segment. I figured if I could kill time for about three minutes, that would give them time to get situated and mic'd and ready to interview the publisher of The Shepherd's Guide, my wife Patti. I had rehearsed ahead of time and did a good job of explaining the purpose of The Shepherd's Guide, what viewers could look forward to that evening, just your typical stuff. Everything so far, so good. I got the cue from the camera guy they were ready in the other room, so on live television for all to see and hear I gladly and confidently said, "And now, with a very special guest in the atrium, let's send it back out to Jonas and Marky!!" *What??* "Er, I mean Marcus and Joni!" That had to be one of the funniest gaffs of my broadcast career! Here I was concerned about the TV folks making mistakes, and I blow the names of the station owners on their own TV station. Ha!

Of course Marcus and Joni were very gracious, and honestly, the rest of the night went off without a hitch. The whole evening was a success, but most importantly, we sent a message to the advertisers we were going to run a business that was different, and that we truly supported them and wanted their businesses to succeed. Patti and I knew after that first night we wanted to do it again next year, bigger and better. We would end up doing the event for nine consecutive years on Daystar.

THIRTY-ONE

Changes

———— ✧ ————

A round 1996, the radio business got de-regulated by the federal government, and one of the biggest changes was the number of radio stations one particular owner could own in a single market. This literally changed the landscape of the industry in just a few years. Salem began buying stations, and picked up the 94.9 frequency in DFW, which had a great signal. They put their teaching and talk format on that station, and hired away Scott Wilder to do an afternoon talk show. KLTY promoted me to Operations Manager over the three stations we owned, which was 94.1 FM KLTY, Praise 104.9 (which was a combination of teaching programs and praise music), and we had an AM station on 1190 that was nothing more than an outlet for paid programs. It had one bright spot, a syndicated sports show hosted by a then up-and-coming Jim Rome. Being Ops Manager gave me the opportunity to work closely with Jon on the sound of KLTY, and we worked well together.

One company in particular, Clear Channel, which was based in San Antonio, began buying up stations very quickly. The deregulation drove up the price of radio stations, and our owner, Marc Rodriquez sold KLTY at an opportune time. Sunburst Media, headed up by a legendary

Texas broadcaster named John Borders, paid Marc just over $63 million
for KLTY. To date, that is the second highest price ever paid for a radio
station in the Dallas-Ft. Worth market. Sunburst then sold the 94.1 frequency for a huge amount to a big Hispanic company, which meant 94.1
would become a Spanish-speaking station. Selling the station at this time
was a very smart move on Marc's part, but it ushered in a very difficult
season for the KLTY brand.

Sunburst was building its own group of stations, and had acquired
the rights to move a station in from Bowie, Texas, to Highland Village, a
Dallas suburb. The idea was to put KLTY on this new frequency, which
was 100.7 FM. The tower location was north of the DFW Metroplex in
Collinsville, Texas. One of the upsides of the move was that the new company was building us new studios and offices in North Dallas. Jon and I
went by the new facility before it was finished, and it really looked great.
We were in the North Dallas Bank Building, and we had management
and sales on one floor, and studios and programming were up some steps
on the second floor. Our on-air studios overlooked a garden area, and it
really was a neat place to go to work. We only had one problem, and it
was a big one. The radio signal.

I was now Program Director of 100.7 FM KLTY, but just prior to
the switch when we were still at 94.1, we had a very good ratings book.
I scored the #1 rank with 25-54-year-old women in my afternoon drive
shift, which I believe was a first for our format in a major market. This was
a big deal, because that group of people is called 'the money demo.' When
advertising agencies buy commercials on stations, the higher your rank,
the more money they will pay. The key is to not be at or near the top once,
but consistently. I was excited that we seemed to making inroads into the
heritage Adult Contemporary station in town, KVIL. But after the move
to 100.7, things went downhill quickly.

When the audience can't hear your radio station, there's really not a whole lot you can do! Because our frequency was licensed to Highland Village, our tower site in Collinsville did not allow us to have a signal that blanketed the market like being on 94.1 did. We did our best to try to make the most of the situation, and our General Manager at the time, Donna Fadal, wanted to try to turn a negative into a positive. She had some very good jingle singers do a knockoff of The Jeffersons TV theme song, but instead of having them sing "moving on up to the east side," they sang that KLTY was "moving on up to 100.7." It was very clever and well done, but it was more than evident that we had a serious problem when we launched the switch with our 'Moving on up Party,' which was appropriately held at the top of the Reunion Tower in downtown Dallas. We catered in fancy food, drinks, and invited clients and artists in to our big bash.

There was only one small problem. When the promotions team from the station got there to set up the sound, they couldn't pick up our own radio station! Talk about a nightmare. We had to play CDs at the event because if you lived south of Interstate 30 in the Metroplex, KLTY had pretty much disappeared off the face of the earth. Our phones were ringing off the hook. People from Arlington and points south were complaining they couldn't hear the station, meanwhile we got calls from people in Oklahoma saying that they loved the new station! God bless those nice folks in Oklahoma, but I needed listeners and ratings in Dallas-Ft.Worth!

There was one big positive that was developed during this time at the station that continues on KLTY to this day. We had hired Mike McVay as a consultant, and since Mike and I worked together in Orlando, working with Mike again was an easy fit for me. We were Mike's first Christian format client, and we began to expand our thinking on the reach of

KLTY. Rather than target the audience as entirely Christian, we began to think out of the box on how we could reach people who might not be overtly Christian, but could potentially become listeners. The whole idea was how do we reach more people, and make the needle move up on the ratings. I was convinced we needed a new positioning statement, something that would include our core Christian audience, but broaden it to reach people who could possibly listen to us because musically and on the air we obviously promoted conservative family values.

For years we ran a bumper sticker campaign, and it seemed like if you ever came across a family in a van with a mom, a dad, and kids, they probably had a KLTY bumper sticker. I came up with the idea, 'The Station for the Whole Family,' and announced it in a meeting with Borders, McVay, and Donna. Everybody loved it, especially Mike, who had just named me McVay Media Major Market Program Director of the Year. This was cool because Mike had many mainstream stations as clients. To have a guy who was programming a Christian station win this award was a first. I came away from the meeting proudly feeling like I was some sort of programming genius. God was about to humble me in short order!

A gentleman named John Frost had become a friend, and John was now programming a station in my hometown of Orlando, called Magic 107.7. John used to program here in Dallas, and had become a fan of KLTY. I knew him as a very smart programmer, and he had taken Magic in Orlando to #1 with a secular Adult Contemporary format, but doing it promoting family values, and a safe listening environment. They even had 'The Magic Promise,' which was a written document and on-air statement promising that they would never do anything on the air to offend you, or anything that you wouldn't want your young children to hear. John was in town one week, and during lunch I shared with him my 'genius' idea on the new positioning statement. We hadn't rolled it out yet on the air but we were close. We had a great visit, talking about our faith and the nuts and bolts of radio programming. When it was time for him to leave, I walked him to the front door.

As he was leaving, literally walking out the door, he looked back at me and whispered the words "One word."

"What?" I said, as I was straining to hear what he said.

He said it again. "One word."

I questioned again. "What? One word? What is it?" I leaned my ear in his direction so I was sure not to miss it.

"Safe," he said. "Safe for the Whole Family."

I was stunned. What a Godsend. That slogan is still used by KLTY to this day, and is now trademarked by Salem for use at other music radio stations in our group around the country.

We launched the new positioning statement, complete with our own version of the 'KLTY Promise.' We had the station in position to make a move. All we needed was a signal.

In May 1999, our daughter Hope Kathryne arrived. Patti chose the name Hope because she told me when we met, I brought hope to her life. I think I'm an encourager by nature. God gives us all certain gifts, and I probably have an extra dose of hope and mercy. I'm also an optimist at heart. I'm definitely a 'glass half full' guy. (Patti reminds me she is the realist!) Now that I'm a parent, it's scary to think I almost missed the blessing of children in my life.

When Patti and I were dating, we went to California for a few days to visit her brother, Chris, and his family in California. We visited the Monterey peninsula, Pebble Beach, and Carmel. I actually thought the beach at Carmel might be a good place to propose to her. The trip went downhill when I shared with her that since I was older, I wasn't sure I wanted to have children. With God's help, I worked through those issues, and now I can't envision life without our Ryan and Hope. They are such a gift. I can't imagine not being there to see Ryan get his 3rd degree black belt in Tae Kwon Do, or Hope singing 'Tomorrow' in a production of 'Annie.' Having children also gave me a whole new perspective on God as my heavenly father. I love my kids so much, if a truck was barreling down the street heading for my children, I would without hesitation jump in front of the truck to save them, even if it meant losing my own life. There would be no debate in my mind. I wouldn't have to think twice about it. God could have easily intervened to save his own son, but did not because of his love for you and me. I never looked at it from that perspective until I had kids of my own. Something else about Ryan and Hope that I never saw coming and has been an incredible blessing is that they keep me young. They have forced me to stay active. I may be in my 60s, but old dads are not allowed in our family!

Being a dad also gives me kinship with other fathers, and I remember being sympathetic to a dad who kept sending me emails at KLTY about his son who was a new artist. Being a dad myself, I 'got it' about wanting to help your boy. The man's name was Connie, he lived just east of Dallas in Grand Saline, and even though we weren't playing his son's songs yet, I enjoyed the little connection we were having via email because just like me, he was just a dad who dearly loved his son. I was the Program Director at the time, so I was the ultimate decision maker of what songs we played. I could tell the young man was very talented, and since he was with Sparrow Records, I knew it was only a matter of time before we would be playing his songs.

I got the biggest kick out of finally sending an e-mail to Connie Tomlin to tell him that KLTY was now playing the song 'Forever,' by his son, Chris. The rest, as they say, is history.

THIRTY-TWO

No Coincidences

As I recount the milestones in my life, I am most amazed at God's timing. We have that saying on the KLTY morning show that we often say together: "You just can't make this stuff up!" I sort of look at my life that way. When God is directing it, it becomes an amazing adventure. Since we are all different and unique, I believe God customizes the experience for those who are seeking his direction.

One of the ways I've been assured of God's guidance in my life has been the way circumstances have fallen into place. When I left Orlando to move to New Jersey, my GM at the time, George Toulas, was initially not pleased that I had resigned and was leaving his station. He got over it, and the station even gave me a nice send off. Of course I didn't know it at the time, but our paths would eventually cross again.

Often times when there is an ownership change at a station, management will call a big staff meeting, the new owners will be in attendance, and the announcement of the ownership change is made to the entire staff. In May 2000, we had such a meeting. Salem Communications was acquiring KLTY from Sunburst, and Salem's president, Ed Atsinger and a group of executives from the home office flew in for the meeting. In the group that day was none other than my old boss from Orlando. Salem was rolling out some Christian music stations in other markets, and they hired George to help facilitate that project.

After the announcement was made and the meeting was over, I took George aside. I was almost giddy at reconnecting with him again.

"George, do you realize you are one of the reasons I'm here?" I said. "Had you not been out of pocket the day I resigned, we probably would have struck a deal, and I never would have moved to New Jersey, which eventually led me to Texas!"

George agreed and we reminisced for a few minutes about our time together in Orlando. That day and the decision for Salem to acquire KLTY was going to eventually have huge ramifications for the staff and the listeners. And for me, too. Things were about to get better, but not before we would go through a few more bumps along the road.

Just prior to Salem buying the station, I was experiencing some burnout, and I convinced Brother Jon and our GM at the time, Donna, to hire a new Program Director. I had gained some favor with Donna because of my ratings, and I negotiated a really decent salary to just do the afternoon shift. I was also doing afternoons in Atlanta for a friend, Jerry Williams, who programmed a Christian music station called J-93.3. I did this recording from a studio I had set up at home. I would record every morning before I went in to do my afternoon drive shift at KLTY. I had a co-host in Atlanta, a really neat lady named Parks Stamper, and since we did our voice tracks together just hours before the actual airtime, we really sounded great. A funny thing that would occasionally happen was this: I would sometimes get a call from somebody listening to me at the beginning of my shift on KLTY, then they would catch a plane to Atlanta, rent a car, hit scan, stop at a Christian music station, and there I was again! They would contact me and say, "Uh, exactly how do you do that?"

Between my combined salary from both radio stations, and Patti growing The Shepherd's Guide, we were doing very well financially. I didn't have the stress associated with being the Program Director, and I was making a great living just having fun on the radio. While I absolutely love the creative process of being responsible for what comes out of the radio speakers, I am not the best when it comes to managing people. I know my strengths and weaknesses. It's something I can manage and pull off if I absolutely have to, but it's not my favorite thing.

As it happens sometimes in our business, when Salem took over we had some downsizing. Mark Ryder, who we had hired from Nashville to take my place as Program Director, was let go. Jon came to me and asked me to program the station once again. We worked together well when it came to programming the station, but I wasn't crazy about the idea. I loved the freedom of just being responsible for my four hours on the air, not the whole operation. Jon convinced me he had no place else to turn, so I reluctantly agreed.

We ended up re-hiring Mark to work in the production department (these are the people who produce commercials, the station's promotional announcements, etc.), which was a little awkward since just a few months earlier he was my boss, and now our roles were reversed. Mark and I had a talk about it and he put me totally at ease. We worked fine together before and he was an absolute wiz and genius when it came to producing on-air things for the station. He was one of the best I had ever heard. It was a very sad day for all of us when Mark took a break, and suffered cardiac arrest while sitting in his parked car in our parking lot. A security guard called the office to say there was an emergency with one of our employees, and sales rep Keith Nelson was the first to get to Mark, with Bonnie Curry just a step behind. They had tried their best to revive him, but he was gone.

We were all dumbfounded, stunned and shocked. It was so sad. His sweet wife, Laurie worked part-time for us on the air, and the station really rallied around her. Even though Mark hadn't worked for us that long, he and Laurie were like family, and I'm grateful to work with a company and group of folks who really care about people. Laurie was overwhelmed by people she didn't even know sending her checks in the mail. Mark was well known and loved by many in our business, and it was a loss to us all professionally because he was such a great radio talent, but I think even more so personally. Mark just had a certain way about him. I don't think I've ever worked with a more likable guy. We all knew he would be missed.

Since Salem already owned 94.9 FM, the decision was made to move KLTY to 94.9, and the Salem teaching and talk station, KWRD 'The Word,' would move to 100.7. Since KLTY needed to compete for ratings, we could recapture the audience we lost by moving to 94.9. It was a 100,000 watt signal, and with our tower in Cedar Hill, we could once again cover the entire market. Also, since The Word was mostly talk, they could make the signal mono instead of stereo, which gave it a farther reach. It made perfect sense. Ironically, the 94.9 address is where KLTY initially launched back in 1985, just before they first called me about a job. It was now coming back full circle. Our new General Manager, John Peroyea, knew that we would have only one opportunity to make the switch and do it right. We brainstormed out of the office at a hotel for a few days to put together a game plan.

Patti continued to grow The Shepherd's Guide, and moved the office out of our home and into office space in Colleyville. We finished the remodeling project on the Victorian and sold it at a nice profit, giving us the chance to relocate to a bigger home. We loved Colleyville, and opted to stay in the same town in a newer development. We came across a spec home that had been on the market a while, and Patti did her negotiating magic and got us a good deal. Since Patti had more responsibilities at home with the kids, she was now managing the business more on a part-time basis. She had hired some strong people, and The Guide continued to hum right along. I continued to do her radio commercials and coordinate the client appreciation dinner. Our lives had developed a certain rhythm between our faith, our home life, our businesses, and church.

I had read 'The Purpose Driven Life,' by Rick Warren, and came away with the desire to get plugged into a local fellowship. We picked First Baptist Colleyville because they had a strong program for kids. Even though Patti and I don't really care for labels or denominations, it seemed like a good fit. We connected with other couples who were professionals who had young kids. One of the things I've felt strongly about is the need for Christians to be involved in a local fellowship. We weren't created to be an island, but to be part of a local body. When you invest your time with others, they will be there for you when your life hits a bump in the road or a crisis.

We know that life will have its share of hard knocks and heartaches. It's good to know if anything was to ever happen to me, Patti has a group of friends who would rally around her and get her through it. I have to credit my wife for helping me to branch out as a person. I spent a good portion of my life being very independent, and even kind of a loner and introverted when I was off the air. My social circle revolved mostly around the radio business, which in retrospect led to a lot of dysfunction. Now that I had a family, I was forcing myself to experience new things, including reaching out to others, and I knew that was good and healthy emotionally. Since Patti did not have much of a home life growing up, we determined early on to start family traditions we could pass down to Ryan and Hope. I did my best to strike a healthy balance between work and family. We started doing things like taking an annual ski trip to Colorado, and traditions like spending Thanksgiving weekend at Pine Cove Christian Camp just outside of Tyler. We also fell in love with the beaches of northwest Florida on the Gulf. And since the Clermont lake home we still owned was 1,200 miles away, I had the dream of owning another waterfront property someday where I could pass on my love of the water to our kids.

THIRTY-THREE

Radio Revival

——— ✑ ———

"**9**4.9 KLTY is back!" That was the marketing message when we made the switch on the dial from 100.7. We were on a mission to get the word out and recapture our audience, and add some new listeners at the same time. The on-air lineup was strong; Jon and his team in the morning, Bonnie Curry from KVIL in middays, I did afternoons, and Andi Jaxson did nights. We ran a double full-page ad in the *Dallas Morning News*, which was very clever; Jon and the morning team on one side, and Scott Wilder and his co-host Lauren Lintner on the other, with what appeared to be moving chairs sliding from one side of the newspaper page to the other.

As good as that was, the TV campaign was even better. Steven Curtis Chapman and Michael W. Smith each cut separate commercials for us, announcing that KLTY was back, and then they actually wrote out 94.9 on the TV screen to drive the point home. It was exceptional. The attitude around the station was upbeat and positive. Thankfully, the 100.7 era was behind us.

Patti and I were on a ski trip in Breckenridge with the kids when I got the call from my GM John Peroyea, along with our regional VP, Rob Adair. The ratings came out, and we were back. We offered a prayer of thanksgiving together on the phone. I remembered back to my thoughts in Orlando when I made the move to Christian radio. I was now employed by a major broadcast group that had great resources; I was programming a 100,000 watt Christian music radio station 24/7 in the 5th biggest market in America. I dreamed one day of our Christian format competing in a major market with the secular counterparts. We were now in a position to do just that.

KLTY has an annual free concert event right around the 4th of July called Celebrate Freedom, and in the summer of 2001, with the help of our new full-market signal, we packed out the famous Southfork Ranch with over 100,000 in attendance. We went through a season with the event where each year we would partner with a different record company, and this particular year it was Sparrow Records. Our headliner was Steven Curtis Chapman, and the timing of the event coincided with the release of Steven's new album 'Declaration.' There was a lot of anticipation and excitement as we got closer to the end of the evening. Avalon had a great set, and everybody was waiting for Steven and his band to take the stage.

What happened next was something I'll never forget. Steven had lost his voice due to a paralyzed vocal chord, and it developed into a six-month issue. Though he couldn't sing, he was still able to talk for short periods of time. Brother Jon came out center stage along with Steven, and they sat down on a couple of stools. Jon explained the situation, and he asked the audience if it was okay if he and Steven played some new songs from the about-to-be released CD. He and Steven would talk for a moment about a particular song, and then we played the song right off the CD through the loud sound system that was covering the multitude of people at Southfork. As we played songs like 'See the Glory,' 'Jesus is Life,' and 'Live out Loud,' we had TV cameras scanning the fans in the crowd who were jumping up and down to the songs, and folks could see themselves having a great time on the big screen jumbotron we had set up. People loved it! Even though we didn't have Steven singing live, the crowd was enjoying every song and having an absolute blast. Jon and Steven have had a long friendship, and I doubt that anybody else could have pulled off what they did, the way they did it. Frankly speaking, the idea was pure genius. It was something I'm glad I got to witness first hand.

I was about to celebrate ten years at the station that fall. My previous longevity record was two months shy of eight years at WNBC in New York. Patti continued to have great success with The Shepherd's Guide, and things were good at KLTY. I always had returning to Central Florida in the back of my mind, but as time moved on, I slowly began to consider Texas as our permanent home. Texans are known for their love of the state and independent nature. I got a kick out of the fact that my kids, Ryan and Hope were born Texans. We have a fun saying here: "I wasn't born in Texas, but I got here as fast as I could!"

I've had people say to me on more than one occasion, 'How can you stay at one radio station for so long?' The answer is simple: God hasn't released me to leave. Until my marching orders change, I continue to march and do what I do the best way I possibly can. While I was very certain I was exactly where I was suppose to be, that wasn't the case for everybody.

THIRTY-FOUR

End of an era

"**D**o you know anything about this?" John, my GM, handed me the letter. It was Brother Jon's resignation.

"No, sir," I said. I had been through a lot of change at the station in the past ten years, but this was an earthquake.

Jon Rivers had been the backbone of the station, and was a legend within our radio format. I had my own theories on his decision to leave, but have always felt it was none of my business. I still feel the same way today. I'm not one for gossip or getting into other peoples business. It does nobody any good. Especially yourself.

Salem was building us new state-of-the-art studios and offices in Las Colinas, and we were going to move over the weekend, and be on the air in our new facilities on Monday. Jon resigned the Thursday before the move. I had enough going on pulling off the logistics of a facilities move. Now I needed a new morning guy. John my boss asked me to go on Monday morning until we figured out what we were going to do. I had also asked Jon to do some test run shows with a news lady named Toni Trueblood. Jon and Toni had worked together before at another station, and I thought she would be a good fit. She also was going to start that Monday. Talk about pressure. Move the station. Go on mornings. With a new news lady. In a brand new studio, learning to run brand new equipment.

One thing I've learned about myself is that when the pressure hits, I kind of thrive on it. Rather than retreat from a challenge, I've always had the ability to step up. I owed a lot to Brother Jon. His insistence on me coming to Texas, and not taking no for an answer, is something I'll always be grateful for. I knew I would miss him professionally and even more so personally. We had been through a lot of life together in ten years. But I was ready to do whatever we had to do to keep things at the station intact and moving forward. Going backwards was not an option.

Toni and I hit if off immediately doing mornings together. I had an idea of what I wanted with a news personality, and Toni was quite a journalist. She was very good at finding heartfelt stories at the end of the newscast, the type of stuff that connected with our female-targeted audience. Toni was doing afternoon news with me a few years earlier when I had hit the #1 rank with women in the afternoons, and we had good chemistry. We also hired a very talented African American lady named Starlene Stringer to do helicopter traffic.

I felt a little out of place doing mornings, but it wasn't as if I hadn't done this before. It just felt odd working at KLTY without Brother Jon. Working with the same guy for ten years is a long time in this business. I never, ever envisioned me doing mornings at KLTY. Honestly, I thought Jon would be there forever. I saw me exiting the station someday way before he ever would. It felt odd in my mind that was now in reverse.

As I continued to work at the morning show with Toni, I could tell we were getting some positive feedback on the way we sounded. I think my General Manager, John, was the first to suggest that maybe I should consider doing mornings as a full-time thing. Between the morning show, programming the station, and my commitment to J-93.3 in Atlanta, I was starting to burn the candle at both ends.

Salem ended up launching a music station in Atlanta, called 'The Fish,' and they weren't crazy about the fact that I was competing against them in the afternoon. John went to bat for me with Salem corporate, and I ended up leaving J-93.3 and was now recording voice tracks for the night show on Salem's new Fish station in Chicago for the same money. A few months went by, and it was obvious I couldn't continue at the pace I was going. My own personal standards on what comes out of the radio are very high, and frankly, doing great radio just takes work. John and our regional VP, Rob Adair, sat me down and told me I'd have to decide. Program KLTY full-time, or do the morning show. They wouldn't let me do both. The decision was mine. Knowing I had earned the right to still have input into the sound and direction of the radio station I had invested the past ten years of my life with, I made the obvious choice. I was going to do mornings for KLTY.

But reflecting back on my time as a programmer, some of the best and most meaningful on-air moments have been when we responded to a tragedy. I remember when we lost Rich Mullins, and how KLTY was a haven for fans who loved Rich and his music. There was the heartbreak of Columbine. We had our own local tragedy at Wedgewood Baptist Church in Ft. Worth when a gunman burst into a service on a Wednesday night and senselessly gunned people down. I had the privilege to fly in medical supplies with a private pilot right after Hurricane Katrina and report on the air from the ravaged beach in Biloxi. But I will never, ever forget September 11, 2001.

THIRTY-FIVE

9/11

On September 11th, Toni and I were having a typical good time on the air, a usual Tuesday morning broadcast. Our morning show producer, Ron Taylor and I were excited about the fact that Michael W. Smith was scheduled to fly in that morning, and we were going to have one of our 'brown bag' concerts at Vista Ridge Mall, where Michael would play songs from his first 'Worship' CD. It was releasing that very day. I was actually interviewing Smitty on the phone when I glanced up and saw the second jet hit the south tower on our TV monitor. I wrapped up the phone call quickly and Toni went to work. She is an excellent journalist, so I gave her the spotlight. We were updating continually.

When the first tower fell, I knew we were in uncharted waters for the radio station. Everybody was glued to the TV monitors in our studios. We ended up eventually joining the Salem news network later in the day for wall-to-wall coverage. I knew after the news coverage ended, people would be turning to us, looking for answers and perspective. The thing was, in all honesty, I didn't have any! I was absolutely clueless on how to handle this as a programmer. There was no template on what to do on the air. This was totally new territory. I prayed.

Bonnie Curry suggested an excellent idea. Contact the local pastors in the area, and give them ninety seconds to two minutes on the air to offer their insight and thoughts from a pastor's perspective. It was perfect. We contacted local people like Josh McDowell, Gene Goetz, my own pastor at the time, Dr. Frank Harber, and others. We ran one of these every hour for about ten days. There were some specialty songs that came out of the tragedy, complete with news reports mixed into the songs. 'There Will Come a Day,' by Faith Hill was one that was especially appropriate. One specialty piece in particular, called 'I Was There,' was produced at our sister station in Atlanta, and it would move people to tears.

While responding to tragedy is painful and not easy to pull off on the air, for me, it's the ultimate in what we get to do. It's obvious that God uses the station to bring comfort, and point people to the truth of the gospel during those times. To play even a small part in our response to 9/11 was incredibly humbling and something I will never forget. It reminded me how grateful I am to be a part of this business known as Christian radio.

A few weeks after 9/11, I was emotionally exhausted. We went through moving the station, losing Jon, and then all of the soul searching as a nation after the tragedy of the attacks. I arranged to have guest hosts do the show for a week. We lined up Steven Curtis Chapman, John Tesh, Nichole Nordeman, Mark Schultz, and my pastor, Dr. Harber, along with our worship leader, Paul Smith. Patti and I escaped to Destin for a few days at the beach with the kids. It's almost like God knew what I needed as it seemed we had the whole place to ourselves. I recharged and headed back to the newness of running the station without Jon Rivers.

A couple of months after 9/11, I received an email from Michael W. Smith. We were one of the first stations in the country to put 'Breathe' from the Worship CD in regular rotation on the air, and he expressed his gratitude and asked if there was anything he could do for me. This is the first time I had received an email directly from an artist, thanking me for playing their song, and I was genuinely touched. Usually all of the communication on things like that are with the record company's promotions team.

I emailed back and said, "Come to think of it Michael, yes, there is something you could do!"

Since Jon was the one at the station who had the relationships with the record companies and the artists, we had absolutely no game plan or any idea of what we were going to do for Celebrate Freedom in 2002. I asked Smitty if he would consider being our headliner. Since he didn't get to do any of the songs at the cancelled mini concert scheduled for 9/11, perhaps he could play as many songs as he wanted at South Fork Ranch! He agreed.

With Michael W. Smith as our headliner, we put a young up-and-coming sales executive named Keith Nelson in charge of securing the rest of the lineup. Everything fell into place. Keith continues to produce our event, and also one at our sister station in Atlanta, to this very day.

Later that summer, our son, Ryan started the first grade. Patti had been thinking about home schooling, but was having a hard time making a decision. We had been praying about it, but I really wanted it to be her call, since she was also running a business. When we came up to the enrollment deadline, she was still unsure, so I made the decision to have him start first grade at a very good Christian school that was literally five minutes from home. Ry went to Pre-K there, it was a good experience, and we liked the lower school principal a lot. She had gotten to know us and Ryan during his time there, and it felt at the time like the right thing to do. It was, but it wasn't!

Let me explain. Ryan is 100 percent all boy. He is also first born, and like both of his parents, very strong-willed. Ry was in a class of about twenty kids, which included about four very rambunctious little boys, confined to a very small classroom with a very stoic and straight laced sixty-two-year-old first grade teacher. With the exception of one recess, the kids were pretty much confined to their desks.

Ry began to get into trouble, and the lower school principal we had the relationship with had to resign to take care of her ailing mother in Tennessee. In the interim, the school had hired a principal whose only experience was with senior high students. After a few more incidences, we were told we should probably have Ryan checked out for ADHD. As a dad, this really hit me hard. If you're a parent, I know you know what I'm talking about. Nothing will get you on your knees in prayer quicker than to think there might be something wrong with your child.

I began to research ADHD as much as I could, and found that the diagnosis was very subjective. We met with a very well known psychologist in Plano, and I was a nervous wreck as we headed into the appointment. His conclusion was that Ry was 'just a boy,' and that provided that we were involved and engaged as parents (we were), providing guidelines and discipline when appropriate (we did), he should be just fine. I came away from the appointment relieved, but our issues with the school were far from over.

It was right about this time that God dropped two books into my lap. One was 'Wild at Heart,' by John Eldridge, and the other was 'Bringing up Boys,' by Dr. James Dobson. Wow. Once again, God's timing was perfect. Dobson in particular addressed the frustration of perfectly normal boys being confined to desks all day at a very young age. Patti and I concluded that a lot of the issues at school were a result of the fact that Ryan was just a boy.

It's against the law in Texas for a school to mandate that your child be medicated, but it's not against the law for somebody to subtly suggest it. I told the principal that wasn't an option for us, and we came to an impasse. The interim principal wanted my seven-year-old son to sign a document, stating that if he participated in certain misbehaviors, he would be expelled from school. I told him I would get back to him in a few days, and Patti and I didn't have to pray hard about the decision.

To their credit, the school allowed us to use their curriculum for the remainder of the school year. Patti always had it in her heart to home school, now we knew without doubt that would be the road for us as a family, until God told us differently. Since I was now doing mornings at the station, the flexibility of my schedule after 10am could really help, since Patti was still responsible for the business. Again, in God's perfect timing for my situation, we hired a new program director at the station, which would free up my time in the afternoons. It would also usher in a time of historic growth for KLTY.

THIRTY-SIX

A New Boss

———❧———

"G et on the plane and just make the move!" I jokingly screamed
    into the phone.

I knew from the first time I met Chuck Finney, he was the guy. As
he was contemplating accepting the KLTY programming job, I would
playfully give him a hard time and tell him to just get on the plane and
get down here. Chuck had programmed an Oldies station in Cincinnati,
and I knew I was handing over the reins of the station to the right guy.
Besides his background and experience, I knew he and his wife, Lynda
were seriously seeking God about the move.

God just gives you a sense in your spirit sometimes about things. It's
neat when you have different parties praying about a decision, and God
just brings it all together. This was one of those instances. I was excited
that all of Chuck's radio experience was in mainstream radio. As is often
the case, just like myself he had worked with some very smart people in
the business. Between us, we were in agreement nearly 100 percent of the
time on the direction of the morning show and the station. I made it very
clear to Chuck from the beginning that if I didn't agree with something,
I would state my case to him in private, but once he made a decision, I
would follow his direction wholeheartedly. One of the biggest headaches

of being the boss is dealing with high maintenance radio personalities. I've always wanted to be exactly the opposite.

Chuck was referred to us by our new consultant, Ted Ruscitti. Ted was an absolute wiz with numbers and research, and he is one of the most likable guys I've ever worked with. My boss, John Peroyea came up with the idea of branding the morning show, 'The Family Friendly Morning Show,' and it was absolutely spot on perfect. The name said it all. Between our General Manager John leading the charge and buying up billboards all over town, Ted's research, along with Chuck's collaboration with me and the rest of the on-air staff, things really began to roll.

After Chuck arrived, we went through a period where we worked on 'mainstreaming' the sound of the station. Since we knew we had a loyal core audience, the idea was to broaden the on-air sound to reach more people on the periphery. Especially on the morning show, I began to talk about topics that would not only connect with a Christian audience, but with our target listener (25-54-year-old females) in general. The recorded on-air elements like the music sweepers and promotional announcements became the best in the market under the direction of Bonnie Curry.

I started using a lot of mainstream music elements in the morning show. I came to the conclusion that not everything had to have a 'Christian' label on it. Provided something sounded good, and didn't offend the majority of our core audience, I used it. It really worked. Chuck and I shared the same mantra, "The most important thing is what comes out of the radio speakers," and the station sounded like it. Our goal was to be consistently top 5 in women 25-54 every quarter when we received the ratings report, and we achieved that relatively quickly.

Soon we were consistently in the top three, and often times the morning show would be #2 in our target demo. We were competing with the big boys on the secular stations, and I was absolutely loving it. Every time we would get a good report, I loved reminding Chuck, "Chuck, we are winning and we're doing it playing songs about Jesus!" I relished the thought of confounding the other radio stations. I have to admit even though KLTY is about much more than ratings and revenue, I still loved to beat the competition. In Jesus' name, of course!

John, our GM suggested we do something that next Christmas that has become very special on the station, and to this day, is one of the neatest things I've ever been a part of in all of my years on the radio. 'Christmas Wish' is a promotion that has been done in various forms at different stations down through the years, and it was a perfect fit for KLTY. The idea is to have listeners let us know about individuals or families in need. Folks would write us with their 'Wish,' and once a morning every weekday between Thanksgiving and Christmas, we would grant somebody's wish.

With the help of different sponsors, we could grant things on the air that were expensive and out of the ordinary. We've done a total house makeover for a blind veteran, complete with new furniture, carpet, appliances and even new central air. We've given away numerous vehicles, arranged surprise reunions for loved ones, and done numerous things down the years that have been very emotional and touching.

One wish in particular that I'll never forget was a request from a daughter for her mom who was dying of cancer. The family was big fans of the group Casting Crowns, and they were scheduled to be in concert in our area in February. While we would get requests from numerous people for elaborate and expensive 'Wishes,' all this daughter wanted for her terminally ill mom was tickets for the family to see Casting Crowns in concert before their mom died. After talking with the daughter, we found out that the mom was so ill that she might not make it till February. We contacted Mark Hall from the group, and I had him on the air on the phone with the terminally ill mom.

It was an amazing on-air moment, when Mark said something to the effect of, "Well, ya know, February is quite a ways off, how about if we just fly in and have a concert just for you and your family right there in your living room. Will next Thursday afternoon work for you?"

There wasn't a dry eye in the studio as the mom said, yes, next Thursday would be just fine. Her Christmas Wish was granted with a private Casting Crowns concert just for her and the family who loved her so much. She went to be with Jesus about a month later.

After the first year, Christmas Wish took on a life of its own. We were getting so many requests, we solicited listeners to come to our studios in Irving to help out, and go through binders where we had needs from various listeners categorized. Listeners began adopting other families in need, and contacting them and granting their wish. While smaller needs were handled by individuals or groups, our promotions team at the station searched for needs that were out of reach for most individuals. Every day it seemed we were airing a different 'miracle.' Year 3, we were running out of room for people at the station, so we partnered with Chick-Fil-A and took the show and the binders on the road. Every weekday morning we would broadcast live from a different Chick-Fil-A, with free chicken biscuits and lots of needs that needed to be met!

On the air, my job was rather simple, and it has made for some of the most memorable on-air moments in my career. Basically, all I would do was when somebody would grant a wish, I would ask them to join me on the air, and ask them what prompted them to come in that morning and help out with Christmas Wish. The stories have been amazing. A mom who had lost her daughter found a family who was going through their first Christmas after losing a child. We have the same dentist come in year after year, and search the binders all morning looking for people who can't afford dental work. Office groups, or representatives from Sunday school classes come in and look for that special family that just can't make ends meet.

But probably the most memorable moments are from people who have been touched by Christmas Wish themselves in the past, are now doing better financially, and just want to give back. They explain how they were once having hard times, somebody helped them through Wish, and now they want to do the same. Honestly, if I had my way, we would be the 'Wish Station' 24/7, 365!

In the ten years we've been doing Christmas Wish, we have facilitated well over $6 million worth of gifts and donations. If you think of it, for the station and me, we're really just sort of the 'middle man.' We let people know of the needs, and then God works through his people to meet those needs. It's an amazing thing to be a part of, and something I look forward to every year.

One of the things I've had to work through as a radio personality during 'Wish' is how to handle, or not handle, my emotions. I'm convinced that when I used to drink, one of the reasons was that I didn't want to deal with my feelings. My personality is such that I feel deeply, and I'm easily moved, sometimes to the point of tears. When we started recording the different 'Wishes' that we would eventually air, often times during the stories and with the recipients on the phone, my emotions would get the best of me and I would sometimes break down. Bonnie Curry, who is the absolute best coach and producer ever for 'Wish,' gave me the freedom to just let it go and not worry about it. Often times I would be so overwhelmed, we would have to go back and re-record some of my lines, because my emotions were just too much.

Rather than be embarrassed by this, or worry about presenting some sort of macho image, I've decided that I'm just going to be myself, and it's okay. I have reached a point in my life where I'm accepting of who I am, and the way that God has made me. My insecurities and fear of rejection were now in the rear view mirror of my life. In reality, if I hadn't had the baggage, struggles, and deliverance of my past, I wouldn't have the sensitivity and transparency on the air to react and respond the way that I do. I've actually found the more vulnerable and real you can be on the radio, the deeper your relationship will go with the listener. In real life and on the radio I want to be genuine, transparent, and real. And that's a good thing. Or, frankly speaking, it's a God thing.

THIRTY-SEVEN

David and Barbara

In the fall of 2005, we went through a once-in-a-lifetime experience with my mother-in-law, who we had moved down from New Jersey in the early 90s. Barbara, or Nanny as we call her, was adopted when she was six months old in Great Britain. She knew she had a twin brother, but they were separated as infants. She had tried in vain to track him down, and when she kept running into dead ends, she concluded that he might be deceased, possibly a casualty of World War II.

Now that more information was available via the Internet, she began contacting agencies in England, attempting to get information on her birth mother. On Thanksgiving day, she got an email. This particular agency did not have any news on her mother, but after a few of the case workers compared some notes, they believed they had found her long lost brother! David lived in Shropshire, with his wife, Josie. They had two grown children, Paula and Clive. Mom made the initial contact, and plans were put into place for a reunion here in Texas after being separated for seventy-five years!

Patti reached out to cousin Paula via email, and they immediately hit it off. David, Josie and Paula were going to fly in and stay with us at our home in Colleyville. Cousin Clive would follow later and get a room. Patti's brother, Chris was also going to be coming in with his family. We were all looking forward to the reunion of David and Barbara after being apart for their entire lives. There was only one detail that had us a little nervous about the visit. We found out that Uncle Dave was an elder with The Jehovah's Witnesses. YJCMTSU!

It was a special moment when Barbara and David embraced for the first time at the International Terminal at Dallas-Ft. Worth International. Patti and I were with Nanny, Ryan and Hope, and we picked up our special guests in a limo. There was joy and amazement all around, and everybody was in great spirits.

As a Christian household, we had been praying about how to address Uncle Dave and Aunt Josey about our differences in faith. We determined rather than get into any discussions or debates, we had one mission while they were here: simply be ourselves and love them. We made them feel welcome and completely at home.

Since Paula had abandoned the JW church as a young adult, she had been having some spiritual conversations with Patti via email before the visit. She made it clear that when she arrived she would like to join us on Sunday at church. Sure enough, Sunday came around, and Paula was ready to go. Patti and I were involved with a Sunday school class, but Paula wanted to go to early service, so I went to Sunday school while Patti went with Paula to the first service.

As our class was letting out, Patti found me and I could immediately tell that she was emotionally upset. She had been crying so I was thinking something was terribly wrong. Actually, something was wonderfully right. Paula got saved in the worship service! And on top of that, I needed to go track down Ryan and Hope and get them over to the second service, because Cousin Paula was going to be baptized!

The morning was filled with tears of joy for Paula, Patti and me and the kids. What's amazing was that Paula had heart issues (physically), and that particular Sunday we had a guest pastor who spoke on, "God can heal your heart!" Paula felt that the sermon was just for her, and when they gave an invitation at the end of the service, Patti walked down the aisle to the front with her long lost cousin from England. My wife also prayed for the actual physical healing of Paula's heart. It blows my mind that God brought her all the way to America so she could respond to the gospel message at our church in Colleyville, Texas!

While I was very happy for Paula, this was a neat moment for Patti and me as parents. Our kids got to witness first hand God's sovereignty in the whole experience. As parents, we can tell our kids about the truth of the gospel till we're blue in the face, but nothing beats them actually seeing it in action first hand.

At the end of church we all gathered, and almost immediately it seemed like we all had the same thought at the same time: how do we explain this to Uncle Dave? We stood in a circle and said a prayer of thanksgiving for Paula's salvation, and then prayed that we would have the right words for Uncle Dave and Aunt Josey. We headed home, and Paula was the one who wanted to talk to her dad.

We weren't privy to the conversation, all I know is he retreated to the guest bedroom for a few hours. When he returned, we just continued to love on him and his wife. Their stay lasted two weeks. The whole time was rather surreal. I could tell that Aunt Josey was intrigued by our openness and joy, and I think that also made an impact on her. In retrospect, we were just really being ourselves. If Christ lives in you, it's just naturally going to have an impact on people.

Patti stays in touch with Cousin Paula, and her conversion is one of those things we will never forget. It was as if the David and Barbara reunion was custom designed so Paula could come to America to find healing for her heart, physically and spiritually.

THIRTY-EIGHT

Mr. Mac

A t the radio station, Celebrate Freedom continued to be a highlight every year, and I was really pumped about our lineup for 2006. Casting Crowns would be the headliner, and I knew they would be great, but I was really looking forward to hearing Toby Mac. I was at the Gospel Music Association Convention in 1990 when DC Talk was at the new artist showcase luncheon. Little did I know at the time that they would become such a big deal. The cool thing was, these guys could have gone the crossover route and made their sound more 'less offensive' for a mainstream audience. Rather than compromise their message, their answer to that suggestion was to record the 'Jesus Freak' project.

My son, Ryan had become a Toby Mac fan, and since he would be with me at Celebrate Freedom, he asked if he could meet Toby and possibly get a picture. I told him we would see, but didn't make any promises. Since I know that artists have people constantly bugging them for stuff, I've never wanted to be the radio guy that is always asking artists for favors. Rather, if they see that they will be dealing with me and KLTY, I would hope they would know our desire is to make their visit easy, fun, and hassle-free.

Celebrate Freedom that year would not exactly be hassle-free, as it become known as the Mud Fest!

North Texas had record rainfall leading up the event, and the turf where we would be having the concert was an absolute mess. The stage was at the bottom of huge field, and we had to take golf carts to transport the artists from the greenroom to the stage site. Golf carts were constantly getting stuck in the mud, and Ryan and I and others were a mud-covered mess from helping push people out! We had our broadcast stage set up close to the green room, and I actually had Toby scheduled for an interview, so I was hoping Ryan would get his wish. The problem was, because of the rain and the mud, the entire schedule was thrown off. I ended my on-air shift with no Toby. I could have tracked him down, but I figured it was not meant to be. As I was leaving the broadcast stage, I caught Toby out of the corner of my eye heading toward us. I told Ryan to wait on the stage, and I intercepted Toby right before he got there, and asked if he could take a moment to meet my son. He said sure, but what happened next made a major impact on me.

I introduced Ryan to Toby, and we got a picture, but what happened next was awesome. Toby took at least five minutes, and totally engaged with my son, asking him questions, and in all honesty, just being the kindest person in the world to my almost thirteen-year-old son. When he finally left after his interview and was out of view, my son raised his hands in the air, looked me square in the face and screamed, "Dad, Toby Mac talked to me!"

This really sent a message to me as a radio personality. Toby had put a smile on my son's face, and in doing that, my appreciation of him not only as an artist but as a person went to a new level. If I could put a smile on the faces of the kids who listen to KLTY with their moms and dads, I figured I could have the same affect.

We had started doing a birthday feature on the morning show, and it became a huge hit. Besides kids getting to hear their name on the radio, some of the things parents would write about their kids were really funny, so the feature also had some great entertainment value. We end the segment with anniversaries, and I've found that women especially enjoyed the sentiments expressed in those announcements. It's a fact most women just love to hear about love!

The Toby Mac experience reminded me that whenever I have the opportunity to engage a listener or child personally, I always do my best to give them some time, and just try to be nice. You just never know what people are going through, and how a kind word or a smile could make a difference in their day. I'm surprised at how grateful many people are when you take a minute to just personally engage with them and do something as simple as respond to an email. It might take some extra time out of a busy day, but I've found down through the years it is time well spent.

During that same summer I did a new agreement with the station, and I completely put to bed the idea of returning to Central Florida. Of course with God, I am open to wherever he wants me to be, but I couldn't deny the fact that I was having a very successful run with KLTY, and in this business when it's going well, you just don't want to mess with it. In Dallas-Ft. Worth, having longevity in doing the morning show has worked to my advantage. It's all about just continuing to build relationships with the listeners, and becoming a habit for them when they wake up or commute to work.

Since I still had a desire to live on the water somewhere, Patti and I found a little place on a lake in East Texas called Lake Cypress Springs. It's about two-and-a-half hours from our home, and we began getting into boating and lake fun with the kids. This was a dream come true for me, a true gift. There's a great verse in Psalms that says, "delight yourself in the Lord, and he will give you the desires of your heart." Thankfully, I've never been into stuff or possessions, but having another place on the water somewhere was definitely a desire that had been there for a long time. Just like I get joy as a father by blessing my own kids with a special gift, I'm certain our heavenly father delights in giving us special blessings. I absolutely love this place. It's just a modest A-frame, but we are up on a hill with a great open water view.

East Texas is completely different from the Metroplex as it's very slow and laid back. It's a great place to get away and just relax, and also a great place to retreat to and hear from God. We also enjoy making the place available to friends or people in ministry who just need a place to get away and recharge. The station also graciously let me take a little bit of extra time to go on an extended home school trip with the family. I had actually thought about asking for a leave of absence, but knew that would be difficult to pull off. We flew to Raleigh where Patti's brother, Chris had relocated with his family, and then rented a car for a history trip to Williamsburg, then through the mid-Atlantic states and Boston. I'm extremely grateful for a boss like John and a company like Salem that understand the importance of family.

THIRTY-NINE

Downturn

———— ✍ ————

I n 2008 the downturn hit the economy, and radio was hit very hard. When the economy goes south, one of the first places people cut back is advertising. It was a challenging time for everybody, and KLTY was no exception. We had cutbacks, and my boss, Chuck Finney was one of the people let go. We had become good friends, and his wife, Lynda and Patti also developed a friendship, and his youngest daughter, Catherine became good friends with our little girl, Hope. We even lived in the same neighborhood. The cool thing was Chuck and Lynda had felt led to sell their home months before, and it sold at the full asking price right in the middle of the Christmas season! The timing of them selling their home, along with the timing of his departure, just had God written all over it.

I was actually taking a break in Breckenridge when I was told the news. Mark Harris, who used to be with the group 4Him, just released a new CD, and I was listening to it over and over again. There's a great song on it called, 'Nothing Takes You by Surprise.' Listening to that song, I knew my friend Chuck would be fine. He has since become a very successful radio consultant, sharing his expertise and experience with other Christian broadcasters all around the country. His exit, though, reminded me of how blessed I am to be able to keep doing what I'm doing.

I'm fortunate that we have a pretty good-sized following in the morning, and while I would love to think I could just keep working because the company needs somebody on the air, the reality is without decent ratings I could be expendable. Since KLTY is a commercial station, we are in business to make a profit. While our leadership in the company is unashamedly Christian, it's still a business, and we operate the company as such. Layoffs and cutbacks are a reality. If the morning show I host can bring profits to the station and the company, it just lends to my job security. I rather prefer it that way. My mission is to grow long-term listeners, but I get just as jazzed to work with our sales staff to develop long-term clients. I have a handful of advertisers I do commercials for, and I love partnering and collaborating with clients to help grow their business. I just seem to be wired that way. I receive great satisfaction in helping others succeed. Since I want integrity to be at the center of everything I do, it's a natural fit for me to partner with advertisers who are committed to the same core values. At this season in my life, KLTY continues to feel like a perfect fit even after twenty-two years.

I went through a period early in my Christian radio career where I needed to settle it in my heart that commercial radio was where I was supposed to be. There are many great Christian stations that are non-commercial and listener supported, but in my opinion being commercial gives us the financial resources to reach as many people as possible. I've always reasoned the more people you can reach, the bigger difference and impact you can make. I've always liked thinking big!

I truly believe I have the best job in radio; I get to have some fun, make a living, and make a difference. Every morning I get to practice my craft doing something I truly love that has eternal significance. I am so fortunate that I get to do what I do! Of course, I have no idea what the future holds, but even if it were to end today, I would have no regrets.

My success in the business has far exceeded anything I could have ever imagined. Even so, my desire is to reach even more people with the hope of the gospel, through the music we play and the relationships we continue to build. Even though at the time of this writing I am just past sixty, slowing down or retirement is not on my radar screen. As long as I can stay relevant and connect with people in a meaningful way, there is really nothing else I'd rather be doing. I see no place in scripture where it talks about retirement. Of course, if God says it's time to move on and do something else, I'm okay with that. I jokingly tell Patti because I am such a fan of Costco Discount Warehouse, I would love to be the guy greeting you at the door, asking to see your Costco card! Frankly speaking, I've found that satisfaction in life is finding out what God wants you to do, and then doing it wholeheartedly.

In the fall of 2008, Patti and I celebrated our 17th wedding anniversary. What was cool was that this particular year, some old friends were organizing a WNBC reunion in New York to commemorate the 20th anniversary of the sign off of WNBC. In 1988, NBC sold all of their radio properties, and 660 WNBC would become 660 WFAN, known as "The Fan." It's become one of the most successful sports talk stations in the country. The reunion just happened to fall the weekend of our anniversary, so we booked a flight, dropped the kids with friends, and flew up for the weekend.

We had a blast. I had some frequent flyer miles, so we booked first class seats going up. When we got on the plane, I was surprised to find a gray-haired man sitting in my reserved seat. It was none other than Pat Summerall! I started to approach him about moving, and then I thought to myself, "I bet he prefers that seat every time he flies." It just so happened he was flying to New York for an event with a friend from Prestonwood Baptist Church who happened to be a listener of our show.

He introduced me to Pat, I introduced Patti, and I told him, "Pat, why don't I just sit where you were supposed to sit?" I just couldn't imagine asking Pat Summerall to move to another first class seat! They are all the same anyway.

While I have no desire to ever live in New York City again, if you know how to get around Manhattan, it's an amazing place to go back and visit. We got a great hotel a block away from Saint Patrick's Cathedral, so we were centrally located. The reunion was in a restaurant and bar off Broadway around 50th Street, so it was an easy twenty-minute walk from our hotel.

It was great to catch up with my old boss Kevin, as well as Allen Bebee, who was one of the original jocks who started with me. A lot of the sales and news people were there, but Allen and I were the only attendees from that group that got hired in 1977. Since the number of WNBC alumni is huge, there were a lot of people I didn't know, but we had a great time just the same. A lot of the old engineering staff were there, and I stayed in touch with Bruce Leonard who was my board op, which meant he was the guy who pushed all the buttons for me while I was on the air. Interestingly, Bruce went on to work behind the scenes with David Letterman and then Conan O'Brien. It was fun to watch Letterman at night and know that whenever he threw the pencil through the glass window, that was my friend Bruce hitting the sound effect of the window breaking!

Patti and I also got to see 'Wicked' on Broadway while we were there, and I got up early that Sunday morning to just go for a long walk. The city was quiet, and I walked down to Grand Central Station, then to my old apartment by 38th Street, then down to 3rd Avenue, then all the way up to 82nd Street, then over to Madison Avenue and back about thirty blocks to our hotel. I loved it. Alone in Manhattan on a Sunday morning. The memories were thick. It was a great trip.

In 2009, the company that provides the radio ratings to advertising agencies and radio stations changed their methodology. Prior to this time, listeners who participated in radio surveys would write down in a diary what they listened to, and then mail it in. Now the company was measuring actual listening with electronic devices that a cross section of the population would carry with them throughout the day. The ratings game had changed on us, and initially we did not do well. My new Program Director, Mike Prendergast had studied the new methodology carefully, and suggested to me we make some adjustments in the morning show. I'm very old school when it comes to certain things, but Mike was very certain about the changes. He was right on the money, and it worked. Mike is a very humble guy, so let me state for the record he is very good at what he does. Almost immediately we saw an uptick in the ratings, especially with the morning show. The chemistry between me and the two ladies on the show, Perri Reavis, who does the traffic, and Starlene Stringer, who moved from traffic to news, began to really gel. I quickly concluded having two very confident women on the air with one sometimes clueless older guy was a great combination.

We genuinely sound like we are having a good time on the air, and it's because we are! Perri is completely off the wall and unpredictable, and Starlene is so loved by the audience, I tell people off the air she is my rock star. Both of them sound terrific on the radio. We are at the point where we can just about read each other's minds on the air. Every morning on the radio feels comfortable, like putting on a favorite pair of well-worn jeans. I jokingly tell them, "Nobody leaves this radio station till I die or retire!"

At the moment, we are the second most listened to morning show in Dallas-Ft. Worth, and KLTY is the single most listened to Christian radio station in the country. When I dreamed so many years ago of this format competing with the other mainstream stations, I had no idea God would elevate us to this level. I'm so grateful.

When the downturn hit the economy, we also saw the beginning of a decline in revenues at The Shepherd's Guide. The home office in Baltimore had launched a pretty good website where people could search online for a Christian business, but their bread and butter was still the printed directory. At its peak, Patti had built it to nearly a million dollars in sales a year. She became quite the business woman, though she will tell you her first and foremost mission has always been being my wife and raising our kids. When she was home schooling the work load got to be too much, so she decided to take a step back from the day-to-day operation, and handed the business over to a couple who had been working for her. The idea was to bless them with a vesting situation similar to the one we had been given.

Over a period of time the business continued to decline, as had been the case for the majority of printed yellow page directories around the country. We had some differences of opinion on how we should move forward with the business, and at one point we were even praying about the possibility of buying out her partner and Patti becoming the sole owner. We had poured a lot of sweat and tears into the business down through the years, and we had a genuine love and appreciation for so many of the advertisers. We had fostered and developed numerous relationships. Patti and I knew that her taking over and rebuilding would be a huge undertaking, but she was willing to do it if that was what God wanted.

For a few months we were in terrible turmoil on which direction to go. There seemed to be a dark cloud over the business and our lives in general. It definitely put a strain on our relationships, including our marriage. Patti decided to take a break out at our little lake house with some lady friends, and we both continued to pray about the situation. While she was there, she felt that God had spoken to her very clearly about what to do. She returned home from her little sabbatical and I was shocked when she told me, "I think God wants us to give the business away!"

"You want to do what?" I said loudly. "Are you kidding me?"

She proceeded to tell that God made it very clear to her, and she was totally at peace about it. Of course she knew that we would have to both be in agreement with a decision of this magnitude. At first glance, I really struggled with the thought. For one, it was going to severely affect our income, and two, in the natural, I just could not see it happening. I knew that God could speak to me about the situation, but I was fearful of letting it go. For almost twenty years we were used to being a two-income family. How was this going to work?

There was also a part of me that knew many people would not understand this decision. Would I appear foolish? I quickly got past that, knowing if I heard distinctly from God, I wasn't really concerned with what other people thought. Living by faith had developed a consistent, (if not always conventional), track record in my life. I had heard some exciting stories from people like Robert Morris and Steve Dulin about radical giving (Pastor Robert and Steve are from a neighboring church in Southlake, called Gateway), but I never envisioned myself in a situation like that. Yet here I was.

It took me about a week of praying, but once I got it, I was flooded with joy and peace. This was the answer! When I told Patti I finally had peace about it, we were giddy with excitement. We laughed! What a neat moment this was for us as a couple. Navigating through that decision was timely, painful and difficult, but it was the right move. What I have found is this: if you will seek God and wait on his timing, he will give you direction. The process at times may be messy and uncomfortable, but if you persevere, the answer will come. The key is to not make a decision based on emotions, or jump the gun and get ahead on the timing. The cool thing is when you are seeking answers together as a couple, it's amazing when you both have peace and closure.

I'll never forget our meeting with our partners, Chip and Cathy, when we told them we wanted to give our ownership shares equally to them and the other couple. My friend Chip, after pondering for a few moments replied, "This is not a human thing!" Precisely.

Our exit from the business and the way it unfolded was nothing short of miraculous. We had given away something that was very valuable, yet in reality, because we had heard from God, it felt as if we had received the bigger gift. It was a radical move, and precisely on target. While I knew it would be a stretch for us financially, I was confident that God would provide.

FORTY

Milestones

In 2011, Patti and I celebrated our 20th wedding anniversary, and I took her to a place I've always wanted to stay at least once. Mohonk Mountain House is in New Paltz, New York, about ninety minutes northwest of New York City on the edge of the Catskill Mountains. When I was in the singles group in Long Island, a group of us hiked there one Saturday in the fall. This place is amazing. It overlooks a crystal clear lake, with balconies and porches either overlooking the water or the woods. I got us a great room with a fireplace and a balcony overlooking the lake, and it was perfect. I love surprising my wife, so I told her to line up some places for the kids to stay, and we hopped on a plane without her knowing where we were going.

As I reflect on our years together, we've had our ups and downs like most couples do. The neat thing is that with Christ at the center, the storms of life allow the roots of your relationship to grow very deep. I can't imagine life without Patti by my side. One of the things that I think has kept us together is knowing, without a shadow of a doubt, that God was the one who brought us together. We had both put the personal relationships in our life under his direction, and he led us to one another. When you have that supernatural moment in your marriage, it's like a strong foundation that is immovable. In the heat of a disagreement I can always remind myself, "Hey wait a minute, I know without a shadow of a doubt God gave you to me to be my wife, so how are we going to work this out?"

We also believe in the wisdom from that famous philosopher from Philadelphia, Rocky Balboa who said, "She's got gaps, I got gaps!" We both realize this side of heaven, we will never be perfect. As time goes on, we have learned to accept each other's gaps. That doesn't preclude us from continuing to work on our relationship.

There are so many great resources available for couples. We love ministries like 'America's Family Coaches,' with Gary and Barb Rosberg, and 'Family Life,' with Dennis Rainey and Bob Lepine. Family Life has a video event that KLTY hosts every year called, 'The Art of Marriage,' which is a wonderful resource. Patti and I have led this event a few times, and are reminded every time we watch it that we are called to be 'professional forgivers!' We view our marriage sort of like a garden. For it to remain healthy, it needs to be tended to. You need to be intentional with the maintenance or you are certain to drift.

When I think of our marriage, it's a reminder I never want to stop growing as a person, emotionally or spiritually. When it comes to my relationship with Christ, there's always something new to experience or learn. You never graduate until you leave this earth. I've found in my experience I have had seasons where I don't seem to be growing, or things spiritually seem to be in limbo. However, when I look back on my life in the context of years, there's no doubt I'm not the same person I was. Age has a way of putting things in perspective.

That November I also celebrated twenty years at the station. In this crazy business that's unheard of, but in Dallas-Ft. Worth radio there are actually a couple of other guys on the air who have been at the same radio station longer than me. I just plan on outliving them! The business has changed so much since I started over forty years ago. It's not the business I got into. In many ways, it has lost the magic and mystique it once had. Since the downturn of a few years ago, many people have left the business. I'm fortunate to be a survivor and be able to get up every morning and go to a job that I still love. I remind my team occasionally to glance out the window of our studios in Irving. Every day, people whiz by in their cars or trucks, many going to jobs that they don't really like, or have to accept out of necessity. And us? We get to do radio!

The morning of November 8th, I did something I've always looked forward to doing on the air if I ever had the chance. I knew I could only do it once in my career. At the beginning of The Beatle's 'Sergeant Pepper's Lonely Hearts Club Band' album, they sing, "It was twenty years ago today Sergeant Pepper taught the band to play." I'm sure a few folks must have double-checked their radio when they heard The Beatles at 6am on KLTY!

I clipped the song at the end of the word 'today' and said something like, "I spoke for the first time on this amazing radio station known as KLTY." I talked for a couple of minutes, basically thanking the listeners for their support down through the years. My producer at the time (a wonderful guy named Jack Rothwell) had recorded some nice comments from some artists who had called in advance of the show. We kept it pretty low key because what we do is not really about me, but it was a kick to hear some of the nice thoughts throughout the show from friends like Mark Schultz, Matthew West, Michael W. Smith, Mac Powell from Third Day, and Amy Grant in particular was very touching in wishing me congratulations.

I've been thinking lately that maybe twenty-five years at KLTY might be a nice number to call it a career, but the timing on something like that, of course, is God's deal, not mine.

FORTY-ONE

New Opportunities

After Patti left The Shepherd's Guide, we began to entertain the thought of her doing her own online Christian business directory for Dallas-Ft. Worth. Once again, to not have a conflict with the station, we would set up everything in her name and my involvement would be limited so I had no conflict of interest.

Our home schooling days were over, and Ryan and Hope were now both full-time in a great private school. This would free up time for Patti to go back to work, and we could make up some of the income lost from letting the other business go. She had always jokingly suggested that since I was getting older, perhaps I could slow down and some day she could support me!

I began to work on a business plan for her, and it seemed like a natural fit. We had a lot of connections and relationships from the previous business, and I had numerous friends encouraging us that it would be a smart move. A no-brainer, actually. Since our relationship with our former partners was reconciled, I was hesitant about rushing into anything. I was trusting God on the timing. Legally, there was nothing preventing Patti from starting her own directory, and everything seemed to be falling into place.

I was genuinely excited that we might be able to start another business for her, without the restrictions of a franchise and doing it solo. I even found a great software company that could easily custom build exactly what she was looking for, at a reasonable price. There was only one thing stopping us from moving forward. God had different plans!

Patti had met a lady named Debbie Bannister through a mutual friend. They had connected online, and Patti told her that the next time she came through town to look her up. Sure enough, in December 2011, Debbie was going to be in town with her husband, and asked Patti if she could make time for coffee. I was right in the middle of Christmas Wish, which is a crazy and stressful time for me. Patti asked me if I would like to join them. I knew that I would carve out the time because I was looking forward to meeting Debbie's husband. She was married to the award-winning record producer, Brown Bannister. I'm sure we've passed each other at conventions, and we have mutual friends in the business, but we never connected.

Here's the neat thing about getting to spend a few minutes with Brown. Around 1983, when I was at WNBC and in the middle of figuring out my relationship with God (and still dealing with so many anxiety issues), I came across an album recorded by him. He only did one solo record himself, and then his career took off as Grammy and Dove award-winning producer for Amy Grant, Mercy Me, and so many others. On this particular album, which was called 'Talk to one Another,' he did a song called 'Create in me a Clean Heart.' It is basically Psalm 51 put to music. I used to play that song over and over again on my stereo in Long Island, and God really used that song to minister to me in some very difficult moments. Now it was twenty-eight years later, at a restaurant in Grapevine, Texas and I had the opportunity to personally tell him how God used his song in my life! These are the kind of moments that excite me as a believer in Jesus. Knowing those moments are no coincidence just fuels my faith. Brown was completely gracious and humble, and I got the biggest kick out of sharing that with him.

Just like many families, the Bannisters got hit pretty hard with the financial downturn of 2008. Couple that with the fact that the record industry has been completely turned upside down because of online music and iTunes, and their income was bound to be severely affected. Now that they had successfully raised five beautiful kids, Debbie decided to enter the workforce. The thing was, she didn't really have any business experience at all. A friend had introduced her to a company named Rodan and Fields Dermatologists. They are the renowned doctors that created the very successful Proactiv Solutions, the #1 acne care system in the world. Rodan and Fields is their second generation of skin care, targeting the four major skin concerns. They started out as the number one line in many high-end department stores, but had a desire to reach the masses and give entrepreneurs the opportunity at independent business ownership.

Patti was interested in the products because as she has gotten older, like many ladies, she was concerned about aging. I've always told her that she looks great, but I understand if there are things you can do to improve your skin and delay the process of aging, ladies are into things like that. Debbie asked Patti if she was interested in building a business and Patti politely told her no, she was planning on launching her own business soon, but she was very interested in trying the products, and decided to get started immediately. We said goodbye to the Bannisters, and while I really enjoyed the time with them, I didn't really think that much about it afterward. Until after about a month went by.

"What's up with your face?" I asked.

Patti said, "What are you talking about?" I told her that her complexion looked off the charts. She looked noticeably younger. Her face looked great. "It's those products," she replied.

"What products?" I asked.

"Rodan and Fields, remember? I purchased them from Debbie. I use them two times a day," she said.

"Well, they work!" I exclaimed. I was genuinely impressed. I really could see a noticeable difference. Then my wife threw me a curve. I didn't see it coming.

"What would you think if I did this as a business?" she asked.

"It's direct sales, right?" I asked.

"Yes," she said.

"Oh no," I thought. Not one of those. How many times have I been approached by people about vitamins, shakes, wellness products and electric companies? How many emails do I get telling me I can get rich quick right on my computer sitting at my dinner table! My family in direct sales? I don't think so. "Uh, love you, but I'm really not into the direct sales thing," I told her.

"Well," she said, "I really think maybe God wants me to do this, would you please pray about it?"

I told her sure, but I was skeptical. I made it a point in my prayer time to mention it, but honestly I wasn't sweating bullets over the decision. Of course, if Patti did this that would pretty much shoot the idea of us getting involved with another business of our own. But I knew from twenty years of life with my wife that if she feels God is leading her a certain way, that is something I definitely do not want to discount. She has great discernment.

A week went by and sure enough, she touched base with me and asked me if I had prayed and what I thought. I told her I didn't get any sense that she shouldn't do it, and asked her how much was the investment. She told me they had three starter kits, one for about $300, one for about $700, and one for about $1,000. Knowing if she were to start her own online directory it would have been thousands of dollars for a start-up operation, I asked her what she wanted to do. She opted for the middle package. I figured the worst case scenario was that I was out $700. She felt good about it, so I told her to go for it.

Patti got started and began training on the phone with Debbie. New reps do a business launch, and Debbie and Brown came down from Nashville for the event held at our home. Patti invited a bunch of lady friends over, and I came to this conclusion very quickly: women are fanatical about their faces! Sure enough, at the first event Patti sold a bunch of product, and she immediately had some friends interested in the business model.

Brown opened up his laptop to show me the organization of reps they had built in just a year-and-a-half, and it was very impressive. I knew that someone with his reputation wasn't going to get into something that was not legitimate and first class, so I was cautiously optimistic. He shared a great line with me that stuck in my head, "Once Debbie got a monthly check that had a comma in it, I said, 'Hey, I think you might be on to something here!'"

Now almost two years later, I feel the exact same way. I started out as just the supportive husband, and now I am totally on board with helping her build her business. Everybody wants great skin and additional income, and with so much uncertainty about jobs, health care, etc., people want to be in a position to make a way on their own. This is the perfect vehicle for many families. In God's timing, we got in on the beginning stages of an amazing opportunity. Because of social media like Facebook and Linked-in, she has business partners locally and all over the country; in Florida, California, Arizona, Tennessee, New Jersey, New York, and soon they are launching in Canada. I'm so grateful we set aside our pre-conceived notions about direct sales. Residual income is a beautiful thing. It just continues to grow! The company and its culture really are different, and Patti is the perfect fit for it. She loves to pour into other ladies personally and professionally. At this time she is a Level V leader with the company, and is making significant extra income for our family. After just over a year-and-a-half, she is covering the majority of our son's college expense. She has great earning potential, and will far surpass what she would have made if she had started her own online business. Leaving the other business now made perfect sense. God knew! In all likelihood Patti will outlive me, so this will also provide her with long-term income and employment. The majority of the growth of the company is still in the years to come, so the timing is perfect.

My wife also reminded me of something that has been a desire of hers for a very long time. Twenty-five years ago, she felt that God planted a desire deep in her heart to one day adopt a child. She had traveled on a mission trip to Japan, and the thought of an Asian baby eventually in our household has always been a desire of hers. Because I am older, I could never get on the same page with her. It never became an issue in our marriage, and now in retrospect, it seems maybe God had a bigger purpose in mind. Patti is gladly giving a portion of her business earnings to a ministry called Shaohannah's Hope (Show Hope), which was founded by Steven and Mary Beth Chapman. Giving financially to this ministry gives Patti the opportunity to help place orphans in loving homes. Rather than impact just one child, she has the opportunity and potential to affect many. I am extremely proud of her, and grateful that I married a lady who prays about everything.

FORTY-TWO

The Verdict

—⟡—

True confession: I am a media junkie. It's easy to make the excuse that I am in media and I need to keep up with things, but I confess that I should probably spend my time doing more productive things than constantly checking the news on TV, radio, or the Internet. So the summer of 2013, I was very much aware of the George Zimmerman trial in Florida. Of course I knew where Sanford, Florida was, since it was just north of Orlando. Little did I know at the time that this news event would lead to a chapter in my book. As I was finalizing it during the summer, for some reason I was unsettled about the last few chapters. I believe it was because I was supposed to include this story.

The Zimmerman verdict came down on a Saturday night. I knew that Monday morning on the radio it would be the primary source of discussion for just about every morning radio show. I began to process how we would handle it on the air. The verdict was incredibly polarizing. I felt terrible for Trayvon Martin's family. Having an eighteen-year-old son myself, I can't even begin to imagine their heartbreak. I followed the trial and evidence closely, so I could also see the other side's point of view. I listened to all the pundits and commentators. Monday morning was approaching. What would we do? When in doubt, pray!

Sunday morning, I decided to get a quick workout in at the health club before I went to church. I did not realize it, but when I lift weights, I have a tendency to grit my teeth. That Friday I got some temporary veneers from my dentist for the majority of my top teeth. The permanents would be ready in about a month. I was on the last rep on bicep curls, straining a little bit, and CRUNCH! A bunch of teeth shattered inside my mouth. I had a mouth guard they gave me, but didn't think to wear it. I went home really distressed, and what used to be my teeth looked a mess! I stayed home from church, which was very much unlike me, and just tried to pray.

For some reason, in the midst of all these crappy feelings, I felt led to write about 'The Verdict.' I knew that Starlene would do a good job covering it in the news, but how was I going to comment? It was so divisive; any commentary I made would probably please some, and anger others. If you listen to our show, you know commentary of that kind is not really what we do. I leave things like that for my friend and colleague down the hall, Mark Davis, who is on the air from 7 till 10am on 660 AM The Answer. Yet I felt strongly that God was leading me as I wrote on my i-Pad.

This is what was heard on KLTY and posted on Facebook at 8am, on Monday morning, July 15[th:]

My thoughts on 'The Verdict,' by Frank Reed.

The prosecution continued to make their case. It was quite a team he assembled. The best of the best. One by one the accusations came. It seemed to go on for hours. They had graphics, video. I tried to keep a stiff upper lip, you know, play the poker face thing. But my demeanor sooner, rather than later, had the look of total defeat. Every accusation was true, what could I say, and what could I do? You know the story of the kid with his hand in the cookie jar? Multiply that feeling a thousand times, and it still wasn't close to the way I felt. One by one the offenses were laid out; pride, arrogance, selfishness, greed, lust, envy. The list went on. The weight on my heart felt the size of an ocean liner. I was utterly, totally, helpless. There was nothing I could say. I was guilty, and I knew it. The only thing left was the verdict, and my sentence. I had done my homework; I knew what the sentence was. I knew my prospects of surviving this nightmare were absolutely zero. Just when I thought things couldn't get any worse, the lead prosecutor, the accuser, he stepped up and said, "We're not done yet!" and began his closing argument. This guy made his associates look like school children. Every wrong thought, motive, and action, was told. Then, it ended. "Your honor, the prosecution rests," At that moment there was only one thing I could think of: The Verdict. And then, it happened. A touch on my shoulder. I looked up. It was him. He was there next to me the whole time. "Frank," he told me. "Hold your head up, son, I've got this." With those words, he stood up and approached the bench. His voice was loud, strong, and crystal clear. "Father," he said. "On a train heading into Manhattan, in June 1982, Frank bowed his head and made a conscious decision of his heart to follow me. He has not done things perfectly, far from it. At many times I thought, son, what in the world are you doing? But the bottom line is this: When I died on the cross, I took away his sin. Every single one, past, present and future. It is written, there is now no condemnation for him. He is undeniably, without a shadow of a doubt, one of mine. I paid his penalty." And then I heard it. The words that would set me free. The words that would give me purpose and a reason for living while on earth, and the words that would usher me one day into heaven. It was The Verdict. "NOT GUILTY!" And you can be declared not guilty, too.

I followed with a great song by Matt Maher, called 'I Need You.' I've had similar moments down through the years on the station where I've known deep inside it was a God thing. That morning was one of those moments. With God's leading, I nailed it. The Spirit had empowered me to do something bold and out of the ordinary. The morning before it aired, I woke up early and had some doubts. Was this really what I was supposed to do? Would people think I was nuts? God, is this really from you? That morning I received validation when I read a daily devotional I use. It said: "Never forget that you are unique, possessing talents, experiences and opportunities that no one else has ever had, or ever will have." Since I posted 'The Verdict' that morning on Facebook, in a couple of days it exploded to over 100,000 views. Everybody was sharing it. I was blown away.

A close friend, Bob Christopher, does a thirty-minute radio program called 'Basic Gospel' that airs on some other Salem radio stations around the country. Many years ago, he shared this simple analogy with me: The Christian life is in many ways like playing center field for the Yankees. You get up every day and you are in the game, uniquely qualified for your position. Some innings you see no action. Then somebody hits a line drive to center, and you have the opportunity to make the play. That morning I felt like Mickey Mantle. I was simply and naturally using the talents and gifts that God has given me, to do a job I was uniquely qualified to do. What's neat is 'The Verdict' was written in the middle of me not feeling that great because of the teeth issue. To be honest, that morning I wrote it, I was kind of an emotional mess. Frankly speaking, I've come to this conclusion: God is looking for willing hearts, not perfect people.

FORTY-THREE

Struggles

———❧———

I knew if I were ever to write a book, I wanted to be completely honest, open, and vulnerable. I've always been bothered with the commonly held stereotype that Christians are supposed to always "have it all together." So let me be blunt. I am often a struggler.

The Bible is clear that when you ask Christ to come into your heart, you receive a new nature. The problem is, the old nature is still there! Paul talks about this conflict in one of my favorite books of the Bible, Romans. Struggling with my old nature has often been three steps forward, two steps back. Many times I just feel like I'm in neutral. I know that I have some perfectionist tendencies, so that's probably part of my issue. I get frustrated with myself easily. One of my problems through the years has been to occasionally use food as an escape. I know for some this may sound trivial, but all you need to do is walk through the mall and see that obesity is becoming an epidemic in our country. You hear a lot about diets, but you hear very little about addressing the root issues of why this is a struggle for so many people. I'm certain many suffer in silence, embarrassed that they can't get a handle on issues like this or some other issue where they feel they are 'stuck.' That's one of the reasons I wanted to write about 'struggles.' If you can relate, I wanted you to know you are not alone, and you are perfectly accepted by a loving God in spite of whatever issues you may be facing.

For me it goes back to replacing those uncomfortable feelings. In times of stress, rather than deal with the feelings, often it's just easy to grab something as a diversion. It's convenient, and in our society it's acceptable. Fast food and processed carbs are readily available, inexpensive, and designed to taste good. Today people are more stressed than ever, and food is an easy and inexpensive fix. Rather than face issues in your life, it's easy to just medicate yourself so (at least temporarily) you don't have to deal with it. The problem is that after you overindulge, you feel terrible, and then you just do the same thing again to cover up *that* feeling. It becomes a vicious cycle.

The problem has been more of an issue for me as I've gotten older. The metabolism slows, and it's harder to keep the weight off. I'm grateful that I genuinely love to work out and exercise. I've come to realize that if I don't deal with the root cause, I'll just continue on the merry-go-round of losing and gaining. I came to the conclusion this is a spiritual problem, not a willpower problem. Getting a handle on it has been interesting from a timing standpoint.

Case in point: For years I was afraid to fly. I had prayed about it often, and wondered why I couldn't get over it. I'm sure part of the problem was that I'm a control freak. Flying in a private plane, though less safe, doesn't bother me as much. I actually enjoy it. But in an airliner it was hard to put my life into the hands of a couple of guys I didn't know and couldn't see up in front flying the plane. I would fly when I absolutely had to, but if I could opt out and drive, that was what I would usually do. Then heading to Colorado one winter I had a stressful drive with the family when we hit a storm. I swore off driving long distances, and it's no longer an issue. In his timing, God finally delivered me from the fear. It's like the 'fear switch' in my brain about flying was turned off! This was an instance where I felt like I was divinely delivered from something.

Likewise, I have prayed for many years about the food issues. In many ways I just replaced alcohol with another substance. While I would love to have the 'food switch' turned off, I'm convinced often God allows these things in our lives so we will seek him! I am getting it under control, but it is an ongoing process. The Bible says if you are controlled by the Spirit, you will not fulfill the desires of the flesh. So it's really a control issue, and a choice issue. Every day I make choices. I can choose to walk in the Spirit, or I can do my own thing. I've found I'm more likely to make the right choices when I'm living in community with other believers, and being honest and open about my shortcomings.

I'm convinced that just about everybody struggles with something, but many choose to keep it private. In my opinion, the church should be the safest place for people to go with their issues. (Very much like it was for me in the rooms of Alcoholics Anonymous.) Unfortunately, that is not often the case. I personally think there are countless Christians on the sidelines of an exciting Spirit-led life because they think God can't use them because they struggle with 'whatever.' Nothing could be further from the truth. God can use you in spite of your personal weakness. I am convinced of this; I am allowed to be a struggler. God's love and acceptance of me never changes.

The enemy of your soul wants you ashamed, embarrassed, isolated and sidelined. Don't buy into the lie. If you are a believer, I urge you to get in the game. You have a sphere of influence that nobody else has. Seeing God actively involved in your life is an amazing way to live. We have the awesome privilege of literally being the hands and feet of Christ. Since he is no longer here in the flesh, we have the opportunity of him using you and me. There is absolutely nothing better then having those 'God moments' when you realize you were used to be a blessing to somebody else. It's what you and I were made for! If you struggle as I do and it sometimes gets you down, know it is because of the conflict between your natural bent toward sin, and God's Spirit living within you. Paul himself makes his own 'struggler' confession in Romans chapter 7 when he says, "the things I don't want to do, I do them anyway!" Please understand this: if you are in Christ, you are totally forgiven, loved, and accepted. God can use you!

Let me encourage you to find a fellowship and group of people where you can completely be yourself, warts and all. It seems to me guys especially have a difficult time humbling themselves and asking for help. We want to be self-sufficient and give the appearance that 'we've got it.' Statistics show that online pornography has become a major stumbling block for many men. I've found if you want to thrive spiritually, you have to deal with issues like this head-on. And you have to call it for what it is, which is sin.

You could have issues with substance abuse, anger, out of control spending, whatever. The good news is because of what was accomplished by Christ's sacrifice, you and I don't have to live there anymore. Since a fruit of the Spirit is self-control, a life controlled by the Spirit can help me get through tempting situations with whatever the issue is. As long as I'm in this imperfect earth suit, I'm not going to do things perfectly all the time, but that's okay. Because Christ lives in me, I am slowly being changed from the inside out. My pastor and friend, Craig Etheredge, reminded me that Christianity is not a self-improvement plan. It is a life change. If you have been trying in your own strength to 'live the Christian life,' I have a suggestion: give up! Only Christ 'living through you' can do it.

I've also found when the Spirit is controlling your body (as opposed to it controlling you), you're just going to be more in tune with God. The physical, emotional, and spiritual are all connected. God made us that way. I'm just going to be more sensitive to His leading when I'm eating right, exercising, getting enough rest, and feeding myself spiritually. I also highly recommend using a friend or group to help keep you accountable with whatever issue you might have. It's very biblical, we aren't wired for walking through this journey called life alone. Speaking for myself, I like to surround myself with positive people who can reinforce the message of God's grace and forgiveness to me. We live in such a performance-oriented society, it is easy to get caught up in feeling you have to 'do stuff' for God. When you truly understand God's grace and forgiveness, the Christian life becomes an exciting adventure, not a performance-oriented chore. My identity stems from who God says I am (his beloved child), not in what I do or don't do.

There's a great verse in the Bible that says, "Confess your sins one to another that you may be healed." It's very true that what is done in secret will control you. If I want to get control of something that is not right in my life, if I want to be healthy emotionally, I need to remember first that God's grace covers it, and then get it out in the open. I need to verbalize it to somebody I can trust. What I've found is this: The wisdom found within the pages of the Bible, coupled with God's Holy Spirit working within me, plus prayer and being in community with other believers, is a temporary solution to dealing with my 'struggles.' The permanent solution will be realized when I meet Jesus face to face.

FORTY-FOUR

Endings

———∾———

Like many in my generation, I've put a lot of thought and time in planning for the future. We work hard to provide for our families, and if we are fortunate enough, we do some retirement planning, and maybe have retirement accounts like an IRA or 401K. I personally love investing in real estate. But how much time do we take to prepare for eternity? This life is really just a blip. The Bible says we are like a vapor, here for a moment, then gone. It says in Ecclesiastes that eternity is placed in the heart of every man. We have been given the desire to live forever.

I'm convinced that many people have been so blinded and consumed by the world and its desires, they have missed the simplicity of the gospel. It's as basic and simple as this: God sent his one and only begotten son, that whoever believes in him should not perish but have eternal life. And the greatest discovery for me has been to have the loving guidance of a very intimate God directing the path of my very own life. Frankly speaking, it is the most exciting way to live, bar none. Since he made me, he knows me better than I know myself. I can trust his ways and guidance, even when (as documented in these pages) things don't always seem logical or make sense.

I have shared my story in abbreviated form in front of a live audience many times down through the years, but last year I spoke for the first time at my home church. As I was preparing my notes for this particular talk, I came to the realization that the two things I wanted to control and held onto so tightly when I made a decision to wholeheartedly follow Christ, my relationships with the opposite sex and my broadcast career, are now the two things that bring me the most fulfillment and satisfaction. There is nothing that gives me more joy than my relationship with my wife, Patti (and my children, Ryan and Hope) and getting to serve the thousands of folks who listen to us every morning on the radio. I released those areas, and they were given back to me, but in God's way, and with his abundant blessing. What an incredible gift!

For so many years while I was climbing the ladder to success in my line of work, I was certain that doing things my way was going to bring me joy and happiness. In reality, to paraphrase a great verse in the Bible, John 6:33, if you make a conscious decision to put God first in your life, everything else falls into place. I have found that to be spot on. I've lived life both ways. My way and God's way. Once you've truly experienced God's way and his grace, love, and forgiveness, it's a no-brainer.

Also, as I've gotten older, there's been more urgency in my heart to communicate the truth of the gospel to as many people as possible. That was really one of the incentives for me to finish this book, which was started years ago. When I turned sixty, I began to ponder the fact that I'm at the age where I could be around for a while, or my time left on planet earth could be short. Death is certain. The day is coming for all of us. It could happen in an instant, or we may go through a prolonged illness. Only God knows.

Are you ready for it? I can remember it like yesterday, being in the ambulance on Long Island. I wasn't ready. Today I believe I am. At the time of this writing, I still have so much to live for, and so much I want to do. But my life and the length of it is God's territory. I'm okay with that. I believe in a place called heaven. I'd like you to be there with me. Please take a moment to ponder this thought: The absolute best gift you can give your family, friends, and loved ones is the certainty that when you have left this life, they know where you are.

Finally, I am of the opinion there is so much misinformation today about *true* Christianity. The onslaught of secular media in our fast-paced electronic age has painted a very tainted picture of the Gospel. I was certain in 1982 when I made my decision to put God first that my life would become boring, routine, and religious. Nothing could be farther from the truth. Actually, it's been exactly the opposite. Yet people today are routinely mocked for their faith. Doing what is right is made fun of, and doing what is wrong is celebrated. Christians are labeled closed-minded, old-fashioned, bigoted and worse. Since I'm a media person, that sometimes bothers me, but I realize it is done primarily out of ignorance. People just don't know the pure, unadulterated truth of the Gospel of Jesus Christ, and the amazing, relentless love and grace of God.

You may have encountered someone who was selfish, prideful and arrogant one day, and then all of a sudden you began to see a change in them. A change for the better. Something was definitely different. Or you hear of a high-profile personality or sports celebrity who has made a decision for Christ. They know they will be ostracized, but like me, they can't deny what has happened to them. They stand up for what they believe anyway, knowing in this day and age it could be very unpopular. How do you explain that? Are all these people crazy, or misguided? Far from it. They met Jesus. They have literally received a new nature. Their priorities change.

The Bible is clear that many will see the things of God as foolishness. If the unconditional love of God because of what Jesus accomplished on the cross is something you just cannot grasp, say a prayer that your eyes would be opened. Pursue the possibility with an open mind, untainted by the media, the culture, or any pre-conceived notions. I challenge you do to this! The grace of God can melt even the hardest of hearts. It's not my job to convince you of anything, sway you to my line of thinking, or win any debates. It is my responsibility to testify to the reality of Jesus in my life, to do my best to love God and to love people. As long as I'm clothed in this body, I won't always do it perfectly, but that's okay. I'm also responsible to be obedient to the leading of God's Spirit, which led me to write the book you are now reading. If it has led you to begin an honest pursuit of the truth, it is no coincidence. If you wholeheartedly seek, I am certain you will find.

God completely turned my life upside down. I gladly give all the glory to Him. He is in the continual process of changing me from the inside out, and it has all been for the good. Life still has its struggles and heartaches, but in the long run there is no downside. I have meaning and purpose in living today, and eternity to look forward to when I'm gone. And believe me when I tell you I'm nothing special. You can have that, too.

Acknowledgements

If it takes a village to raise a child, it takes a small army of friends to help Frank Reed write a book! Since I've never done this before, I got a clue very early in the process that the best thing to do was to ask for help. Joe Battaglia, you read the first rough draft and assured me this was not a dumb idea! Thank you for your honesty, insight, and friendship. I love you Joe. John Peroyea, you were an encouragement to me on this project from day one, thank you Boss. Thanks to the numerous friends who reviewed the ever changing manuscript through various phases and offered their input, critiques, encouragement, and suggestions, they are: Tim Dukes, David Alvey, Craig Etheredge, David Sylvester, Susan Lewis, Bob Lepine, John Cicone, Lloyd Parker, Brown Bannister, Bob Christopher, Rick Tarrant, Chad Harbour, Keith Nelson, and Drew Altom. Special thanks to John Bowen, whose office is right across from mine at KLTY. Often I would yell in his direction; "Hey John, look at this sentence, does this make sense??" Starlene Stringer, you are amazing. Thanks for your friendship and all your help on this project. Chris Chamberlain, technical wizard, thank you. Jack Peddy, thank you for the great cover and help with the pics. Thanks also to Allen Beebe and Dave Edwards. Special thanks to David Busch, President and CEO of Hawaiian Falls Waterparks for his infectious inspiration and encouragement. To the team at Xulon;

all I can say is WOW. Chad Nyamp, you have assembled a very talented group. Everybody was a pleasure to deal with. Thanks to Don Newman, Michelle Johnston, Jared Walton, Erika Bennett, Melinda Howard, and special thanks to Karla Castellon and Mimie Auxila. Editor extraordinaire Michelle Levigne, thank you!

Look for 'Frankly Speaking' the audiobook coming in 2014.
Updates at www.FranklySpeakingTheBook.com.

Frank Reed is available for limited speaking engagements. Start the conversation by emailing FrankReedontheair@Gmail.com.

CPSIA information can be obtained at www.ICGtesting.com
Printed in the USA
LVOW13*0913120114

368981LV00001B/1/P